REINVENTING
MANAGEMENT
THINKING

USING SCIENCE TO LIBERATE THE HUMAN SPIRIT

Reinventing Management Thinking

Using science to liberate the human spirit

Jeremy Old

Team Business Development Ltd.

Originally published under the title of "Why organisations don't work" in April 2014, ISBN 978-0-9929104-1-9 in print form and ISBN 978-0-9929104-0-2 in electronic form. The book has now been retitled as "Reinventing management thinking" and updated with extra written material, diagrams and tables.

Published by Team Business Development Ltd
40 Wimborne St Giles, Near Wimborne,
Dorset, BH21 5NF

www.teambusinessdevelopment.co.uk

Published October 2015

ISBN 978-0-9929104-3-3

Cover illustration and diagrams by Mark Starmer

Printed by Create Space

Companies, institutions and other organisations wishing to make bulk purchases of this book can contact Team Business Development direct: 40 Wimborne St Giles, Near Wimborne, Dorset, BH21 5NF. Tel: 0845 0945 819 email: info@teambusinessdevelopment.co.uk

Table of contents

PART I   **The amygdala effect**

1.1 Stress as a management unknown
1.2 How stress impacts decision-making faculties
1.3 Stress generates unproductive behaviour
1.4 How to analyse the real cost of stress to your
       organisation
1.5 The hidden cost of stress – case examples

2.1 A powerful new organising principle - the human
       givens perspective
2.2 A new working definition of stress
2.3 The mechanics of stress
2.4 How low grade stress impairs productive capacity

3.1   Basic overview
3.2   Why stress and high performance are two sides of
        the same coin
3.3   Using the concept of biological needs – the human
        givens to motivate improve performance
3.3.1 Security, including safe territory to develop and

Chapter 4   **Meeting emotional needs liberates organisational potential**   70

List of tables

List of diagrams

14

Preface

Why this book may be important to you

Reinventing management thinking came about from asking the question 'WHY'.

During twenty-five years of management consultancy in dozens of organisations large and small, I am forever asking the question why. After a bit of digging, each 'why' brings it's own answer, but inevitably leads to the next 'why' and so on until I have drilled down to the root cause of a problem. Why aren't you making a profit? Why are you losing customers? Why are there so many rejects? Why are there so many mistakes in production? Why are your people de-motivated? Why are they so stressed? …

Root cause analysis seems out of fashion in management these days. This may be because it is a bit like peeling an onion – you peel off one layer after another and sometimes the process makes you cry. Peeling layers off can be painful for managers as they discover what is wrong with 'their' system. But I have found that the upside to root cause analysis is well worth the pain. As you delve down to the root cause of a problem, you move nearer the truth and a clearer, deeper and broader meaning emerges. From this you can extract a more balanced and sustainable solution.

> Root cause analysis is a bit like an onion - you peel off one layer after another and sometimes what you find makes you cry.

Asking so many different managers and staff members 'why' so persistently (and possibly even irritatingly), reveals that a lot of our business and organisational problems are simply down to the way we habitually like to run things. In turn this habitual functioning tends to arise from poor or degraded thinking. Wherever I see an upward shift in the way managers think and a shift in the quality of their thinking, I witness an effortless transformation in their ability to enhance their organisation's productivity and performance. The experience has been so consistent that I have come to realise that if we could only improve management and leadership thinking generally, we would solve a lot of society's problems and transform our economic prosperity. With this awareness in mind, I set out to share what I have learned about new ways of management thinking from both science and my own observations.

Hopefully, when you read this book you will experience a few of those precious 'aha' moments of realisation that help you immediately discover why your organisation isn't fulfilling its promise and more importantly what you can do about changing direction and fixing the problem. To achieve this aim - I want to get across four salient points.

Point one – Most organisations underperform way below their true potential.

My starting point is the basic supposition that a large proportion of our organisations aren't working very well. Now you may disagree with this generalisation, especially so if you are running one or working in one that you feel is successful. But lets do a check here, because you don't want to waste time reading this book, if you think your organisation is perfectly OK. So before going any further, can you honestly answer the following three general questions in the affirmative?

1. Are you happy in your work? Does it give you joy or are you often stressed? The acid test is this. Do you feel genuinely alive with energy and enthusiasm on a Monday morning when it is time to go to work? Do you feel exhilarated at the end of the week or just simply knackered?

2. What about the people who work for you; are they happy in their work? Are they joyful or are they stressed? Do they feel genuinely alive with energy and enthusiasm on Monday morning when it is time to go to work? Do they feel exhilarated at the end of the week or just simply knackered? Have you asked them? Does it really matter to you?

3. If your organisation is in the private sector, is it making good profits, say at least 10% of sales revenue after interest payments? If you are in the public or charitable sector are your services coping well with the demand for them? By the way, that is from the customer's point of view not some anodyne corporate announcement about achieving targets. Are you proud that your organisation is always fulfilling it's full potential and that you and your organisation are doing something genuinely worthwhile?

OK, so long as you have been honest and have <u>not</u> been able to give a resounding YES to <u>all</u> three of the above questions, then this book may well be able to help you, because you are at least open to the concept that you and your organisation is functioning below par. This book will show you how reinventing your thinking can turn that situation around and a lot faster than you would think possible.

> Management science is work in progress. The more we learn about how the human brain works, the more we have to change the way we run things.

Point two – The prevailing management and leadership culture is based on an outmoded psychological model

I don't mean to be critical here of all the effort put in by tens of thousands of conscientious managers and business owners. People are generally trying to do their best, but the fact is that underperformance of large organisations is hardly surprising when you consider that only a generation or so ago, organisations in general were a fraction of the size that they are today.

The disconnection, between science and management, is responsible for an epidemic of stress in organisational life.

Culturally we have not developed the collective capacity to run so many huge concerns that number hundreds, thousands or even a million or so people. As a result, the type of management structures we use, the elements of management function that we think are necessary and the leadership styles we adopt are still not up to the job of fully exploiting human and organisational potential.

Management science is very much work in progress. The more that neuroscience and psychology learns about how the human brain actually works, (and there has been a cascade of new findings in the last thirty years or so) the more we have to change the way we run things.

The plain fact is that too many of our standard management practices and some out-dated theories are completely divorced from the new scientific reality of how the brain works and how people like to function in groups. Currently our preferred leadership styles, management structures and management functions very often trigger the stress response among both employees and management alike. This disconnection, between science and management, is responsible for an epidemic of stress in organisational life.

Point three – Organisational stress debilitates productivity, creativity and decision-making.

Leading on from the above point, I aim to show you through research and my own observations that many of the problems inherent in our organisations are due to endemic stress. Modern science recognises all too clearly that stress corrupts thinking, demotivates people and supresses those talents and qualities needed for a competent and coherent group effort. At present, the underlying causes of stress and the real cost of it in terms of organisational performance are way beyond what the average manager, leader and business owner recognises or can even imagine.

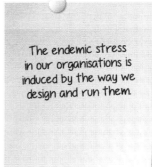

The endemic stress in our organisations is induced by the way we design and run them.

Point four – The antidote to organisational stress is to redesign the system in a way more sympathetic to human nature.

Currently, attempts to remedy stress in the workplace are mostly left in the realm of the HR department. Managers and HR people tend to focus on individual stress management techniques as a means to reduce individual stress and so improve personal performance. This approach is only a palliative at best.

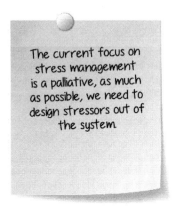

The current focus on stress management is a palliative, as much as possible, we need to design stressors out of the system.

A far more productive approach is to tackle the root cause of the stress. Most of the time in most organisations, stress is generated by the system itself, by which I mean stress is triggered by the way the organisation is run, designed and structured. Changing the way you think about the system and redesigning it to suit the inhabitants rids it of pernicious 'stressors'. If you can achieve this, you can largely reduce the need for stress management palliatives. Stress is a toxic constraint on the effectiveness and efficiency of an organisation. Eliminating stress in the system liberates the human spirit as it frees up the innate human resources that often lie dormant or at least underutilised in any stressed organisation.

What you will get from this book

In essence this book is about helping you to massively improve organisational performance by working on the organisational ecosystem to make it less stressful for yourself and for everyone working for you.

In this respect, the book has one main function: To use the latest findings from neuroscience and psychotherapy to help you design stress out of whatever organisation you are running. An organisation is more than just the sum of its parts. If you learn to remove the stress from an organisation you will not only get the best out of all those you seek to lead and manage, you will also optimise the performance of the overall system.

This book transcends many conventional assumptions about stress as well as a lot of established management psychology and takes you on a journey of exciting knowledge that will make both you and your group far more successful in your work.

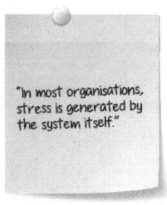

"In most organisations, stress is generated by the system itself."

In general terms this book gives you:

- Useful research insights into the nature of the human brain. You will see how working against the brain's true nature obstructs the progress of both individuals and the groups they work in, whereas learning how to work with the brain's innate nature galvanises your people's energy, intelligence, creativity and engagement

- Dozens of ideas, methods, and techniques to prevent you from de-motivating your team and your colleagues and obstructing their progress

- A systematic analysis of why certain management structures, functions and styles create 'organisational stress' and why such stress generates dysfunction and suboptimum performance from people in your working environment

- Practical case studies of how a working knowledge of organisational stress can transform thinking, learning and overall performance in the workplace

- Clear guidelines to adapt organisational design and your leadership style to optimise the brain functioning and productivity of everyone in your work group

- Precise methods to enable you to pinpoint the exact causes of stress (stressors) in the work environment; assess the impact that each stressor is having on the organisation and more importantly, remove them.

How to use this book

As a means to reinvent your thinking, the book describes in detail **'thirty organisational stressors'** each with its own problems, impact and relevant remedies. But I would like to recommend that before you get into the actual stressors, you read the introduction and the first four chapters (Part 1) as these provide you with a coherent analytical approach to guide you along the path of successful leadership, system design and management.

When you understand the principles, laid out in Part 1, you will make better sense out of Part 2. You will then be able to more fully utilise the proven methods, techniques and ideas that ameliorate or remove the thirty stressors.

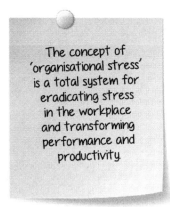

The concept of 'organisational stress' is a total system for eradicating stress in the workplace and transforming performance and productivity.

It is important to understand that the concept of organisational stress is a total system, not just for eradicating stress in the workplace, but also for stimulating far higher levels of productivity, performance and enjoyment for both you and your workgroup. By fully understanding the total system you will not only be able to follow all the techniques, methods and ideas that are provided in Part 2 you will also create and invent your own as the need arises.

Reading the book from cover to cover will change your thinking and provide you with a clear overview of what our natural brain state is, how it is harmed by organisational stress and how to avoid or remove the pernicious influence of stress. In the final chapter, entitled 'Pulling the various strands together', you will find Table 18 - Integrating collaborative leadership into the system. This table schedules the various management techniques and structures mentioned in the previous chapters along with their reference points in the book. The idea is to help you return again and again to the relevant techniques and methods as and when you need them, so, in time you can acquire mastery over their use.

As a further attempt to provide you with a clear overview, you can read Table 19 in Appendix 1. This table comprises a comprehensive summary of collaborative leadership in contrast to its top down command and control counterpart. I depict the contrasting characteristics of the two regimes under six main headings including, management structure, motivation, qualities of leadership, decision-making, culture and management and leadership ethic. Hopefully this depiction of 'darkness and light' will help shift you in the right direction towards a more collaborative and scientific approach to your everyday management challenges. This table more than anything else demonstrates why, what I advocate, is a reinvention of current management thinking.

Introduction

Science based leadership approach

The key message of this book is that modern psychology and neuroscience tells us that we come into life with a rich heritage of inherent survival skills. These qualities and abilities include enthusiasm, conscientiousness, compassion, enterprise, curiosity, group loyalty, creative problem solving, teamwork, focus and intuitive thinking.

Where organisations fail to express these natural human attributes, it is because their employees' thinking and behaviour are being harmed by stress. If more than a few employees suffer from stress they have an adverse impact on the whole organisation and its objectives.

These new scientific findings offer an opportunity for leaders everywhere to improve organisational performance enormously.

Diagram 1

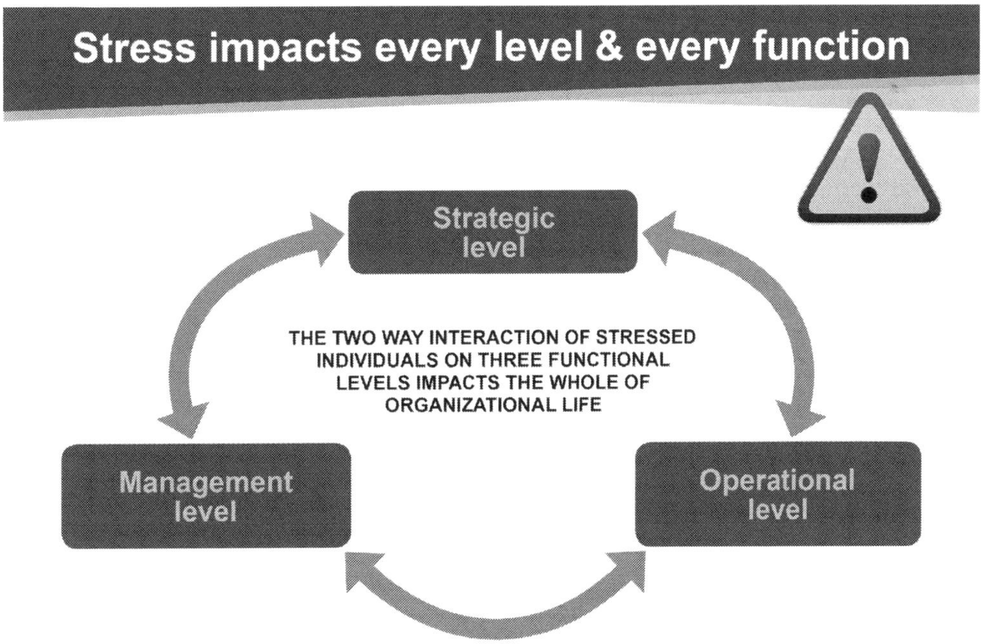

Stress impacts every level & every function

Strategic level

THE TWO WAY INTERACTION OF STRESSED INDIVIDUALS ON THREE FUNCTIONAL LEVELS IMPACTS THE WHOLE OF ORGANIZATIONAL LIFE

Management level

Operational level

IF AN ORGANISATION EXPERIENCES STRESS AT ALL THREE LEVELS THEN IT WILL SERIOUSLY MALFUNCTION

Typically, organisations underestimate both the cost and prevalence of stress at work by a huge margin. The received wisdom is that stress and its costs are limited to absenteeism, sickness and the risk of compensation claims when someone falls ill. These factors are bad enough, but the real problem with stress is much greater.

Misunderstanding stress drives managers unwittingly to create structures, cultures, procedures, processes, protocols and controls that trigger the stress response in their employees. Where this happens, managers in effect create inhospitable working environments that generate massive costs in terms of waste, low productivity and poor performance. The stress problem can intrude at every level and across every function.

- **At strategic level** stress contributes to poor judgement, insatiable greed and power lust, destructive competitive rivalry and incompetent, reckless and unethical decision-making.

- **At management level** stress drives rushed and inadequate operational planning, corrosive 'impression management', defective analysis, flawed problem solving, faulty decision-making, unethical and controlling behaviour, weak relationship building and de-motivating leadership.

- **At operational level** stress provokes employee disengagement, inauthentic working relationships, personal conflicts, poor communication, compassion fatigue, insensitivity to customers' and other colleagues needs, accidents, costly mistakes and rework, lethargy, low creativity, waste, resistance to change and incoherent teamwork.

If an organisation experiences stress at all three levels then it can seriously malfunction, as the interaction of stressed individuals between these three functional areas will always compound the problems.

The importance of organisational stress

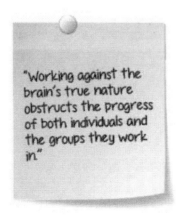

"Working against the brain's true nature obstructs the progress of both individuals and the groups they work in."

The stress phenomenon goes a long way to explain why many of our larger organisations are not working nearly as well as they should be and why there is always a risk that the larger an organisation is, the more it degenerates into a self-serving sclerotic bureaucracy. Unlike healthy individuals, such organisations find it difficult to cope with change, become insensitive to customers' and junior employees' needs and are often incapable of motivating or controlling people in the performance of sophisticated or complex work processes.

Of course, many senior managers will disagree with the idea that there is a pattern of systemic failure with organisational leadership. But this attitude flies in the face of the evidence. The fact is that during the last decade or so, western economies have been battered by a succession of government and corporate failures, insolvencies, and scandals. Most notorious have been the calamitous bank failures across the USA and Europe. But there is also a pattern of corporate corruption, scandals and insolvencies affecting some of the largest and most wealthy economic concerns in the world. Incidentally, all of these organisations employed the very best outputs from our leading business schools and management training.

The elapse of time can obscure this pattern of failure. Although large corporate scandals make headlines when they occur, most become a blur in our memory as the years go by, until they are entirely eclipsed from view by later events. So as a refresher, below is a sample of notable corporate failures, scandals and disasters in the last fifteen years or so:

- Fraudulent accounting at WorldCom – 2001
- Bethlehem Steel bankruptcy – 2001
- Swiss Air, national icon nicknamed the 'Flying Bank' collapses in 2001 after pursuing an aggressive acquisition strategy
- The implosion of HIH, Australia's second largest insurance company – 2001
- Enron's concealment of large losses and subsequent collapse – 2001
- Arthur Anderson's criminal obstruction of justice relating to the Enron scandal – 2002
- Royal Dutch Shell overstating oil reserves – 2004
- The collapse of MG Rover, the UK's leading car manufacturer – 2005
- Refco Brokering's concealment of bad debts from investors – 2005
- The collapse of Lehman Brothers triggering a global financial market meltdown, with Bear Stearns, Northern Rock and the Royal Bank of Scotland all collapsing in 2008
- General Motors formerly the most powerful car manufacturer in the world, filing for bankruptcy – 2009
- The collapse of Washington Mutual, America's largest Savings and loan association and the largest bank failure in history to date – 2008
- Nortel's excessive executive pay scandal – 2009
- News corporation phone hacking scandal leading to the demise of the "News of The World" – 2011
- BP's catastrophic oil spill – 2011

- The Co-operative Bank rescue by hedge funds – 2013
- The manipulation of profit figures at Tesco, The UK's largest supermarket chain – 2014
- Volkswagen emissions scandal – 2015

The problem is not isolated to just the commercial sector. In recent years we have seen a range of public sector scandals in both the US and UK. Notable examples in the USA are the Fannie Mae (FNMA) and Freddie Mac (FHLMC) bailouts for a massive £250 billion.

"A high level of stress among employees and management is very often the reason why organisations don't work."

In the UK, among many public sector scandals, there are ongoing revelations about the distressing standards of care in the UK National Health Service[1] (sometimes covered up by the health services own statutory regulator the Quality Care Commission). There have been equally unacceptable outbreaks of appalling incompetence, neglect and chronic overspending in UK social service child protection[2]. At the time of writing, the latest revelation has been about the sexual exploitation by gangs of predatory men of 1,400 children at Rotherham. Apparently, the social services and police already knew that about a third of the children were at risk, but despite this fact, reports of rape, torture, abduction and sex trafficking were ignored or disbelieved by management in both agencies[3]. (You can find an explanation as to why this institutional disbelief can happen in chapter 11 section 7). In addition in the UK we have witnessed the bizarre farm payments scandal and just recently hard pressed taxpayers woke up to the astonishing news that the Government has tipped £500 million of taxpayers money into the 'Global Fund' a Swiss based charity of rather dubious reputation paying its employees an average salary of $150,000 per year. The indecent rush to dispose of the cash was to meet some target about giving money away in overseas aid.

Globally, these and multiple similar incidents are damaging the safety, security, finance and welfare of millions of ordinary citizens, employees, savers and investors by losing billions of pounds, costing millions of jobs and generating unknown hardship and suffering. In some cases, as with the banking crisis, failures in corporate and public sector management are impacting whole economies and have plunged the western world into a prolonged period of economic turbulence and recession.

"In our natural brain state we are highly socialised, collaborative problem-solving mammals. This innate talent is hardwired into our DNA and if we are prevented from utilising it we become stressed"

But service failure and macroeconomic problems are not the only consequence of organisational stress and mismanagement. The daily experience of hundreds of millions of employees is reflected in record levels of work-related depression and anxiety[4], high unemployment levels[5], falling average standards of living for those in work and the burgeoning long working hours culture that harms individual health and family life. The common experience is that organisational life seems to suppress the human spirit.

The nature of stress in organisations

To fully understand why we have such a large-scale problem with our organisations we need to look at the core element of every organisation – the human physiology. Specifically we need to study the human brain physiology and its instinctive reaction to threat, known as the stress response.

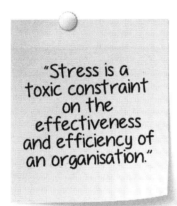

"Stress is a toxic constraint on the effectiveness and efficiency of an organisation."

In essence, the stress response is the emotional arousal we experience as the fight or flight reaction. This impulsive reaction occurs in two types of circumstances.

Firstly, our brain physiology triggers a stress response whenever we cannot meet or perceive we cannot meet innate physical and emotional needs such as our need for security.

Secondly, the fight or flight response can spark off when events or circumstances stifle our innate resources and so prevents us from doing something that helps meet our emotional needs.

In many working environments a number of our emotional needs are being smothered or violated. The resultant stress is an emotionally driven response that progressively shuts down a variety of normal and high value faculties of the brain such as empathy, self-awareness and rational thinking. Even low-grade stress experienced mildly in ways such as anxiety, resentment or embarrassment begins to inhibit these valuable faculties in seemingly random ways. As a result stress drives a whole range of sub-optimum behaviours and impulsive activity that is harmful to individual work output, working relationships and general organisational coherence. Essentially a high level of stress among employees and management is very often the reason why organisations go wrong.

Transforming group performance

Leading high performance organisations requires removal of the 'organisational stressors' that prevent people meeting their emotional needs and holds them back from expressing their superb innate survival skills. Remove the stress and you remove suboptimum behaviour and impulsive activity and instead establish a focussed, energetic and high performance work culture.

Diagram 2

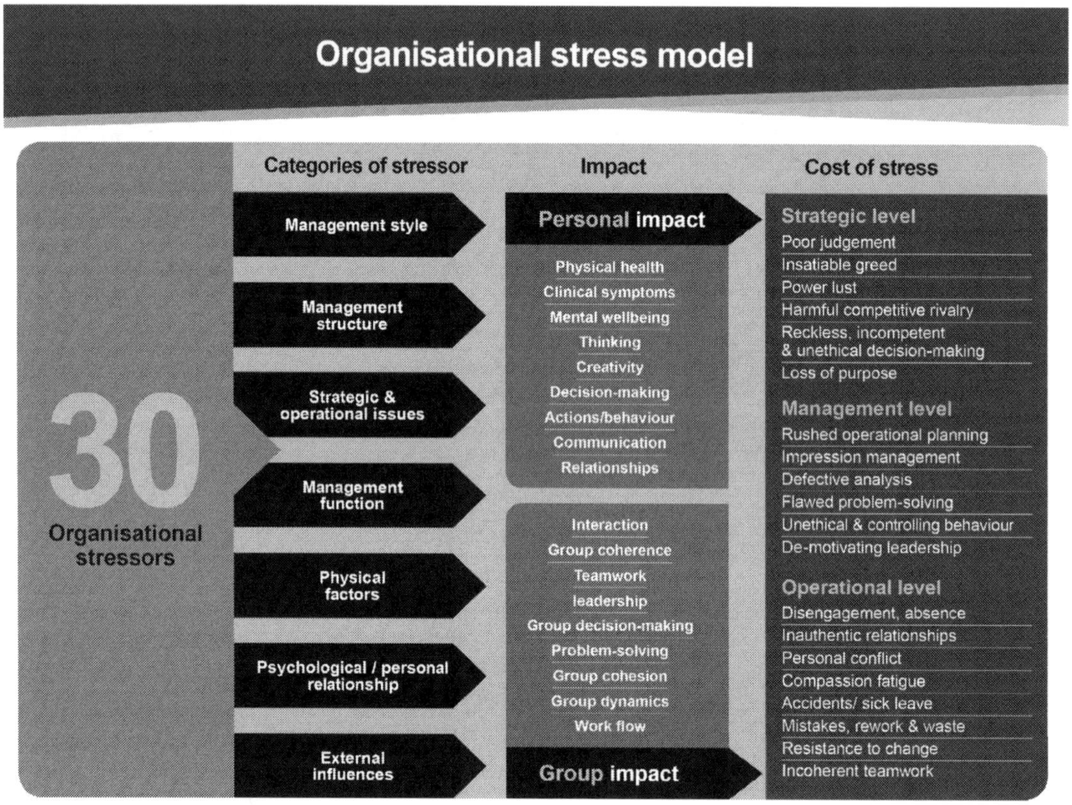

Organisational stress model

Categories of stressor	Impact	Cost of stress
Management style	**Personal impact**	**Strategic level** — Poor judgement, Insatiable greed, Power lust, Harmful competitive rivalry, Reckless, incompetent & unethical decision-making, Loss of purpose
Management structure	Physical health, Clinical symptoms, Mental wellbeing, Thinking, Creativity, Decision-making, Actions/behaviour, Communication, Relationships	**Management level** — Rushed operational planning, Impression management, Defective analysis, Flawed problem-solving, Unethical & controlling behaviour, De-motivating leadership
Strategic & operational issues		
Management function	Interaction, Group coherence, Teamwork, leadership, Group decision-making, Problem-solving, Group cohesion, Group dynamics, Work flow	**Operational level** — Disengagement, absence, Inauthentic relationships, Personal conflict, Compassion fatigue, Accidents/ sick leave, Mistakes, rework & waste, Resistance to change, Incoherent teamwork
Physical factors		
Psychological / personal relationship		
External influences	**Group impact**	

30 Organisational stressors

Removing or at least alleviating typical organisational stressors is the key to reducing stress and enabling employees to meet their emotional needs. During the next three hundred or so pages, I identify thirty different stressors (See table 1 over) and study the harmful influence each one has on organisational performance and the impact each has on people's needs and performance.

What emerges from the study is that a core attribute of every healthy employee is the ability and willingness to participate in activity that will improve the group's performance. As human beings we have survived as a species because in our natural brain state we are highly socialised, collaborative problem-solving mammals. This innate talent is hardwired into our DNA and if we are prevented from utilising it we become stressed.

Reinventing management thinking is about harnessing this raw human potential for collaboration and problem-solving by empowering people to drive improvements and organisational excellence as a means to get their own emotional needs met.

The benefits to you and your organisation

If you can adopt the principles and practical guidelines outlined in the following chapters you will create a low-stress and more collaborative style of leadership that enables everyone involved with you to meet crucial emotional needs.

When leaders help people meet their innate needs, or when they at least avoid violating them, they enable a natural brain state in their employees where the normal mode of functioning is focus, enthusiasm, loyalty, initiative taking, creative problem-solving and commitment to their work and their organisation's values. The result of everyone working in their natural brain state is a surge of benefits across the organisation that accumulates to a transformation in productivity out of all proportion to the costs involved.

What you get with a low-stress working environment includes:

- Rapidly improved information flows between functions and individuals
- Improved planning outcomes
- Enhanced decision-making
- Spontaneous and creative problem solving at every level
- Infectious enthusiasm and support of the work group towards colleagues, customers and the organisational goals
- Employees totally engaged and committed
- A healthier, happier working environment
- Compassion and creativity otherwise repressed by stress
- A significantly lightened load of stress for the people at the top

Table 1: The thirty organisational stressors

Caution

Management styles adopted by organisations
1. Top-down command and control management
2. Institutionalised atmosphere of mistrust that
   poisons relationships and performance

Types of management structure
3. The imposition of goals or targets from a higher authority
4. Unclear boundaries of functions and responsibilities
5. Organisational units that are too large

Strategic and operational issues
6. Major strategic change
7. Onerous externally imposed deadlines with insufficient time to do the task.
8. Functional specialisation creating boredom and monotony
9. Low quality performance

Elements of the management function
10. No clear short-term goals for staff and managers to work towards
11. Responsibility without the necessary authority or means to fulfil a task
12. Career uncertainty often a result of short-termism
13. Insufficient or inappropriate support from management or colleagues
14. Loss of a natural routine
15. New functions being allotted without adequate training and guidance
16. Disagreement with organisational values or philosophy
17. The unequal treatment of equals or the equal treatment of "unequals"
18. Fast track career paths

Physical factors in the working environment
19. Environmental factors such as excessive noise and inadequate equipment
20. Stale air, electromagnetic fields and artificial day lighting

Psychological or personal and relationship factors
21. Negative Relationships
22. High internal competitiveness in the work culture
23. Incompatibilities
24. The presence of a socialised psychopath
25. Organisational straight-line thinking
26. Drug misuse
27. Botched decisions due to defective thinking patterns
28. People bringing their own stresses to work

External influences that constrain success
29. Excessive government regulations and intervention
30. High taxation

PART I

The amygdala effect

PART I

The amygdala effect

Chapter One

Stress as a constraint to thinking

1.1 Stress as a management unknown

Managers, policy planners or accountants are not trained to perceive or understand the biological mechanics of the stress response and so have very little idea as to the true cost of a stressful workplace. As a direct result, organisations are unable to identify the symptoms of stress that occur on a daily basis and also lack the means to measure the real damage that stress has on organisational effectiveness.

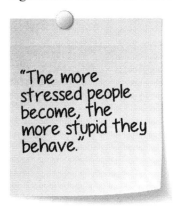

"The more stressed people become, the more stupid they behave."

Typically, stressed thinking and stressed behaviour occur at every level of organisational activity. In fact stressed functioning is so common that we tend to take it for granted at a huge cost to our society in general, our organisations, our relationships and our health.

In effect, stress is so prevalent at work that it is something we have learned to live with. This void in management thinking about the real nature and true cost of stress is perhaps the prime reason why so much of what managers do generates stress for themselves and their employees and so actually harms the organisation they are running.

In broad terms, the stress response impacts organisational performance in four ways:

Firstly, stress distorts or impairs our thinking faculties that in turn impinge our ability to make decisions, analyse, problem-solve and plan.

Secondly, stress provokes a variety of unproductive individual behaviours (See table 2).

Thirdly, in a group setting, stress inhibits the free flow of interaction, communication and coherent activity required to pursue shared goals successfully.

Fourthly, prolonged stressful episodes damage the health and wellbeing of the workforce.

Where many individuals and groups of individuals are involved in a constant process of interaction with one another, making decisions, problem solving and planning then, where it exists, stress is like grit in a machine. Grit that jams everything up creates random breakdowns and causes extra wear and tear on every element in the system.

Blinded by the obvious

Perched on a rock at the bottom of the sea, sat a wise old crab who was teaching some young fish the ways of the world. He started his talk by saying:

"So, when you leave the water, you enter into a strange and wonderful world very different from our own. An amazing thing is that when you leave the water you can move much more easily, it seems warmer and you can see much further in the distance. When you leave the water things seem much clearer and colours much brighter.

Also out of the water there are strange creatures moving about including some two-legged types with funny tufts on their heads."

The old crab went on like this for a while until the end of the lesson when he asked: "So, do any of you have any questions?"

"Yes I do." Piped up one little fish. "What's water?"

From a story told by Ivan Tyrrell of the Human Givens Institute[1]

1.2 Stress impacts decision-making faculties

The number of decision-making faculties impacted by the stress response illustrate on their own why maintaining a low stress environment at work is important for high productivity and performance. Stress impacts:

- Our ability to think and reason clearly and rationally
- Our ability to distinguish between intellect and emotion
- Our ability to make sound judgements
- Our positivity, optimism, curiosity and enthusiasm and sense of humour
- Our willingness to empathise with others and their problems whether they are colleagues, subordinates, customers, patients or clients
- Our ability and willingness to listen and receive input from others and collaborate supportively with them
- Our willingness to share information
- Our ability to access complex long term memory patterns
- Our ability to access our imagination and creativity
- Our ability to focus
- Our ability to problem-solve including the desire to investigate and evaluate alternative solutions

The five steps to stress-driven mistakes

Psychotherapists now recognise that the more stressed people become the more stupid they behave. When in this impaired brain state, decisions tend to be crass and simplistic. This may seem odd at first, but nature renders us stupid during a stressful crisis for a very good reason.

The stress response is designed to instigate instant, dynamic even violent action for the immediate purpose of survival through indomitable defence, overwhelming attack or speedy withdrawal to a safe place. In essence we are programmed to react instantly and perform unthinkingly in times of physical danger.

Stressed decision-making is a C-R-I-M-E

This programming has an important bearing on organisational management wherever decision-makers are stressed. Where we don't need a primeval reaction to protect ourselves, an inappropriate stress response simply gets in the way.

By definition, stressed decision-makers are emotionally charged. As a direct result stressed decision-makers manifest defective thinking that is pretty ruinous when the circumstances require a rational, well thought through, and balanced appreciation of a problem, and the careful evaluation of alternative detailed and imaginative solutions.

Typically stressed decision-making goes through five steps. These are:

Step 1. Crass oversimplification of the problem - When emotionally aroused we tend to jump to a drastic oversimplification of the problems at hand. Things appear very dramatic, black or white and extreme. There is little room for subtleties and we tend to 'catastrophise', such as thinking that missing our train is suddenly 'the end of the world'.

Step 2. Rapid broad-brush solution - one grand idea - We tend to come up with just one grand simplistic idea to solve things. It can seem at the time vividly brilliant but there is always a vagueness ascribed to this potential solution. We overlook or lose sight of the detailed picture. Complexities and subtleties are avoided. Crucially, second or third alternatives are overlooked or instantly discounted. Steps one and two mean that when stressed we can easily try and tackle the wrong problem with the wrong solution.

Step 3. Inability to listen or consult, we are 100% right - Perhaps most disastrously we have an unshakeable belief in the absolute correctness of the solution that we have decided upon.

Nature designs stressed thinking to give us an overriding confidence in our own sense of direction; taking immediate dynamic action is the priority in a life-threatening event. So when stressed there is a strong emotional tendency to believe we are right and everyone else is either wrong or, at least, their views become irrelevant to us. Unfortunately this overconfidence is less than useful when the requirement is to make a rational assessment of the situation, partly based on an ability to listen to other points of view and patiently glean the precise facts upon which to base a decision.

Step 4. Mad rush to act – "Do it now" syndrome - Compounding the last catastrophic feature, we feel compelled to make immediate decisions or take immediate action. This is the classic knee-jerk reaction to events. Stressed thinkers are impelled towards making a 'quick fix' solution. The stress mechanism compels them to act before they can take a more considered, rational, researched and consultative approach.

Diagram 3

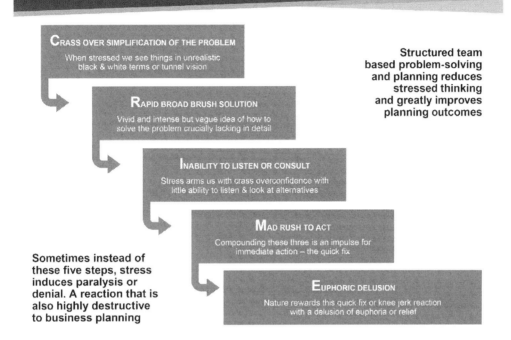

Stressed decision-making is a C-R-I-M-E

CRASS OVER SIMPLIFICATION OF THE PROBLEM
When stressed we see things in unrealistic black & white terms or tunnel vision

RAPID BROAD BRUSH SOLUTION
Vivid and intense but vague idea of how to solve the problem crucially lacking in detail

INABILITY TO LISTEN OR CONSULT
Stress arms us with crass overconfidence with little ability to listen & look at alternatives

MAD RUSH TO ACT
Compounding these three is an impulse for immediate action – the quick fix

EUPHORIC DELUSION
Nature rewards this quick fix or knee jerk reaction with a delusion of euphoria or relief

Structured team based problem-solving and planning reduces stressed thinking and greatly improves planning outcomes

Sometimes instead of these five steps, stress induces paralysis or denial. A reaction that is also highly destructive to business planning

Step 5. Euphoric delusion – After the quick fix comes the euphoric feeling of success. Unfortunately this high is entirely delusional. This emotion is simply a biochemical event and is nature's way of rewarding the decision-maker for arriving at a quick decision. The elation in no way reflects the poor quality of the decision just made.

There are variations to these five steps of emotionally-charged thinking.

Sometimes, instead of speed, stress provokes the impulse of procrastination and even paralysis in the decision-making process, like the rabbit petrified into inaction when caught in the headlights. In other cases the stress surrounding a problem can provoke denial of its very existence. This is the classic head in the sand response.

Whatever the reaction, a stressed response to the sort of problems we are confronted with at work is almost universally useless.

Although when at work most of us are hopefully not experiencing extreme states of panic, many people do get weighed down with low-grade stress and anxiety. Even this low state of anxiety can provoke sufficient emotional arousal to have a corrosive influence on the thinking process with these negative characteristics beginning to come into play.

1.3 Stress provokes unproductive behaviour

But stress debilitates more than just executive decision-making.

Where we don't need a primeval reaction to protect ourselves, an inappropriate stress response simply gets in the way.

In our natural brain state we have a wide range of superb faculties for problem-solving, relationship-building and team-working.

In contrast to this happy brain state however, the stress response gives rise to a wide range of negative emotions, unproductive behaviours, sub-optimum thinking and unhelpful attitudes that impact every category of organisational activity.

You can clearly see this contrast between the two brain states by comparing tables 2 and 3. Hopefully even a casual study of these two lists will dispel any doubt as to which type of brain state you would prefer your people to be in when working for you.

Generally it is now accepted that people's thinking and performance is impaired if say they are intoxicated or under the influence of drugs. As such, it is unacceptable for an employee to arrive at work drunk.

However, management has not reached the same level of awareness about the corrupting influence of stress on behaviour and thinking. As a result of this blind spot, culturally there is too cavalier a view of the whole issue. Stress can even be seen as a 'good' thing. This is a serious mistake.

If we want high performing organisations, such a lenient attitude to stress has to change. Table 3 demonstrates clearly why stress is not a useful state of mind for productive activity, harmonious teamwork and coherent decision-making.

Different people react to stress in different and often random and contrasting ways and with greatly differing degrees of intensity.

Different people react to stress in different ways

The tendency to take stress for granted is reinforced by two further factors.

Firstly, different people react to stress in different and often random and contrasting ways. For instance intrinsically nervous people, when under stress, may tend to become deceitful, forgetful, overly sensitive, procrastinate or lose focus[2]. The hotter more passionate types may become perfectionist, critical, angry, hostile or over-competitive. The steadier types, when stressed may become stubborn, lazy or overly attached to the existing ways of doing things[3].

Secondly, different people react to stress with greatly differing degrees of intensity. What seems to stress one person doesn't necessarily stress another nearly so much. For instance research shows that people with a high degree of self-empowerment or who are optimistic in the face of challenging demands react more positively to potentially stressful events[4]. In other words, some of the time, stress can be subjective. Those people who are able to reframe or perceive things in a positive light or have developed successful coping strategies minimise their stress arousal and can seem immune to stress triggers, whereas other people may flare up at the slightest provocation.

The net result of this variable response to stress is that it is often difficult to identify exactly which of the behaviours we may be witnessing is actually stress driven. A lot of stressed behaviour, if it is recognised at all, is mistaken for idiosyncratic behaviour or personal character traits.

But, whatever the underlying reason for the complacency in dealing with stress in organisations, it is costing us dear in terms of simple cash and lost performance.

Table 4, at the end of the chapter, provides a checklist of the type of costs to look for when stressed behaviour erupts in a working environment. The list helps identify precisely how, where even low-level stress exists, it has an insidious effect on every significant personal transaction or encounter between staff and management and between staff and customers and suppliers.

Stress disrupts flow

In particular, stress in the workplace obstructs the flow of communication between people, functions and departments and blocks the coherence required to generate a smooth integration of all the diverse factors in the management of any complex organisation.

Just as stress is known to obstruct the natural flow of activity and information in the individual brain physiology, so stress in the collective system also obstructs the flow of information and quality of group activity.

Table 2: Motivated functioning at work – Our natural brain state

Adaptable	Logical
Alert	Loyal
Awake	Light hearted
Attentive to advice and feedback	
Able to handle delegation	Mentally agile
Balanced - a sense of proportion	Non-critical
Caring	On top of everything
Coherent	Open to change and new ideas
Collaborative	Open to negative feedback
Committed	
Communicative	Peaceful
Compassionate	Present
Competent, professional	Proactive in problem-solving
Connected, centred	Productive
Conscientious, dedicated	Positive minded, upbeat
Creative	Proportionate sense of urgency
Curious	
	Quick to learn
Eager to learn new things	
Empathetic	Rational
Energetic	Reliable
Enterprising	Responsible
Enthusiastic	
Ethical	Sensible
	Sensitive to others
Finger on the pulse	Stimulated
Flexible	Sociable
Flow	Supportive
Focussed	Self-motivated
Friendly	Self confident
	Solution orientated
Happy	
Healthy	Tranquil
Honest	Trusting
Hopeful	Time efficient
Humorous	
	Vibrant
Imaginative	Vivacious
Initiative taking	
Inspired	Well balanced
	Willing

38

1.4 How to analyse the real cost of stress to your organisation

As an exercise, think of an instance where a stressful episode has arisen or is arising at work or with an organisation that you are familiar with. Then, using the information in table 3 and the checklist in table 4, reflect for a while on both the direct and <u>indirect</u> consequences that are being incurred for that organisation. For instance try and answer the following questions:

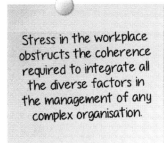

Stress in the workplace obstructs the coherence required to integrate all the diverse factors in the management of any complex organisation.

- What are the costs of the behaviour in terms of management and staff time?

- What other costs are there, measured in terms of money or other resources?

- What are the costs in terms of customer or client satisfaction?

- What are the costs in terms of negative relationships within the organisation? Did those negative relationships result in time-wasting conflicts that took mediation, negotiation and meetings to resolve?

- What are the costs in terms of the achievement of the organisations objectives?

1.5 The hidden cost of stress – Case examples

Mistakes – Long working hours are a powerful stress trigger especially when exacerbated by fluctuating night-shift patterns. As such, the typical routine of twelve-hour shifts in many health services can be debilitating to accurate and caring work. One research study indicates that 33% of medication errors in intensive care units are due to heavy workloads, stress and fatigue[5]. The consequences invariably lead to medical complications and so can be fatal in such a sensitive environment.

Accidents – A breakdown in family relationships is well known as a potent stressor. However, less ackowledged is the impact this type of domestic problem has in the workplace.

A case in point involved a van driver at a small manufacturing company. The man was experiencing a very stressful episode at home, as he was heading for a divorce. The stress distracted his attention enough to provoke three traffic accidents over a two-month period.

To make matters worse for him, he tried to hide the last accident from his managers. The resultant cost to his department amounted to £20,000 in increased insurance premiums on the fleet of vehicles and about £6,000 of management time spent identifying the culprit and going through disciplinary proceedings. Although the driver was a long-term employee with a previously exemplary track record he was fired for this episode.

Resentment – Dysfunctional management can often provoke stress unintentionally and this is very often experienced as some sort of anger. As an example, an experienced local authority office administrator became resentful and disgruntled when his prior IT experience and pro-active problem solving were casually taken for granted by managers who had co-opted him onto a newly-formed project team. In a fit of pique, the administrator withdrew his input from a series of project meetings making excuses that he was far too busy to attend. Without the benefit of his prior experience the project ran up unnecessary costs of approximately £140,000 in extra labour and IT consultants.

Reckless and unethical decision-making – Stress can make people behave unethically. In one case, fear of not meeting the monthly wage bill, led the managing director of a small loss-making printing company to submit invoices to his finance company for payment before the relevant work was even completed. Although in the short-term this trick enabled him to obtain some ready cash, it prevented him from invoicing for the full amounts due for the printing work. The drawback was that these premature invoices were prepared and submitted from the original job estimates and so did not take into account a variety of extras that accrued from client requests as the job passed through the protracted design and production process. What started out as a one off crisis management strategy became a monthly habit every time he had to meet the next wage bill.

Typically the extras being excluded from the invoicing amounted to approximately 3% of sales turnover. Effectively, this meant that the company failed to recoup something like £150,000 annually from the extra work carried out. As it happened this sum was roughly equivalent to the losses the company was experiencing at the time. When the finance company finally realised what was happening they suspended the finance facility. So not only did the managing director's rash and impulsive behaviour lose him essential revenue, the loss of this crucial financing facility put his company into liquidation.

Table 3: The many ways stress impacts functioning at work

Mood/ Emotion

Anger, hostility, aggression, rage
Fear, anxiety, panic
Stubbornness
Loss of empathy
Greed, possessiveness
Embarrassment
Irritation, annoyance
Gloom, despondency
Resentment
Sense of humour failure
Loss of enthusiasm, exhaustion, burnout
Mistrust
Fragile emotions (Sensitivity)
Impatience
Undue pessimism or optimism

Behaviour

Hypersensitivity to criticism
Ease of taking offence
Over ambition and competitiveness
Workaholic behaviour
Tyrannical or controlling behaviour
Evasiveness, prevarication
Procrastination, denial
Lack of commitment, apathy, lethargy
Malingering, slow working
Fickleness, changeability
Unreliability, recklessness
Mistakes, errors
Silliness, flippancy, petty point scoring
Unethical behaviour, dishonesty
Depersonalisation of clients, patients, etc.
Intolerance, self-righteousness
Disloyalty, secrecy, mild paranoia
Negativity towards customers, fellow
colleagues and the organisation
Negativity towards new initiatives
Impatience awaiting outcomes
Clumsiness and accidents
Lack of confidence, over caution
Crass overconfidence

Thinking

Stupidity, irrational thinking
Extreme, black and white thinking
Tunnel vision
Undue perfectionism, obsessiveness
Dullness in creative problem-solving
Short-term thinking
Quick-fix impulsive thinking
Poor judgement with relationships
Poor judgement with planning
Obsession with detail, loss of big picture
Inattention to detail, loss of focus, distraction,
forgetfulness and amnesia
Absentmindedness
Judgemental attitude, emotional criticism
Confusion as to priorities

Activity

Unnecessary interpersonal conflicts
Wasteful turf wars, politicising
Hidden agendas, sabotage
Attachments to the status quo
Obstruction to change
Chaotic activity, disorganisation
Absenteeism, sick days
Early retirement due to chronic stress- related
illnesses
Departure from the organisation
Overzealous or malicious compliance to rules
& regulations
Non-compliance with rules & regulations

Communication

Harsh and critical language, sarcasm
Tactlessness, course language
Guarded speech
Inability to listen and consult

Clinical

Insomnia, loss of libido
Onset of clinical depression
Psychosis, neurosis, paranoia
Substance abuse
Suicidal tendencies

Unnecessary conflict, chaotic activity and disorganisation – Stress can make people lose the ability to collaborate and communicate effectively. An example of this problem occurred when a production scheduler found himself failing to cope with competing and sometimes irreconcilable pressures that were largely outside of his control. The obstacles to the smooth flow of work included inadequate staffing for the different shifts he had to schedule for, last minute customer demands disrupting his plans, excessively tight deadlines and arbitrary interference into the planned schedule from senior management. Lack of understanding about his predicament by management meant he felt isolated and powerless to coordinate the efforts of the different production departments.

As time went on he became increasingly aggressive and uncooperative towards colleagues in other departments and his language became famously caustic. So much so that colleagues and subordinates were reluctant to work with him. This, in turn, led to fractious behaviour and lack of cooperation between the various departmental heads. Before the situation was resolved the resulting mistakes and inefficiencies added about £350,000 in extra agency staff, express delivery costs to compensate for delays in production, scrap rates and rework.

Time off for sickness – Prolonged stress is seriously bad for your health, yet is still largely ignored by many busy executives as a valid risk to avoid. A project manager at a shop-fitting firm was regularly under extreme pressure to meet tight deadlines. The job involved long hours and usually meant working away from home for weeks at a time. After years of this gruelling regime he suffered from a heart attack and had to take months off for surgery and convalescence. The firm suffered unacceptable delays to their projects, as other members of the team tried to fill in for his absence. The immediate cost to the business was the loss of a valuable client and significant extra costs in salaries and overtime.

Stress can be infectious – Dealing with people who are in a stressed state can confuse our ability to think and communicate. As an example people ringing into an ambulance emergency call centre are often in a highly-stressed state if not in actual panic. This means that the callers' thinking and ability to communicate are impaired which makes obtaining coherent information in the limited time available very difficult. This difficulty is further worsened if the circumstances are harrowing enough to trigger the operator's own stress response.

Under this sort of pressure it is easy for things to go wrong, such as operators despatching ambulances unnecessarily for less acute calls or sending vehicles to the wrong address. When this happens scarce resources are deployed to low priority patients while critically ill patients are left waiting for help or are ferried into hospital by police cars[6]. In addition, prolonged exposure to this sort of stressful encounter has its own detrimental effect on the operators' health and helps account for the high level of time off due to sickness in this profession.

Fatal loss of business momentum – Prolonged stress can often result in depression and a consequent loss of enthusiasm and energy.

A good example of the debilitating impact of depression occurred in a small start-up business. The entrepreneur was fully engaged in developing his business but was working from home to save money on overheads. To help reduce costs further, at a time when there was still no cash coming in, he took in a lodger. After a few months he complained that his enthusiasm for his big new idea was waning and that he was gradually losing direction and momentum. Despite tangible success with prospective blue-chip clients he reached the point where he was ready to pack the whole enterprise in.

As it turned out, this depression stemmed from an on-going conflict he was experiencing in his own home with his new tenant. Frequent and largely unresolved disputes over late rent payments, apportionment of bills and noisy late night behaviour threatened his feeling of security, privacy and his need for a healthy routine. The resultant on-going tension and tiredness precipitated the depression. The problem was instantly cured once he was aware of the cause of his malaise and had asked his tenant to leave.

Mistakes and depression – The senior management at a busy print firm had invested in an expensive new gluing machine for the finishing department. The objective was to help speed up the binding operation. Unfortunately during the procurement process, they failed to confer with the finishing manager about how he was to integrate this new machine into the overall operation. As a result, they set him a budget that only allowed for one person per shift to be trained up on the new machine. What they did not know was that the actual need was for two or three trained operators. Inevitably the lack of skilled labour led to delays and bottlenecks in scheduling whenever one of the trained operators was away or involved with other machines.

The stress of trying to reconcile deadlines and conflicting work schedules led to the finishing manager trying to compensate for his 'failure' to cope by overworking. He gradually became more and more stressed.

The result was a series of sub-optimum decisions and costly mistakes. Apart from the risk of losing a major client who spent £800,000 per year with the company, the extra costs per annum for running the machine inefficiently were estimated at £25,000, a figure that was way over the cost of training three more operators. Feeling unable to cope and being increasingly criticised for 'underperforming' the finishing manager was eventually laid off sick with depression. His absence created even more strain on the department and accelerated the falling standards of customer service.

Table 4: Current state cost analysis of stress

	Indirect	Direct	Quantifiable or measurable as:
Customer			
Lost sales, lost customers			
Low customer satisfaction			
Rejects or complaints from customers			
Reduced repeat business			
Damaged reputation with clients & referrers			
Poor quality			
Labour			
Absenteeism and sick leave			
Poor discipline/ disciplinary hearings			
Additional labour hours, overtime			
Extra training expenses			
Low morale, attrition of quality staff			
More temporary labour, agency fees			
Production			
Lower throughput and capacity, delays			
Outsourcing production			
Slower throughput, disruption to schedules			
High Work in Progress			
Shorter equipment life			
High equipment downtime & maintenance			
Increased materials & consumables costs			
Higher tooling costs			
Higher transportation of materials			
Higher movement of people			
Scrap, errors, mistakes and rework			
Overproduction, duplicated effort/ handling			
Unnecessary paperwork			
Energy & space wastage			
General			
Litigation/ compensation/ insurance claims			
Damaged relationships, cost of conflict			
Low gross margins and productivity			
Management time sorting problems out			
Time wasting doing extra tasks			
Increased administration/ supervision			
Irrational health and safety compliance			
Unnecessary accidents, breakages, injuries			
Increased insurance premiums			

Chapter Two

The need to demystify the term 'stress'

Modern neuroscience is clearing up a number of common misunderstandings about stress. In particular we have a much clearer definition as to exactly what stress is and what actually triggers a stress response.

2.1 A powerful new organising principle - The "human givens" perspective

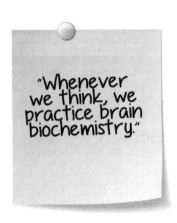

A wealth of new insights into the brain gained by modern research have led to a new concept in psychology known as the "human givens" approach.

This new approach delivers consistently successful interventions in the psychotherapy arena. For instance, using this approach, therapists are now able to handle mental health problems such as depression, phobias and post-traumatic stress disorder (PTSD) particularly effectively and in very much shorter time spans than in the past. Time spans measured in hours and days not weeks, months and even years of therapy.

The relevance to management is that these breakthroughs in the human givens treatment of mental ill health are based precisely on a clearer understanding of stress and the impact that stress has on thinking and behaviour. As such these insights are proving to be a seriously powerful organising principle that can help optimise the design of management structures, modify management functions and determine management styles in a way that will improve morale and all round performance throughout any organisation.

2.2 A new working definition of stress

The human givens approach defines stress in the context of two factors:

1. A range of physical and emotional needs such as security, being part of a wider group and a need for attention

2. The innate resources used to meet those needs such as our rational left brain, imagination, and communication skills

(See table 5 in chapter 3 for a full list of these human needs and table 6 in chapter 4 for a list of human resources).

To quote the authors of the human givens approach:

"We are all born with a rich natural inheritance – a partially-formed mind containing a genetic treasure house of innate knowledge patterns. These patterns appear as physical and emotional needs that must be satisfactorily met if our minds are to unfold and develop to their fullest potential. How they connect with the world, and unfold in it, determines our own individual character, the clarity of our perceptions, our emotional health and happiness, and that of our family – as well as the maturity and humanity of the society we create around us." Joe Griffin, Ivan Tyrrell, Human Givens.[1]

The three basic triggers to the stress response

Leading on from this understanding about the existence of biological needs and innate resources we can now be certain that there are three basic situations that trigger the instinctive physical reaction or trance-like state known as the stress response. Basically we are liable to get stressed when we:

1. Are unable to meet one or more of our physical or emotional needs, or
2. Believe, perceive or imagine that we are unable to meet our biological needs, or
3. Are unable to utilise our innate resources to get our needs met.

Failing to nurture or provide for these human needs not only induces stress-driven poor performance, but these needs can also expand into destructive impulses. We can be consumed by a ravaging desire for "wants" rather than a rational pursuit of our legitimate "needs". These subliminal urges can then contribute to the range of sub-optimum behaviours seen earlier in table 3.

The human brain is designed to problem solve

An important point here is that normally and when we are otherwise healthy, we rise to everyday challenges to meet our own needs. But, when we start to feel that we cannot cope, because we feel too overwhelmed by a challenge, or we feel unsafe, undervalued, bored or perhaps purposeless in our work, that's when our brains can start to experience the stress response. And when this happens we can quickly switch into an instinctive survival mode and start to act impulsively.

Unfortunately although our instinctive survival mode serves us well in physically harsh and hostile situations it is less than helpful in a modern work environment. Unhappily, the ancient mechanisms that panic our bodies for "fight or flight" in the wild, still create similar, albeit milder, trance states and mental and physical sensations when the threat is nowhere near as dire or immediate.

2.3 The mechanics of stress

Although mild, the mechanics driving these sensations are exactly similar to those that drive us into the extreme forms of stress such as panic or rage. For this reason, it is useful to know what happens when we are confronted with a really terrifying situation.

Diagram 4

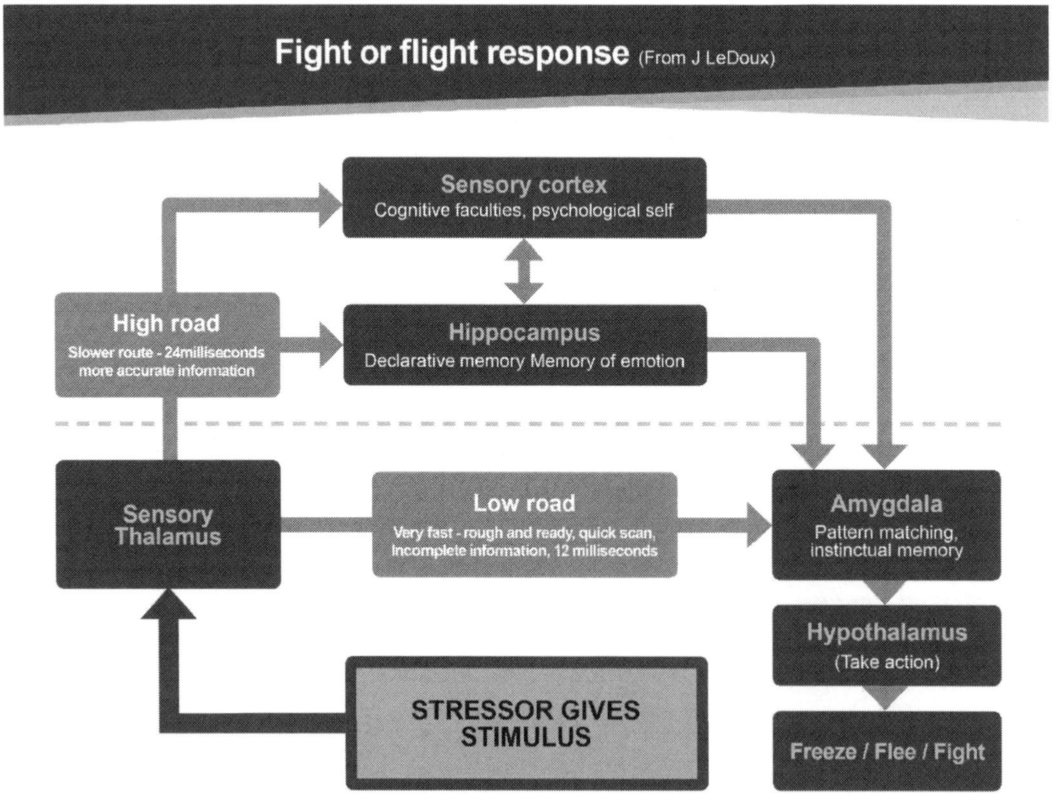

Fight or flight response (From J LeDoux)

```
                    Sensory cortex
                    Cognitive faculties, psychological self

  High road                Hippocampus
  Slower route - 24milliseconds    Declarative memory Memory of emotion
  more accurate information

  Sensory        Low road                    Amygdala
  Thalamus       Very fast - rough and ready, quick scan,   Pattern matching,
                 Incomplete information, 12 milliseconds    instinctual memory

                                             Hypothalamus
                                             (Take action)

           STRESSOR GIVES
           STIMULUS                          Freeze / Flee / Fight
```

In essence, the human brain is programmed to react and function instinctively or emotionally in times of danger[2]. When one of our senses perceives a threat it is actually recognised as such by a part of the brain called the amygdala. This tiny organ embedded in the centre of the brain is a powerful early warning system. It is constantly on the alert for life-threatening events through a rather rough and ready pattern-matching process. Basically the amygdala stores instinctive memories of past threats and traumas in the form of basic patterns and its role is to identify similar patterns as and when they arise.

Diagram 5

The A-P-E-T model of stressed thinking[4]

Whenever we think, we practise brain biochemistry. As such, just like any other mental process, the stress response is a biochemical event. During the stress response, the amygdala triggers an emotional arousal (biochemical event) by automatically preparing the body for an immediate, dynamic and physical reaction to a potential threat. And this happens before the threat has been bought to our conscious awareness. This emotional arousal is well known as the fight or flight response. In the process a number of normal and high value faculties of the brain such as empathy and rational thinking are progressively shut down (See table 3). The higher the emotional arousal the more our field of response is constrained by primitive emotional thinking patterns.

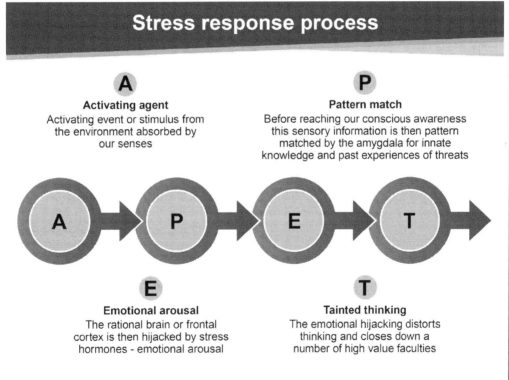

Stress response process

A
Activating agent
Activating event or stimulus from the environment absorbed by our senses

P
Pattern match
Before reaching our conscious awareness this sensory information is then pattern matched by the amygdala for innate knowledge and past experiences of threats

E
Emotional arousal
The rational brain or frontal cortex is then hijacked by stress hormones - emotional arousal

T
Tainted thinking
The emotional hijacking distorts thinking and closes down a number of high value faculties

At the point the amygdala perceives a situation that pattern matches with a previously stressful incident it automatically fires our body into immediate overdrive by first overriding the frontal cortex. Crucially, in the context of a study on the impact of stress on performance, this process occurs before the information reaches our conscious awareness (see diagram 4). As a result we basically slip into a trance state. Our logical, intellectual and rational faculties are immediately and progressively diminished according to the level and intensity of the perceived threat, releasing our primitive, unbridled, emotional side. The resultant change in our thinking process is summed up neatly by the A-P-E-T model in diagram 5.

In other words, we become emotionally aroused and this high emotional arousal swamps our ability to think straight. This process, sometimes called 'hijacking'[3], is designed to help us take more impulsive and dynamic action and so prepare us to either attack or runaway. Hence the term, often used to describe stress, is the fight or flight response.

Broadly speaking, we experience this mechanism emotionally as either anger or fear although the body also experiences a full range of changes to make us ready for action (See diagram 6).

Diagram 6

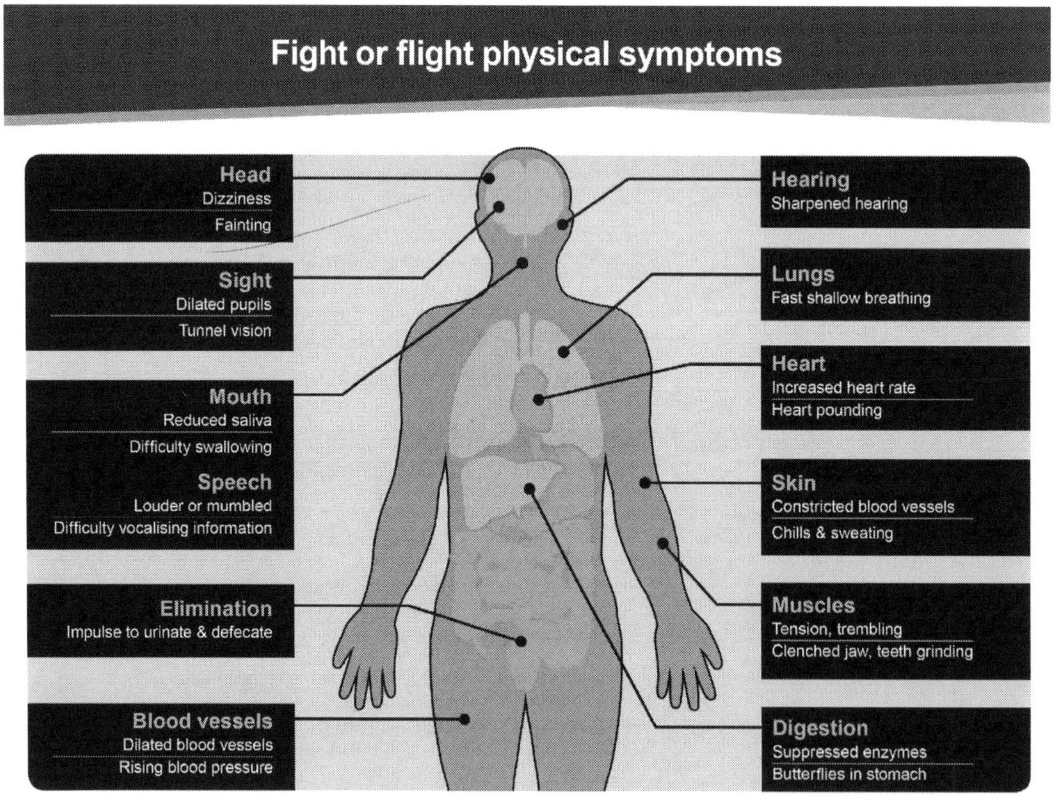

Fight or flight physical symptoms

Head Dizziness / Fainting	**Hearing** Sharpened hearing
Sight Dilated pupils / Tunnel vision	**Lungs** Fast shallow breathing
Mouth Reduced saliva / Difficulty swallowing	**Heart** Increased heart rate / Heart pounding
Speech Louder or mumbled / Difficulty vocalising information	**Skin** Constricted blood vessels / Chills & sweating
Elimination Impulse to urinate & defecate	**Muscles** Tension, trembling / Clenched jaw, teeth grinding
Blood vessels Dilated blood vessels / Rising blood pressure	**Digestion** Suppressed enzymes / Butterflies in stomach

So, under extreme threats, we are left with no aptitude for negotiation or diplomacy. There are no shades of grey, no planning or analysis about deciding what to do. The body-mind kicks into action with a flood of stress hormones or bio-chemicals such as cortisol, adrenalin and so on. These hormones gear the muscle tissues, blood circulation, oxygen flow, heartbeat, and even our elimination system for a massively strenuous and life-saving effort.

What would typically follow in a real life-threatening event is that, in the process of running away or fighting for your life, all these stress bio-chemicals in the system are burnt up and flushed out through the normal process of strenuous activity. That is if you are lucky to survive the event. But herein lies one of the problems.

A violent response to stressful stimuli is not helpful

Today, in a working or business environment, most of the time, the stressful stimuli that we experience provoke only a low-grade stress response. Happily, not many of us are actually experiencing life-threatening events at work. We are simply being confronted by situations where subtle emotional needs are threatened, or where we perceive we cannot cope, or where we perceive or believe our needs are under threat. In the latter cases it is this perception or belief that gives rise to our stress response, not the actuality of the circumstances.

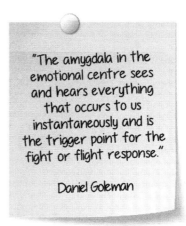

"The amygdala in the emotional centre sees and hears everything that occurs to us instantaneously and is the trigger point for the fight or flight response."

Daniel Goleman

Generally this type of low-grade stress is experienced not as raw panic and destructive rage but more as fears, worries, anxiety, resentments, doubts, antagonisms, irritations and so on. In other words, in today's working environment the typical "threats" we experience do not warrant violent and exhilarating action. Instead we have to adopt a subtler response and *find more cerebral means to resolve stressful situations*. The last thing to do is to give in to rampant, black or white emotions or resort to some sort of spirited physical reaction.

2.4 How low-grade stress impairs productive capacity

Now, these stressful or perceived stressful situations might well be described as low-grade, but the problem with them is that they are also widely prevalent. In fact the reality of everyday life in so many working environments is that stressful threats to our emotional wellbeing seem interminable.

A state of stress arousal can continue indefinitely

Not only are the stressors sometimes interminable, the fact that there is no dynamic or physical way to take evasive action means we can get stuck in a state of emotional arousal. For some people this state of arousal can continue almost indefinitely. There is a twofold significance of this unnatural and long-term state of stress.

Firstly, this type of stress arousal diminishes our mental and emotional functioning for as long as we are experiencing it. All the while we are in this semi-trance state we are not acting rationally and spontaneously to the reality of the situation around us. Instead we may be instigating a pre-programmed stress response to traumas and stressful situations long past; situations that are no longer relevant to the current circumstances.

Secondly, long-term or chronic stress damages our health. Prolonged stress can lead to a number of conditions such as:

- High blood pressure
- Heart problems
- Depression
- The suppression of the immune system with stress even being implicated in the growth of tumours[5]

Diagram 7

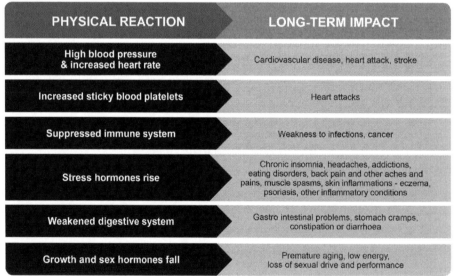

PHYSICAL REACTION	LONG-TERM IMPACT
High blood pressure & increased heart rate	Cardiovascular disease, heart attack, stroke
Increased sticky blood platelets	Heart attacks
Suppressed immune system	Weakness to infections, cancer
Stress hormones rise	Chronic insomnia, headaches, addictions, eating disorders, back pain and other aches and pains, muscle spasms, skin inflammations - eczema, psoriasis, other inflammatory conditions
Weakened digestive system	Gastro intestinal problems, stomach cramps, constipation or diarrhoea
Growth and sex hormones fall	Premature aging, low energy, loss of sexual drive and performance

Chronic stress has also been shown to harm a part of the brain known as the hippocampus by reducing the number of synaptic connections between communicating neurons. This reduction in communication between neurons effectively results in memory loss and this loss can be permanent.

As we have seen the root cause to stress is the actual or perceived threat to our emotional and physical needs. So the next step is to identify what these needs are. When handled correctly these needs also provide managers with a powerful motivational tool. The next chapter reviews our main emotional needs and the implications of these needs for management and leadership.

Chapter Three

A new psychological model based on human needs

3.1 Basic overview

Management theorists have understood the significance of emotional needs for a while now. Elton Mayo was perhaps the first to touch on the idea of certain social needs being an important causal factor in work performance with his studies at the Western Electric Company's Hawthorne Plant in Chicago during the 1920s.

But the concept really got off the ground in 1959, when Abraham Maslow's hierarchy of needs made the idea famous[1]. Since that time, Maslow's version has become standard knowledge for any aspiring manager and leader.

Similarly the concept of two different sets of factors that cause either dissatisfaction or motivation at work have become well established in management circles since Frederick Herzberg's research in the late 1950s[2]. Herzberg also helped establish the idea that people are intrinsically motivated. The implication being that leaders don't have to motivate their people, they should just avoid de-motivating them.

Importantly though, however good these theories were at the time, research has moved on since then. In particular the "human givens" model of emotional needs has built on the numerous advances in neuroscience, research-based psychology and clinical experience that have developed since Maslow and Herzberg's ground- breaking work.

Maslow's original hierarchy depicted a set of five needs. These included physiological needs, safety (security), social, esteem (ego) and self-actualisation. (Incidentally John Adair has added in a sixth level, that of transcending the self, a concept that he believes Maslow also adopted later on in his life[3]).

"The freedom to fulfil our own needs can inspire levels of individual performance that collectively transforms organisational performance."

The human givens model has built on this concept

and its catalogue of needs is another step in the evolution of our knowledge of human nature.

3.2 Stress and high performance - two sides of the same coin

The concept of emotional needs enables us to see that stress and high performance are two sides of the same coin.

The downside: Where our needs are not met or where they are threatened, or even perceived to be threatened, then the debilitating stress arousal can be provoked.

The upside: On the other hand where we can freely engage in the pursuit of our legitimate needs at work, we find it wholly motivating. Our enthusiasm soars, our commitment and loyalty becomes reinforced and the organisation has access to our full range of mental and emotional resources.

Table 5:
Our physical and emotional needs as defined by the human givens approach to psychotherapy [4] (See 3.3 for fuller explanations)

- Security – including safe territory to develop and work in
- A good degree of autonomy and control over our immediate environment
- Emotional connection to others
- A degree of status or recognition within the social group
- Some sort of meaning in life often associated with having an overall purpose bigger than yourself
- Regularity of routine

- Attention including the need both to give and receive it from at least one significant adult in our lives
- Enjoyment, friendship and fun including peak experiences
- The need for a challenge and to problem solve
- A sense of achievement and a feeling of competence
- A degree of privacy to reflect and think and share intimacies
- Close connection to a wider community

Significantly, several human needs also work on a reciprocal basis. The best example is the need for attention, which we can hardly achieve as adults without also providing it for someone else. Similarly, if we want to meet our need for feeling part of a community, we also need to embrace the others in our host group. Many of the peak experiences we enjoy involve participation with others and so on.

3.3 Using the concept of biological needs – the human givens - to motivate improved performance

In a leadership role it is best to use a piecemeal approach when gauging how to convert needs from a negative stress factor to a positive motivational drive. Where stress exists in your organisation, review the situation in the context of each need in turn and identify which ones are not being met. Once you find the gap, where a need is not being met, it is usually relatively easy to find a remedy.

The following review of the human givens' needs provides useful material to help you recognise ways to avoid or remove stress in the working environment and so motivate improved performance.

Diagram 8

Human Givens - Our key emotional needs

3.3.1 Security - including safe territory to develop and work in

In the context of organisational leadership, the need for security involves freedom from fear of a range of potential threats at work. These threats include redundancy, technological change, major changes to work processes, chaotic routines, physical intimidation and bullying, arbitrary adverse decisions

56

affecting one's personal welfare, insensitive autocratic management behaviour, simple physical safety and so on.

However, this need for security extends beyond just the individual need.

Human beings have an innate sense that their own security is closely interrelated with their host group. This manifests as a natural loyalty and a desire to collaborate with group problem solving (See chapter 4.3.10). Where people's ability to make a group contribution is impeded they can become uneasy. Instinctively people become aware that the group security is subtly threatened in such situations.

3.3.2 The need for attention, both to give and receive it

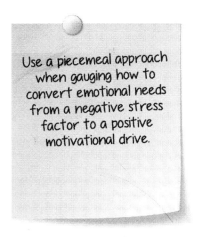

Use a piecemeal approach when gauging how to convert emotional needs from a negative stress factor to a positive motivational drive.

The need for attention involves the need to both give and receive it. In the management context this need was identified as far back as the 1920s during the Hawthorne[5] research experiments mentioned above.

Over the eons we have evolved as "social animals", as we have to a large extent depended on collaboration with one another to meet our physical and emotional needs. Over time, this interdependence has literally been hardwired into our psychophysiology and this is manifested in our innate ability to both give attention to other human beings and our need to receive it from others.

When we lack attention from other human beings, this stress registers in our physiology on an emotional level as "loneliness". A feeling of loneliness is nature's cue that we are not getting this need met.

Scientists now recognise that being isolated from friends, or feeling lonely can be as harmful to our health as smoking and can be a sure predictor of ill health[6]. Loneliness leads to higher cortisol levels, weakens the immune system, raises blood pressure, upsets sleep patterns and so increases the risk of depression[7].

Importantly, if we don't satisfy this need to interact regularly and fruitfully with others, then the stress we experience can manifest in a wide variety of behavioural and other problems.

Psychotherapists have known for a long time that the simple act of giving close attention to a patient can help to relax them. The very act of giving attention is healing to a certain extent in its own right.

Attention as motivator

The therapeutic power of giving attention is an opportunity for leaders to utilise listening skills. Lending an attentive ear in the right circumstances can diffuse heated conflict, act as a persuader and motivate people to greater efforts.

Also in management terms the need for attention has important implications for the necessary feedback required to motivate people.

In terms of motivating higher performance, it is well known that the most effective feedback is positive feedback. But it is perhaps this need for attention that determines that 'zero feedback' is the most debilitating in terms of motivating people and influencing their performance. For this reason, providing 'zero feedback' is more harmful than providing negative feedback in the context of relationship building.

Incidentally part of this attention-need means that avoidance of conflict can also be harmful to performance. Conflict, where handled through collaboration or group participation in a problem-solving process, can allow this natural human tendency of giving and receiving attention to enable a mutually satisfactory solution.

The 150 rule

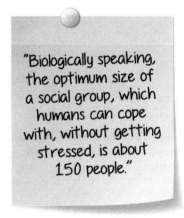

"Biologically speaking, the optimum size of a social group, which humans can cope with, without getting stressed, is about 150 people."

An important subset of the need for attention in organisational structures is the 'Law of 150'[8]. It appears that, biologically speaking the optimum size of a social group, which humans can cope with without getting stressed, is about 150 people. Beyond this figure, the necessary interchange of attention between people that is required to maintain good mental health (and therefore good performance) is weakened.

The larger the unit, the more the benefits of loyalty, cohesiveness, close community support, and co-operation are increasingly lost. (See chapter 7, section 3 for further details).

This fact has major implications for organisations that are structured in large work units. The 150-rule may be a big part of the reason why large organisations become so sclerotic and bureaucratic.

3.3.3 Autonomy and control

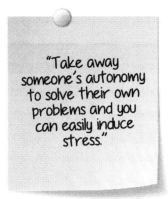

"Take away someone's autonomy to solve their own problems and you can easily induce stress."

People require a sense of autonomy and control over their immediate environment and relevant tasks. This need is of profound importance to management thinking and organisational design, as when met it is powerfully motivating[9].

From infancy onwards, and unless hindered, we progressively develop the means to handle and enjoy a high degree of independence; by doing things for ourselves we become more self-sufficient as we grow up. We could go so far as to say that part of growing up *is the desire* and ability to attain a level of control over our environment and take on more responsibility for our own lives. Where our independence and freedom is curtailed, it goes against the grain and this gives rise to anxiety and depression.

This is a common experience at work where we are habitually excluded from the decision-making process about activities that directly affect us. The same applies even when we are simply denied relevant information about our own situation and the situation of our social or work group.

Addressing this need is of particular importance if you are leading a group in a

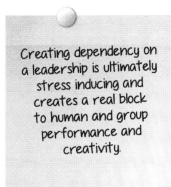

Creating dependency on a leadership is ultimately stress inducing and creates a real block to human and group performance and creativity.

rapidly changing environment. As such, meeting this need has important implications for change management practices (See chapter 8, section 1 – Achieving buy-in for strategic change).

The key point to remember here is that once we feel we have an element of control we feel more positive about our ability to cope with challenges and change. This feeling of control in itself can have a significant impact on our actual ability to cope and consequently has an impact on our performance.

3.3.4 The need for a close connection to a wider community

The human race has survived as a species by evolving into highly sociable, collaborative, problem-solving mammals. We have grown to become dependent on our respective groups for individual survival and so much of our fulfilment in life stems from group involvement. This is so much so that this need for group membership and active participation in the group can have a determining effect on our health.

> "As a rule of thumb, if you belong to no groups but decide to join one, you cut your risk of dying over the next year in half."
>
> Robert Putnam[10]

In this sense, _loyalty to our host group is a natural survival mechanism_. This loyalty can remain even though the group may be under threat and often loyalty is actually reinforced under these circumstances[11]. Despite this, any threat to the group will have some impact on our own stress levels as instinctively we become aware that our own individual survival is also threatened.

Reflecting on this point I was struck by a finding from a UK Mass Observation Survey carried out at the start of the Second World War. One journal entry made during the very first week after the declaration of war referred to the effect of collective stress. During this first week no other adverse event had occurred, no bombs had been dropped and as yet no British lives lost but, nonetheless, people were assimilating the dire predicament the nation had just got itself into. At this time there was the simple journal entry "Everyone seems to have aged ten years this week" (premature ageing is a symptom of chronic stress).

Equally, it isn't just a threat to the host group that is stressful. Any perceived threat to our membership of our host group or isolation from it is also stressful. Examples of this predicament are threats of redundancy or simple exclusion or non-participation from group contact. Similarly, so far as people are prevented from participating in running an organisation, they tend to loosen their feeling of connection to it. This exclusion from active participation can have a consequential impact on stress levels and performance, often in the form of apathy, slow working and acts of irresponsibility.

> Enforcing equality creates stress, as it cuts across our need to feel valued for our specific and unique contribution and our unique sense of being who we are.

3.3.5 A degree of social status within the group

The need for status implies being given appreciation for who we are and for our contribution to the common good. This need is closely connected to our need to be part of a host group and our need for attention. We have a need to feel valued by the group and the people around us, so motivational leaders will show clear recognition of our worth or value to the organisation that we belong to.

Importantly, status in this context doesn't necessarily mean having a title or a position of authority. Even more significantly this need for a degree of status does not mean having to have "equality" with others. Interestingly, although the desire for equality has become a driving force in political policy, this seems to have little validity from a psychological perspective.

Whereas equality in respect of the law may be important from the point of view of ensuring security and recognition of status within society, from a psychological perspective people simply do not have a "need" to be socially equal to others.

In this sense the political emphasis on enforcing equality creates stress, as it subtly cuts across our need to feel valued for our specific and unique contribution and our unique sense of being who we are.

The biological need for social status is perhaps the determining factor as to why, during the course of a reprimand, it is best to avoid judgemental criticism of a person's worth or value. (See chapter 9, section 4 about the pivotal role of management support and encouragement).

3.3.6 A degree of privacy to reflect and think and share intimacies

Even at work people still need private time and space to self-reflect and think about their own needs as well as just think about their work or the business. For a leader the need for some degree of privacy is essential.

Positive introspection can reduce stress levels. Techniques such as a "journaling" where one can explore in writing thoughts and feelings about life and events all help to develop critical self-awareness, clarify problems and get life into perspective[12]. As such, facilitating an appropriate amount of introspection improves operational effectiveness.

Without adequate private time and a safe space to reflect and introspect, people fail to acquire the essential capacity for objectivity and learning. And this includes the receptivity to other people's ideas and observations, an important feature of both good teamwork and effective leadership.

"In quietness and confidence shall be your strength."

Isaiah

Reflection is also important in order to learn from experience. We may not be able to control external events but we can at least control our own state of mind. We can achieve such control by long-term practice of inner reflection. Such self-reflection can also help leaders recognise the awful truth that they don't have all the answers.

Cultivating this type of humility can be very empowering for the rest of the team. The open, or at least tacit acknowledgement by the leader that he or she does not know everything helps break the team's dependency on the leader for answers. Such an attitude makes the rest of the group feel that they can make a valuable contribution too. In turn this reinforces three other needs, the need for autonomy, a feeling of competence and a degree of status.

Healthy introspection helps:

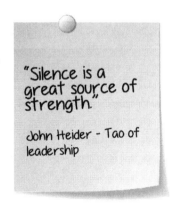

"Silence is a great source of strength."

John Heider - Tao of leadership

- Develop self-confidence and self-analysis
- Master the fear of uncertainty and ambiguity that is a significant driver in rushed and impulsive decision-making (See chapter 11, section 7 on competent decision-making)
- Foster both social and self-awareness
- Hone creativity
- Cultivate intuition

There is one other important outcome of successful introspection. Managers who practice this are far more likely to adopt a better work-life balance. And this is so crucial to attaining <u>sustainable</u> success.

The implication here is that of course all this takes time and space and a degree of privacy. As a leader, taking time out from your hectic schedule and building into your working routine (or for that matter the routine of your co-workers) some private time to think and reflect will harvest countless benefits.

3.3.7 The need for a challenge, achievement and a feeling of competence

People need a challenge to exercise their rational brains. Human beings are hard wired to be able to problem solve as an instinctive survival mechanism and this is why we also have the need for a consequent feeling of achievement and competence. So, importantly, from both a therapeutic point of view and a management perspective, one of the factors required for maintaining a healthy and active human brain is actually having problems to solve. Take away people's autonomy to solve their own problems and you can easily induce stress.

This stress manifests in a wide range of symptoms such as a dissatisfaction with life, lethargy, greed, resentment and even anger and depression. The physical brain actually needs new challenges to keep it healthy. Cut off the supply of challenges and it is like cutting off the oxygen supply. The brain's neurons literally atrophy when the brain isn't being stretched[13].

According to Matthew Crawford, the more concrete and tangible the challenge, the more therapeutic it is. In his book[14], Crawford makes the case that competence in manual skills, as opposed to purely intellectual ones or the usual office skills, actually makes you feel and behave better. And part of this satisfaction derives from the sense of autonomy and usefulness achieved by doing something with your hands that accomplishes something practical and useful to others. Without the ability to actually make or fix things we tend to become somewhat passive and dependent. Learning to meet rigorous practical challenges with measurable outcomes, including having to deal at times with what he calls "unambiguous failure", is necessary to hone our sense of practical reality about things we have the power to control and things we don't.

People get a real sense of flow and fulfilment from taking and overcoming challenges. You have probably heard people talk of being 'in the zone' or of having a feeling of bliss or euphoria, and even ecstasy when overcoming insuperable odds, finally mastering a new skill or successfully uncovering an eternal truth. Hopefully you will have experienced these feelings yourself. These feelings are all nature's biochemical pay-off for meeting the need for a challenge.

This human given has far reaching implications for top-down command and control style leadership. Creating dependency on a leadership is ultimately stress inducing and creates a real block to human and group performance and creativity.

3.3.8 Some sort of meaning in life

Closely related to the need for stretch and challenge from the human givens' perspective is the need for meaning.

"Neurobiology, psychology and sociology all show that there are inner patterns of perception that seek to connect with the greater world and, when they do, allow for greater refinement and progress as human beings. ... Life always seems more significant when we stretch ourselves" - Joe Griffin and Ivan Tyrrell[15].

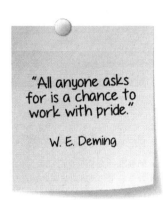

"All anyone asks for is a chance to work with pride."

W. E. Deming

As such, having something significant or meaningful to do at work can go a long way to satisfy this need for meaning.

The search for meaning is integral to us and when we find it, anxiety is reduced. For instance, according to new research from the University of Toronto a belief in God can help block anxiety and minimize stress. The researchers have discovered distinct brain differences between believers and non-believers[16].

But in the human givens' perspective, the search for meaning is not limited to a belief in the divine or being stretched. A sense of meaning can also be satisfied to some degree from supporting or sharing the wider goals or values of the organisation, group or society.

For healthy individuals it is about more than just money

Our core experience as a social mammal makes us dependant on a wide ranging interactivity with others for survival. The instinctive understanding about this dependency means that healthy, well-balanced people find a greater fulfilment knowing that their work involves a benefit to the wider good.

Dr W. E. Deming, the famous quality guru, recognised that even the pursuit of total quality or continuous improvement is stress reducing. In this way, the quest for customer-focussed total quality can provide a level of meaning in the workplace that is truly motivational for those involved[17].

Basically, to satisfy this need, work has got to be about more than just money.

A certain amount of money is required to help satisfy other basic needs such as security and so on. But, much beyond that level, pure moneymaking may be indulging our egos, fantasies and vanity. So, working for an organisation that is just obsessed about the "bottom-line" and nothing else is ultimately dissatisfying for healthy individuals.

The stress engendered by this dissatisfaction manifests in a variety of ways including the sub-optimum performance of a wide number of the less qualified staff and the excessive greed of senior executives accruing vast salaries and bonuses.

Many observers and leaders have testified to the point that for significant meaning to be generated in a working environment, profit alone cannot be the prime motivating force of the organisation. As an example, Archbishop John Sentamu, states that in order to satisfy the sense of meaning, profit has to "have a purpose beyond itself"[18].

In this context, public sector organisations should have an innate advantage over purely commercial concerns as their raison d'être imbues them with essential meaning for their employees. This is one of the reasons that cost-cutting in public services can provoke so much anger. The employees are not just doing the work for money. Part of their daily motivation is the belief that their work is meaningful and making a genuine contribution to the common good. Where cuts are seen to endanger this purpose they threaten this sense of meaning and provoke the stress response.

Whether private or public sector, a greater sense of meaning can be instilled at work if the leadership takes a more holistic view of their responsibilities as managers and a more holistic view of the objectives of the organisation. For teamwork to fulfil the true meaning of the word, it has to embrace more than the collection of all the parts in a narrowly focussed venture. To avoid being alien to the human condition, teamwork must be infused with a sense of wholeness in that the objectives of the team embrace the wide range of human needs. In this sense, true teamwork spontaneously upholds life-supporting values both via the team's objectives and the activity of everyone within it.

We are becoming slaves to our work

In direct violation of the need for meaning, the profit motive in modern commercial enterprises, especially the large PLCs, and the financial sector has become paramount. But it is not just an obsession with profit that violates this emotional need. Even in the public sector narrow goal-driven operational procedures can easily displace this wider sense of meaning.

As an example, in the UK thousands of NHS nurses are routinely working twelve-hour shifts that risk overwhelming them with tiredness. Such fatigue impairs the ability to collaborate effortlessly with colleagues, maintain focus, think straight, access a memory bank crammed with clinical knowledge and empathize with patient needs. When they get home it is no better, emotional and physical exhaustion from work degenerates family and social relationships and often precludes participation, at a satisfying and nourishing level, in family and community responsibilities.

Over time, this erosion of the core competencies to do the job and the growing disconnection from the wider host group saps the vocational meaning traditionally associated with the nursing profession. Dragging oneself through this sort of hell, the question inevitably arises 'if I can't do the job properly what is the point of doing it at all?' Perhaps this is why staff turnover in vocational professions such as nursing, teaching, the police and social services is so high.

Even in the narrow context of seeing work purely as an economic activity, we are slaves to our economy rather than the economy being our servant for the purpose of addressing our material needs. If you disagree with this proposition, ask yourself why it takes the average family the best part of thirty years, or most of their working lives, simply to buy a house to live in. This cannot be anyone's definition of a free society or for that matter a wealthy or healthy one.

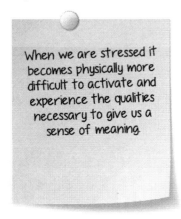

When we are stressed it becomes physically more difficult to activate and experience the qualities necessary to give us a sense of meaning.

Shifting this emphasis from pure profit or other narrow goals to wholeness is within the remit of every leader. Such a shift will help provide a greater and wider meaning to life at work. The payoff is that stress levels will go down. Ironically, shifting the emphasis away from a narrow definition of productivity and cost saving to wholeness can only enhance individual motivation, commitment and performance. The outcome enhances organizational success.

How the stress response physically impacts our sense of meaning

To be fully functioning, the prefrontal cortex, that part of the brain that differentiates us from the rest of the animal kingdom and makes us human, needs to have a high level of "brainwave coherence". In this context, coherence means there is a highly dynamic integration of activity between the different brain cells.

A good degree of brainwave coherence is required for sincere motivation, self-control and competent decision-making. But brain wave coherence is also needed to perform the complex functions needed to develop meaning. These functions include:

- Having a true sense of self,
- Spontaneously holding to genuine values,
- Thinking conceptually
- Undertaking moral reasoning.

Basically when we are stressed the connections between the cell-structure of the pre-frontal cortex are weakened and we tend to become less coherent. When this happens it becomes physically more difficult to activate and experience the above qualities necessary to give us a sense of meaning. In other words, stress can diminish our sense of meaning.

3.3.9 Regularity of routine

The emerging new science of chronobiology recognises that the human physiology functions according to specific natural rhythms and regular cycles[19]. The implications of this growing body of research are that when we synchronise our various activities with natural rhythms we optimise our long-term performance. On the other hand pursuing a frenetic lifestyle and engaging in unnatural routines will:

- Weaken the immune system
- Upset sleep patterns
- Disrupt the digestive system
- More likely provoke unnecessary stress responses to mild stress stimuli

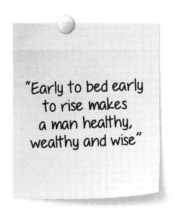

"Early to bed early to rise makes a man healthy, wealthy and wise"

Unhealthy routines therefore have a variety of practical implications for effectiveness at work. For instance, people perform better in the afternoon if they have had a break for a proper lunch. By that is meant actually taking time out from their machine or workstation, stopping work and sitting quietly and eating something nourishing, preferably in company with other people. Similarly, people can focus more in meetings if there is a break every hour and a half or so. People are more alert, more energetic and work more productively when they regularly get a good night's sleep. This means going to bed by 10pm and getting up at around 6 am. What this need implies is that it is best if people stop work in the late afternoon, not late in the evening. Going home on time gives them an opportunity to wind down in the evening in order to get settled rest at bedtime.

This is not exactly rocket science and was all part of our folk wisdom seventy years ago. But somehow this sort of simple and natural way of thinking has been almost lost, at least in the UK. This natural understanding is becoming further and further eclipsed by the long work-hours culture currently prevailing in our economy and our reliance on information technology such as emails that intrude more an more into our after-hours home-life.

The UK works longer hours than most European countries but has one of the lowest levels of productivity. Part of the answer to this low productivity may well lie in this vital need being insufficiently met. The question has to be asked are too many British workers too tired to do their jobs properly.

Take into account your employees' biological need for regularity of routine, and it will have an impact out of all proportion to any cost associated with the effort or disruption required. Don't be blinded by today's management obsessions with improvements driven by technology and targets, at the expense of neglecting such straightforward practicalities. This key topic is discussed further in chapter 9, section 5 – A natural daily routine – the backdrop to productive organisational activity.

3.4 Case example - The human givens model at an RAF base

Engineering support units at an RAF base were due to merge. Typically, the merger was based on cost calculations that it would save money by exploiting economies of scale[10].

The thinking behind the proposed merger was that a combined engineering unit, serving three or four squadrons, would be more efficient in terms of personnel and facilities than separate units attached to each squadron.

Unfortunately no one had consulted the relevant engineers and non-commissioned officers about what they thought would be the best options. Years of direct, on the ground experience were overlooked in this rather radical shake-up.

So, a remote Group Command was setting out to "modernise" the engineering units on a more industrial scale without having an intimate knowledge of what really made the units work effectively. The fact that this move was creating a lot of disgruntled staff was considered unimportant as the senior officers reckoned that this upset simply reflected a typical aversion to change.

At a distance the high command could not see that what was really upsetting the engineers. In psychological terms the proposed merger threatened at least four emotional needs.

Autonomy and control: The engineers on the ground felt they were powerless to avoid this drastic step backwards. Currently pilots and engineers work together as a team. The engineering ground crew look after the aircraft right through to the mission and back. As a result the ground crew have a high degree of accountability and a very real sense of responsibility for the safety of their flight crew as well as the means to provide an excellent service. They felt that the merger was, in effect, seriously threatening their ability to provide an excellent service to the flying crews.

Recognition and status: With a close working partnership between aircrew and ground crew, the engineers benefit from direct feedback as to the quality of their work. As a result, the engineers feel a very real sense of ownership. In effect the success of a mission becomes a joint enterprise. Under the existing regime, this responsibility and the recognition that goes with this teamwork are all very motivational for focus and commitment.

Competence and a sense of achievement: The engineers could see that separating the two functions would reduce both valuable operational feedback and motivation with an almost inevitable drop in quality of work. They could also see that peacetime efficiencies would cause the squadrons to lose their 'sprint capacity' and cause catastrophic bottlenecks when the squadrons were in action and at full stretch.

Meaning: By destroying the sprint capacity the efficiency created by the proposed merged system would have restricted the air squadrons' capability at the very time when they were serving their real purpose and needed maximum output.

Fortunately, the concept of emotional needs as a motivating factor was brought to the attention of the air force high command. The potential damaging consequences were duly noted. As a result the intended merger was reversed and the ground crew teams continued to serve their individual squadrons.

Chapter Four

Meeting emotional needs liberates organisational potential

Managers, particularly those with a technical or accounting background, tend to view employees as though they were set pieces in a chess game with fixed "moves" or predetermined capabilities. This simplistic view holds that our employees' capability, level of energy and enthusiasm is somehow a given and can be relied upon no matter what else is going on.

To improve the organisation or gain competitive advantage and "win the game" these types of managers just move their chess pieces about the board and rely on strategy, tactics, process improvements and new technology to achieve their goals.

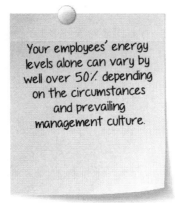

Your employees' energy levels alone can vary by well over 50% depending on the circumstances and prevailing management culture.

This attitude misses out on an incalculable opportunity. The reality is that the way we structure the system and the way we lead and manage our people hugely influences their ability and even willingness to contribute to the success of an enterprise.

Your employees' energy levels alone can vary by well over 50% depending on the circumstances and prevailing management culture[1].

Just think how much easier it would be to beat an opponent in chess if you could somehow bend the rules and unilaterally enhance the power of your own pieces by 50%. What would be the outcome if you could convert each pawn to have the power of a knight or castle whilst your opponent was still stuck with eight pawns? If you can imagine the outcome would be a walk over, then you can imagine the significance of removing stress in the workplace.

4.1 The human givens' model of innate resources

Create a low stress environment and work with low stressed people, then essentially you are working with individuals who, in their settled state of mind, have access to a range of superb qualities.

Importantly these qualities include the ability to collaborate creatively and problem-solve on behalf of their work group or organisation. Redesigning the system to facilitate these particular skills can transform the achievement and success of any group or organisation.

Table 6: Our natural problem-solving faculties or 'given' resources

* A rational intellect that enables us to discriminate, check out emotions, ask questions and analyse
* The ability to handle uncertainty
* An innate curiosity and enthusiasm
* A natural desire and ability to problem solve
* Communication skills that enhance group collaboration
* A dreaming brain that helps us de-stress
* The ability to learn and the ability to learn how to learn
* A natural and innate desire for our own group to survive and prosper

* Empathy and a natural aptitude for collaborating with colleagues
* A long-term memory that can draw on past experiences
* The ability to learn from experience
* A creative imagination that can visualise solutions and can allow us to focus away from our emotions to problem solve more effectively
* The ability to understand the world unconsciously through metaphor and complex pattern matching
* An observant-self that can separate our core identity from the problem at hand and recognise itself as a unique centre of awareness.
* The ability to form habits both good and bad[2]

4.2 Redefining motivation

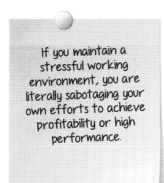

If you maintain a stressful working environment, you are literally sabotaging your own efforts to achieve profitability or high performance.

The driving principle here is that motivating a leap in performance and productivity is a matter of converting stressed behaviour into unstressed behaviour. Motivation isn't just about satisfying human needs. Motivating high performance is about creating a climate where low stressed human beings naturally and spontaneously start interacting and functioning at their full potential.

Where stress infests our organisations it is responsible for suppressing people's ability to access and use their innate resources. And it is these innate resources that, when unleashed, can so quickly transform a mediocre or even failing organisation into a world-class wealth generating enterprise or a truly superb public administration delivering an excellent service. Quite simply if you maintain a stressful working environment, you are literally sabotaging your own efforts to achieve profitability or high performance.

The sections below elaborate on eleven of the innate resources outlined in table six above. I have tried to detail their potential impact on an organisation and the sort of problems that can arise when stress prevents these innate resources from being activated effectively. As such I have limited the discussion to those elements that:

1. Are directly relevant to generating higher performance.
2. Can be influenced by a leader's ability or inability to foster the right environment.
3. Are often currently overlooked as relevant, or at least aspects of them are obscure from a management perspective.

4.3 Eleven innate resources

4.3.1 A long-term memory

The ability to develop complex long-term memory patterns is the core ability that enables us to retain skills from our training days and call on past knowledge and experience. I have lost count of the number of times in team workshops I have heard people say, "In my last job we used to solve this problem by …"

This faculty could be made so much more use of if management adopted a more collaborative style, involved employees in problem solving and idea generation and therefore asked them about their prior experience. Too often managers overlook this strategy by ignoring or neglecting the experience of longer-term employees.

When stressed, people can experience an impaired long-term memory for the prevailing period, specifically it can become distorted to suit the dominant emotion at the time. You might well have experienced this yourself that when angry with someone you can only remember their negative traits not their positive ones. So under stress, this faculty becomes less reliable and less able to help the process of improving any given situation.

Diagram 9

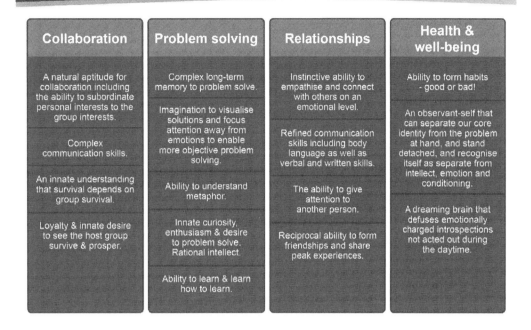

Human Givens - Innate resources

Collaboration	Problem solving	Relationships	Health & well-being
A natural aptitude for collaboration including the ability to subordinate personal interests to the group interests.	Complex long-term memory to problem solve.	Instinctive ability to empathise and connect with others on an emotional level.	Ability to form habits - good or bad!
Complex communication skills.	Imagination to visualise solutions and focus attention away from emotions to enable more objective problem solving.	Refined communication skills including body language as well as verbal and written skills.	An observant-self that can separate our core identity from the problem at hand, and stand detached, and recognise itself as separate from intellect, emotion and conditioning.
An innate understanding that survival depends on group survival.	Ability to understand metaphor.	The ability to give attention to another person.	A dreaming brain that defuses emotionally charged introspections not acted out during the daytime.
Loyalty & innate desire to see the host group survive & prosper.	Innate curiosity, enthusiasm & desire to problem solve. Rational intellect.	Reciprocal ability to form friendships and share peak experiences.	
	Ability to learn & learn how to learn.		

4.3.2 A creative imagination

Our creative imagination enables us to dream up new ideas and visualise solutions. But our imagination has another very valuable use too.

We can use our imaginations to focus away from any intrusive emotions and this enables us to utilise our rational brains to problem solve more effectively. Life coaches and psychotherapists already use this faculty to focus a client's thoughts away from the negative and towards creating a positive reality. Otherwise, visualisation, or the use of imagination to create a picture of what you want to achieve, is still a largely overlooked tool in leadership. This is an important oversight, as the imagination can have both a positive and negative impact.

"Whatever is possible is first imagined. What the mind imagines, the brain spontaneously tries to construct."

Whatever is possible is first imagined. Neuroscientists now know that what the mind imagines the brain spontaneously tries to construct and tries to find ways to bring about. This can happen unconsciously. So if you fantasize negatively about the outcome of an event or activity then you are invariably setting yourself up for failure. This does not mean that you should avoid thinking about anticipated problems. But, where you have prudently anticipated negative outcomes, you can use your imagination as a powerful tool to visualise positive or constructive scenarios to over come the difficulties.

This factor underlines the importance of leaders:

- Being clear of stress themselves
- Retaining a positive outlook and avoiding feeding people's negative imaginings
- Communicating this positivity to everyone around and inspiring them with a vision of a positive outcome to the situation

4.3.3 An innate curiosity and enthusiasm

Have you ever wondered at the contrast between people working for say a large corporation or government department on the one hand and working for themselves, or perhaps for a small community or charity project on the other?

"The imagination is literally the workshop wherein are fashioned all plans created by man."

Napoleon Hill

On the one hand you might see employees who look very much as though they are just going through the necessary motions without any apparent enthusiasm – roll on Friday and the next payday. Such employees, especially those in the more humdrum jobs have to be beguiled, regulated, threatened or bribed to make a special effort or sometimes any effort at all. Recently we have even seen the arrival of the "attendance bonus", an extra reward for just turning up!

Yet these same individuals when they clock off from work can throw

Nature ensures that we are naturally enthusiastic and curious. Boredom, lack of curiosity and apathy are all counter-evolutionary.

themselves wholeheartedly into a project, perhaps building their own house extension or coaching juniors at the local football club, going on charity marathons, giving pastoral care at their local church, participating in parent teacher association fund-raising activities and so on. The contrast is enormous with those same people's everyday work behaviour. Nothing seems too much trouble and they will bend over backwards to do whatever is required to achieve the project's goals, often at some sacrifice to themselves and usually without getting paid.

This level of enthusiasm is our natural state. If as a manager or leader, we are not seeing this at work then be sure that somehow our leadership is at fault. The system is breaking down their enthusiasm.

Nature ensures that we are naturally enthusiastic and curious. Boredom, lack of curiosity and apathy are all counter-evolutionary. Such symptoms have never contributed to the survival of the species and, as such, are a sign of stress and malaise.

All you have to do to fire up enthusiasm, commitment, loyalty and conscientiousness is be sensitive to the emotional needs of your employees.

Enthusiasm and curiosity are an infinitely valuable resource that you can tap into in an organisation. All you have to do to fire up enthusiasm, commitment, loyalty and conscientiousness is be sensitive to the human givens' element – the emotional needs of your employees.

4.3.4 A natural desire and ability to problem solve

The brain is primarily a problem-solving organ. Nature has designed this organ to solve the problems associated with everyday existence. Use it or lose it as they say. The more we use this problem-solving faculty, the better it is at it.

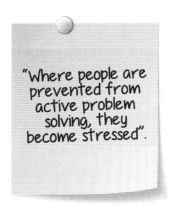

"Where people are prevented from active problem solving, they become stressed".

In short, we have survived as a species by solving the myriad of problems that have challenged that survival. As this problem-solving faculty is such an integral part to our survival, the need and ability to use it is hardwired into our DNA. In fact, the brain is so attuned to problem solving that it will do so even to relax and have some fun. Just as an example of this phenomenon, next time you are on a commuter train after work, look around you and what do you see? Tired and stressed commuters worn out by the day's activity and frustrations, but still doing all kinds of problem-solving activities like the newspaper crossword, Sudoku, computer games and so on.

On the other hand, if the environment or some other factor prevents us in some way from problem solving, or if we just simply don't use our brains for this crucial purpose we get stressed. Active problem solving meets the need for stretch and a challenge and when we do it well it also meets our need to feel competent or attain achievement. In addition, being enabled to problem-solve at work is likely to mean that the management is going some way to meet our need for a degree of autonomy and control over our life. The problem-solving role gives us some meaning, provides recognition and makes us feel we are making a contribution to the group effort.

This faculty has important implications for any organised group where there is a culture of the leadership doing the problem solving and the rest doing as they are told. Trying to work or live in such an atmosphere will be intrinsically stressful.

The net result of making everyone dependent on the management to make decisions is a general lowering of productivity and overall organisational performance. Although this stress may be at a low level of arousal, one other problem with it is that it is almost perpetual in such a climate and therefore there is no relief. The impact of such stress accumulates in the physiologies of the subjects over time, with ill-health being the ultimate outcome as seen in diagram 7.

4.3.5 A conscious rational mind

Our conscious rational mind or intellect enables us to perceive our emotions in a detached way. This unique human faculty enables us to check out whether the emotion is appropriate for the circumstances and whether it is useful or a hindrance to the need of the time.

Having a good degree of presence of mind and not submitting to inner emotional turmoil is fundamental to successful leadership.

As with all the other inner resources, although it is termed a given, the raw potential of the rational mind to function effectively requires developing. Only when we have developed this quality, can we have a detached insight into our emotions and so have a clear perception of our own strengths and limitations.

Maintaining a calm rational outlook promotes a true and realistic view about ourselves and our aspirations. In our rational mind we are able to understand and hold onto realistic and meaningful goals and intuitively use this faculty to guide our path in life no matter what else is going on around us.

Having a good degree of presence of mind and not submitting to inner emotional turmoil is fundamental to successful leadership. Presence of mind is a prerequisite for effective self-management, and the focus required to achieve challenging goals despite distractions from stressful situations and stressed colleagues or clients. A symptom of poor self-management is the expression of volatile emotions both negative and positive. At work this volatility in a leader confuses and demoralises colleagues and subordinates.

Beyond techniques

The leader's ability does not rest on techniques or gimmicks or set exercises. The method of awareness-of-process applies to all people and all situations. The leader's personal state of consciousness creates a climate of openness. Centre and grounding give the leader stability, flexibility and endurance. Because the leader sees clearly, the leader can shed light on others.

The Tao of leadership[3]

As a leader you cannot hope to enhance the performance of others if you erupt into a rage at every frustration and descend into panic or maudlin depression at every set back; succumbing to this sort of emotionalism drives up your colleagues' own stress levels.

4.3.6 The ability to create rapport and connect with others

Empathy and rapport are underlying competencies in social awareness. As such they are fundamental faculties in our innate ability to collaborate with one another and a key requirement of the coaching style of leadership.

Where leaders lack these qualities or at least fail to display them, as in "straight line thinking" and psychopathic behaviour, (see chapters 11.4 and 11.5) they generate significant stress levels and therefore underperformance within the group.

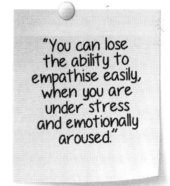

"You can lose the ability to empathise easily, when you are under stress and emotionally aroused."

As with our other resources, healthy individuals are born with a natural talent for striking rapport and with a natural ability to empathise. Even as babies we have the instinctive knowledge of how to look for human facial features and almost from the start we can imitate other people's actions. We seem to come into the world with an innate knowledge that we are like other people and other people are like us[4].

This innate knowledge is driven by our need for security and attention. Now, although hardwired into our anatomy in readiness for infanthood[5], obviously we have to nurture and develop empathy if it is to continue to be effective in getting the attention we need in adulthood.

The therapeutic power of empathy or a good "bedside manner" is well established[6]. People's physiology and stress levels literally change when subjected to an empathetic response or when they are experiencing a strong rapport.

Where leaders lack these two core attributes, far from inspiring and motivating people they have a dissonant impact on their working environment. Leaders who lack the ability to empathise tend to jar people's nerves or get their backs up. On the other hand, where a leader can empathise they are able to listen easily to other people's points of view, sympathise with their feelings, and tune in to their needs. They are then able to respond or act in careful consideration of these feelings and needs and both encourage and motivate colleagues and subordinates alike. An appropriate amount of empathy and rapport provides a powerful lubricant to working relationships. Empathy allows the cogs and wheels of working collaboration to run smoothly. Empathy and rapport between people puts them at ease. As a result they can more easily access their mental and emotional faculties.

Another contributing factor here for enhanced group performance is that empathetic leaders are more likely to retain talented employees. One factor that demoralises talented staff is "tuned out, dissonant leaders"[7]. The added cost is that departing talent and experience disrupts and depletes the organisation's wealth of knowledge, the organisational memory and group cohesion.

"Giving attention takes time, failing to give it takes up a lot more."

The important point to remember is that you can lose the ability to empathise easily when you are under stress and emotionally aroused[8]. Impatience, frustration, anger or anxiety cloud our perception of other people's needs, prevent us listening to other points of view and force us into tunnel or extreme black and white thinking. It is this style of stressed thinking that excludes the broader picture or misses out on essential detail.

4.3.7 Communication skills

As we have already seen in the chapter on human needs, the giving and receiving of attention is a powerful human need. Communication skills are somewhat pivotal in being able to facilitate this. In a leadership role being adept at communication is essential whether to convey instructions, persuade and inspire, empathise and express feelings in an appropriate manner, find things out, listen for feedback or to provide performance feedback.

Again we see that succumbing to the stress response is debilitating to effective and motivational leadership. As we have already noted in chapter two, one aspect of stressed thinking is the inability to listen to other people's points of view. The stress response is designed to shut down this faculty in order to ready us for instant and impulsive action.

4.3.8 An observant-self

The observant self is that part of us that can step back from external events, our emotions and even our thoughts, and recognise itself as a unique centre of awareness. It is that faculty that can see us as separate from our intellect, emotion and conditioning.

Awareness of the self or consciousness is the purest form of awareness as it transcends both thought and emotion and enables us to get in touch with the very core of our being. Transcending thought and emotions means to literally experience awareness of ourselves without the effort needed to think thoughts or feel emotions.

In point of fact these two elements, thoughts and emotions experienced in the normal waking state of consciousness may actually inhibit a deeper experience of self-awareness. Certainly, in a state of stress and excitation where we experience many vivid thoughts and powerful emotions this observant self is progressively lost or clouded over, leaving us disorientated and preventing us from getting a true perspective on things. When calm and relaxed, this faculty of 'being' or awareness of the self or consciousness, gives us the ability to separate our core identity from the problem at hand[9].

At the level of awareness we are intimately connected to one another

The new understanding of the observant self as a faculty may have profound implications for the future direction of leadership, management and organisational behaviour. These implications are born out by modern physics. Physicists are now theorising that at the level of pure awareness we are intimately connected to one another.

The logic derives from the discovery of four fundamental force fields or energy fields. Quantum physicists who have been mapping out these four fields are now attempting, with the aid of theoretical mathematics, to merge these four fields into one overall field of intelligence. These 'unified field' physicists predict that all the diverse aspects of material nature across the entire universe, including all other laws of nature, are in their essence derived from one unbounded field of energy or field of creative intelligence.

By implication this unified field governs all the material and non-material aspects of nature and equates to a field of pure awareness or consciousness.

> *"By getting to smaller and smaller units, we do not come to fundamental units or indivisible units, but we do come to a point where division has no meaning."*
> Werner Heisenberg (From God and the new physics by Paul Davies)[10]

The relevance to group leadership is that as terrestrial beings we are an integral part of this unified field. As this common experience is something we all share, it provides us with a close, even intimate connection with everyone else in our group.

The concept of the collective consciousness

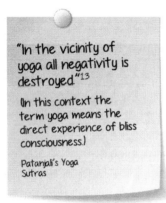

"In the vicinity of yoga all negativity is destroyed"[13]

(In this context the term yoga means the direct experience of bliss consciousness.)

Patanjali's Yoga Sutras

This intimate non-material connection between us has implications for group work, as it leads on to the possibility of a concept known as the 'collective consciousness'. Individual consciousness is intertwined with collective conscious, and that means that the collective consciousness influences individual thoughts and actions within the group, at the same time as being influenced by the individual consciousness of the group members.

These ideas, although they represent a paradigm shift in contemporary thinking, are not exactly new and correspond closely to what has been understood over the ages by various spiritual and mystic traditions particularly in the East[11].

For example, the ancient Vedic tradition of India holds that at our simplest state of awareness, where we have transcended thought, ego and emotion, in other words where we are in close touch with the observant self, we are actually in touch with or are experiencing directly this unified field or field of consciousness. According to this tradition, the human physiology can experience the unified field during deep meditation in the form of what it terms as bliss consciousness[12].

Diagram 10

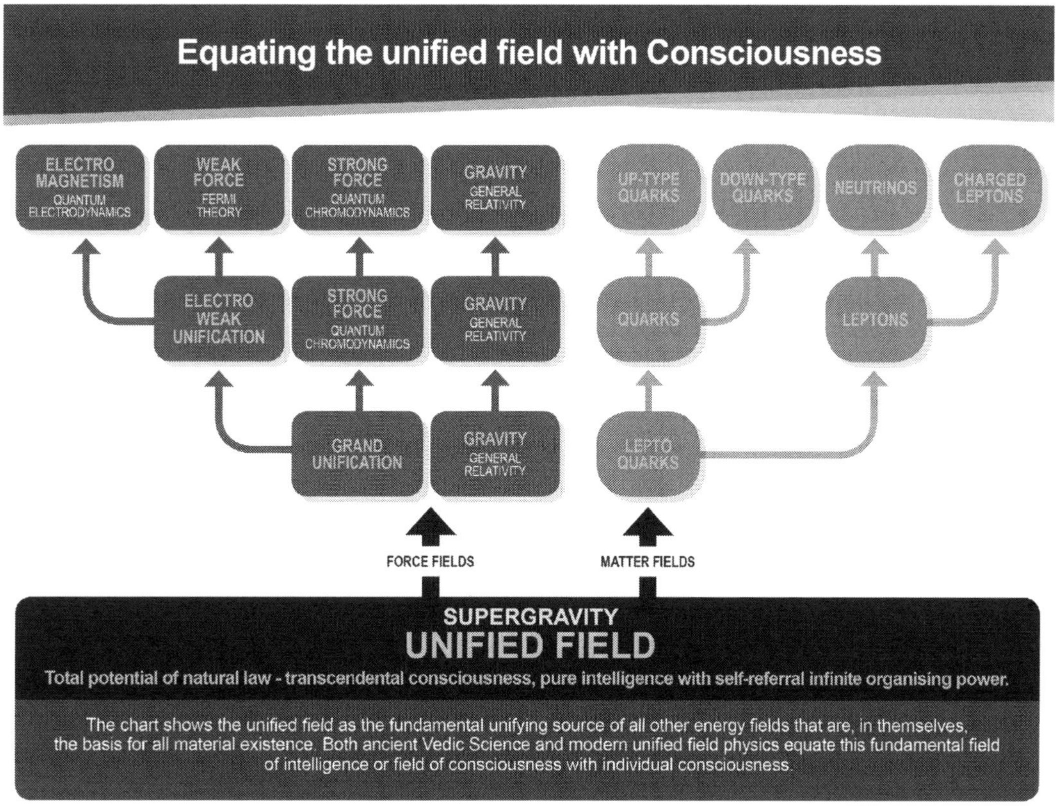

Equating the unified field with Consciousness

SUPERGRAVITY
UNIFIED FIELD
Total potential of natural law - transcendental consciousness, pure intelligence with self-referral infinite organising power.

The chart shows the unified field as the fundamental unifying source of all other energy fields that are, in themselves, the basis for all material existence. Both ancient Vedic Science and modern unified field physics equate this fundamental field of intelligence or field of consciousness with individual consciousness.

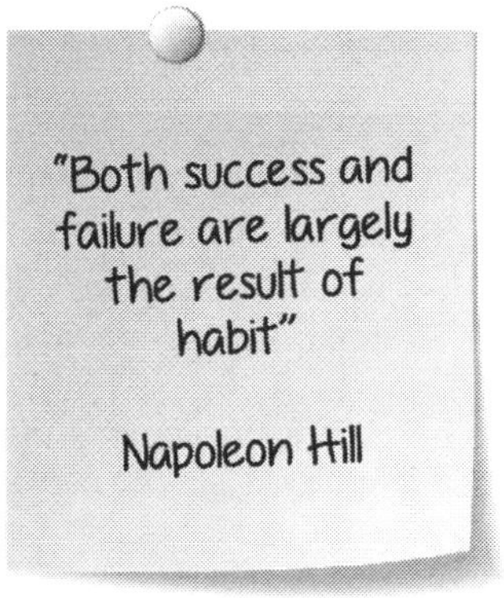

"Both success and failure are largely the result of habit"

Napoleon Hill

Significantly anyone who experiences this profound state of bliss consciousness is not only benefiting themselves but is also transmitting, through the medium of the unified field, tangible measurable benefits to other people in their vicinity.

Modern research is validating this traditional view and indicates that negative thoughts and behaviour tend to dissipate in the proximity of people who are directly experiencing unity or bliss consciousness.

A form of meditation known as Transcendental Meditation has been subjected to study into the broadcast effect of the individual experience of bliss consciousness. The research shows significant reductions of behavioural indicators of stress such as changes in cortisol and serotonin in non-participating people at a nearby distance from the experimentation group of meditators[14] and similar results from even twenty miles away[15]. Two other studies show synchronised changes in EEG patterns generated by meditators on non-meditating subjects[16 17].

81

Although not widely known yet, there are a number of studies relating to the impact of Transcendental Meditation on whole communities published in peer reviewed academic publications including The Journal of Conflict Resolution edited at Yale University[18], Psychology, Crime & Law [19] and The Journal of Mind and Behaviour[20][21]. The implications of this body of research are that the leader of any organised group can make use of the phenomenon of the collective consciousness through the medium of this type of meditation to reduce the stress levels within their group.

4.3.9 A dreaming brain that helps us de-stress

Our dreaming faculty plays an important part in the natural release of stress from the day's work and activity. The dreaming brain preserves the integrity of our genetic inheritance every night by metaphorically defusing emotionally arousing introspections not acted out the previous day[22].

As such any activity or behaviour that interferes with our natural sleeping patterns also disrupts our dreaming. And when our dreaming faculty is disrupted it impairs our ability to handle and assimilate the stress we experience during the working day.

Long working hours, artificial stimulants, alcohol, heavy evening meals remaining undigested at night, unremitting anxiety or the intrusion of excessive negative emotions during the day are all capable of causing problems with our dreaming brain. If the dream state (REM or Rapid Eye Movement state) is over activated due to stress this can quickly displace the more restful and restorative slow wave sleep.

As a direct result of this displacement we get up in the morning feeling tired instead of refreshed and rejuvenated and so are even less able to cope with whatever stresses are confronting us during the following day. The implications for leadership are that the consequence of inadequate dreaming is impaired efficiency the next day and subsequent days if the problem is not remedied. This aspect is covered more fully in chapter 9, section 5.

4.3.10 An innate desire for our own group to survive and prosper

This resource is manifested as a natural loyalty, affinity or attachment to our host group. This is the case whether it is our family, tribe, employer, locale or our country and even our world family or species. As healthy human beings we instinctively wish the best for those around us and also for our host group. We will spontaneously strive to solve group problems as a means to ensure our own survival. We will do so even at some personal cost to ourselves[23].

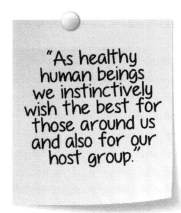

"As healthy human beings we instinctively wish the best for those around us and also for our host group."

Time and time again I have seen this faculty kick in and come to the rescue in some problem-solving session. Their boss may have mucked around the participants on innumerable occasions. They may have been ignored, disregarded and abused. The whole shaky edifice may be creaking towards collapse because of the senior management's reckless ignorance of the organisation's needs or poor strategic direction. But when sat down together in a calm and relaxed, friendly atmosphere, with a brief to find some explanation to the cause of the problems and how to solve them, I have seen middle managers, supervisors and staff all just click into group problem-solving mode. Up come ideas, solutions and suggestions to help the organisation out of the mess it's in.

Recent advances in Game Theory have begun to reverse the long held Game Theory view that people behave for purely selfish reasons. A systematic study of "Team Reasoning", led by Professor Andrew Colman of Leicester University School of Psychology, indicates that "in some circumstances decision-makers cooperate in their collective interests rather than following the purely selfish predictions of orthodox game theory"[25].

The importance of this inherent resource derives from the need, discussed earlier, for a sense of belonging. And this need stems from an innate understanding that we can only survive and prosper if our host group survives and prospers. In a healthy individual this innate need is expressed as family loyalty (at its most basic level), organisational loyalty at work, civic pride at community level, and a natural sense of patriotism at national level.

"There in Szeged, (a town in former communist Hungary) with people who had lived their lives in the greyest of environments, who had no objective basis to believe that life should promise anything different, I witnessed a flare ignite in each and every one of them as they came to believe in the possibility of something better.

What this tells me is that the drive to connect to one's fellow man, to strive to create a better world for all of us to live in, is not a function of environmental conditioning, but is innate to each and every one of us."

The Hidden Game[24]

The concept of patriotism here is entirely distinct from jingoism, nationalism or chauvinism and does not imply any "we are better than you" attitudes or any racial purity theories or religious intolerance. Furthermore the feeling of close connection with say your family, town or country does not have to exclude the emerging perception that the whole world is our family and the growing consciousness that to survive as a species our self-interest now has to stretch way beyond narrow national boundaries.

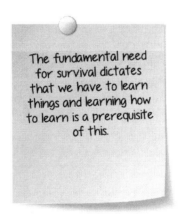

"If ever time should come, when vain and aspiring men shall possess the highest seats in government, our country will stand in need of its experienced patriots to prevent its ruin."

Samuel Adams

It is simply a fact that we have hard-wired into our DNA the instinctive recognition that we can only survive and prosper if our group survives and prospers. Group loyalty is an emotional drive that is part of every healthy individual's natural survival mechanism. When tapped into it is highly motivational.

This emotional need has important implications for the qualities required of a leader. It indicates that one of the prime qualities of leadership is a healthy love of, or at least loyalty to the host group. Following on from this, needs to be the subjugation of any narrow self-interest, ideology or self-belief when in pursuit of the group interest. We should be naturally suspicious of any leader or aspiring leader who expresses disloyalty to or dislike of our group. Such people are a potential threat to our emotional well-being and survival.

4.3.11 The ability to learn and to learn how to learn

The fundamental need for survival dictates that we have to learn things and learning how to learn is a prerequisite of this.

We come into life endowed with all the above innate resources. But at birth, of course, they mostly exist as potential. The very act of growing up is about nurturing and developing these inner resources. Even an ability as touchy and feely as being able to empathise requires improvement as we get older, in order to be of any real use. A gurgling smile will do wonders for our prospect of food in the arms of a doting mother at the age of three months; it is hardly a sufficient tactic in the boardroom is it?

Even a faculty as basic as perception is now understood to be something infants have to actually learn. The capacity to make sense of incoming an stimulus and ascribe meaning to it can only be achieved through active interaction with the environment both inanimate and human at an early age. Although we grow up

84

to think that we always knew how to see things and make sense of them, the fact is that this perception is learned.

So, the fundamental need for survival dictates that we have to learn things and learning how to learn is a prerequisite of this. We may wish to learn something from a book, but before that we learn how to read and even before we acquire that simple skill we learn how to distinguish marks on a page. It is a simple imperative that we nurture this faculty of learning how to learn continually in order to maintain health.

Part of the learning how to learn faculty is nature's inbuilt reward system for learning new things in order to adapt to the changing environment within which we live. This is why learning something new gives us joy. That euphoric 'ah ha' moment at the point when the penny finally drops or that feeling of satisfaction when we are honing a new skill to perfection are nature's ways of stimulating the learning required for meeting changes, growing and developing.

Learning is a survival mechanism and, as such, nurturing the joy and enthusiasm for learning is a sacred part of all teaching, coaching and authentic leadership.

> "Knowledge is the basis of action. Action is the basis of achievement. Achievement is the basis of fulfilment."
>
> Maharishi

Learning how to learn is a valuable resource for leaders to utilise. A well-developed learning how to learn faculty has both direct advantages for an organisation, (development of skills or knowledge) and indirect advantages, (enhanced enthusiasm and commitment to the place of work).

4.4 Good stress management is good management

The key factor to remember about the resource element of the human givens is that when we are calm and relaxed and in a settled state of mind we all have access to this range of resources and superb problem-solving faculties.

Where stress exists, it progressively deprives us of these faculties. Stress therefore deprives us of the very means to alleviate the problems at hand and so further inhibits us from getting our needs met. Part of any therapeutic regime includes stress-reducing initiatives in order to enable a patient to get back to a balanced and clearer state of thinking. And central to this stress reduction is always an assessment of what needs are not being met in the first place, as this is often the trigger for the debilitating stress response.

Management structures, functions and styles, are often the most potent stressors within an organisation.

The high prevalence of stress in the workplace indicates that management would benefit by adopting the same strategy. A low-stress working environment is a powerful means to enable higher productivity and performance. And the best place to start is to study what needs are being neglected, threatened or violated by stress factors or "stressors" in the workplace.

This includes, of course, investigating the prevailing 'system' – the management structures, functions and styles, as these are often the most potent stressors within an organisation. Management stressors not only impact people's needs but they can also suppress or neglect those innate resources, that if utilised correctly, can transform organisational performance. These stressors are the subject matter of Part II.

PART II

Releasing the handbrake

PART II

Releasing the handbrake

Chapter Five

Stress as a handbrake on group performance

5.1 The impact of stress on the system

Organisations behave in many ways like organic systems and seem to suffer from stress in the same manner. In an organism, what impacts an individual cell's performance will ultimately impact the collective performance of the system through the medium of interconnectivity between cells and their mutual interdependence. In the same way, through the medium of interconnectivity within an organisation, whatever stresses the individual human being ultimately stresses the organisation.

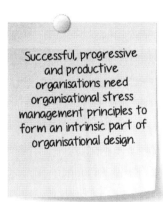

Successful, progressive and productive organisations need organisational stress management principles to form an intrinsic part of organisational design.

Systematically removing stress-inducing factors at work (or at any rate alleviating them) not only transforms individual performance and productivity but also transforms people's ability to interact more freely and productively with the rest of the system. The resulting shift in performance is out of all proportion to any cost of the removal in terms of time, effort or other resources. The speed of change can also be dramatic.

What stresses people out at work?

Whatever induces stress upon the individual is known as a "stressor" or stress stimulus. We can now identify about thirty specific organisational stressors that, in broad terms, threaten our individual needs, induce stress and therefore impinge on our "given" resources. (See Table 1 – The thirty organisational stressors.)

Each of these thirty stressors is a constraint to success as it has the potential to:

1. Disrupt or distort the flow of operations.
2. Block or distort the flow of communication.
3. Generate mistakes, accidents and rework.
4. Dampen the work culture.
5. Reduce individual productivity.
6. Generally make life more difficult for everyone in the workplace.

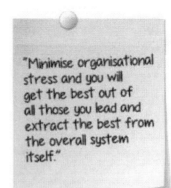

"Minimise organisational stress and you will get the best out of all those you lead and extract the best from the overall system itself."

5.2 The 30 stressors' model as an analytical tool to improve performance

In general terms, the thirty organisational stressors fall into seven broad categories:

1. Management styles.
2. Types of management structure.
3. Strategic issues or operational factors.
4. Elements of the management function.
5. Physical factors in the working environment.
6. Psychological, personal and relationship factors.
7. External influences that constrain success.

In the following chapters we review each stressor in turn by defining the problem and consequences of each one, identifying the impact on the human needs, looking at appropriate remedies and finally reviewing the impact of these on the human givens.

5.3 An introduction to collaborative leadership - the twin benefits

"It is not necessary to change. Survival is not mandatory."

WE Deming

You will read that a number of remedies involve the concept of "collaborative leadership". The stress-reducing benefits of collaborative leadership are reviewed in detail in chapter 6, section 1. But in one sentence, the reason collaborative leadership is such a useful antidote to stress is that collaboration comes naturally to human beings.

Teamwork or collaborating with colleagues tends to meet a number of our biological needs, and it is this factor that makes this mode of working spontaneously stress reducing.

However, collaborative leadership isn't just a remedy for stress.

We live in turbulent times and large organisations inhabit a complex and dynamic environment where customer-demand, technology, cultural, political and economic forces are in a constant state of flux. To survive, an organisation has to be proactive in adapting its structures, processes and its culture to match changes in the environment as and when they arise.

"Everyone shares responsibility for problems generated by a system".

Peter Senge

This requirement for ongoing adaptation necessitates a high degree of variety, complexity and intensity of activity in the decision-making process. And this complexity is best handled by active participation from a wide variety of stakeholders. In a complex and dynamic environment as many people as possible need to put forward different viewpoints, provide fresh angles on things, suggest ideas and supply vital negative feedback as to the full dynamics of the situation.

Relentless change in the external environment underlines the importance of a style and function of leadership that maximises the widest possible level of spontaneous stakeholder participation in the decision-making process. Individual stakeholders deferring responsibility to someone or some group higher up the hierarchy is a contra-survival activity and is no longer a valid option.

Individual stakeholders deferring responsibility to someone or some group higher up the hierarchy is a contra-survival activity.

I use the concept of collaborative leadership as a generic term and this is meant to embrace a number of similar leadership and management approaches. These include, for instance, systems thinking[3], lean management[4], Timpson's upside-down management[5], Team Action Management[6], Kaizen, the Semco experiment[7], The Nordstrom Way[8], self-directed teams, teamwork, Sociocracy[9] and my own collaborative leadership and team planning process, Team Business Development (TBD).

Chapter Six

Management styles

Stressors reviewed in this chapter

Stressor 1   Top-down command and control style management

Stressor 2   Atmosphere of mistrust that poisons relationships and working performance

6.1 Why a more collaborative style of leadership stimulates high performance

The problem defined: Stressor 1 – Top-down command and control leadership

> "The more coercive you are, the more resistant the group will become. Your manipulations will only breed evasions. Every law creates an outlaw."
>
> John Heider - Tao of leadership

So many performance debilitating stress factors arise from top-down command and control management that it is almost the mother of all organisational stressors. This is unfortunate as this type of management is currently the norm in most large private and public sector organisations[1].

What is top-down command and control leadership?

Essentially top-down command and control leadership separates the decision-makers from those who actually do the work. Culturally we are conditioned to understand that the world of work is divided into two types of people. The first lot tell others what to do and the others do as they are told.

We ought to clarify that top-down command and control, authoritarian or autocratic management doesn't necessarily mean the forceful or charismatic domination of subordinates by some raving Hitler type barking out orders. Certainly this sort of despotic control freak would be included within this definition, but most top-down command and control management falls within a much wider classification.

I believe that many managers or leaders reading this would not recognise themselves as top-down command and control or authoritarian leaders. Nevertheless how they run their organisations still falls into the category of top-down command and control if the key feature of their style is that _management decides and others follow_.

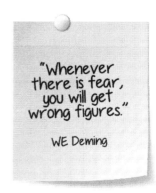

"It's cool for managers to be in command and control - It's the shout culture, but it's not effective."

Professor Cary Cooper

Main characteristics of top-down command and control management

However mild, innocuous or benign the style of top-down command and control management, ultimately it relies on coercion and the deeply embedded cultural expectation of implicit submissiveness evoked by the customary boss/subordinate relationship. This type of deep-seated submissiveness has become the norm whereby:

- Rules and regulations govern employees' activity and procedures and eliminate or at least constrain individual discretion and judgement
- Significant decisions are routinely deferred upwards for a senior authority to decide on
- Functional specialisation and demarcation extends to departments and functional areas and this restricts the information flow across the organisation with very few people outside of senior management having a holistic view of the organisation's circumstances
- Higher authorities pass down directives and targets whether or not the people below perceive that they are effective or useful
- Those in charge impose standardised processes on subordinates
- Managers impose a high degree of functional specialisation that deskill subordinates to a minimum level of expertise; in excessive cases employees are functioning more or less as automatons

"Whenever there is fear, you will get wrong figures."

WE Deming

- Central authority imposes 'best practice' rules or guidance inhibiting the use of judgement and initiative at local level that in turn inhibits continuous improvement initiatives
- Managers, auditors, inspectors, supervisors, etc. routinely monitor and enforce compliance

Authoritarian leadership works against evolution

The basic unit of any organisation is the living outcome of millions of years of successful evolution.

In practical terms this means that any organisation has, as a basic unit of resource, the autonomous, imaginative, intuitive, resilient, highly adaptive, highly collaborative, problem-solving human brain of every one of its employees.

In other words, an overwhelming proportion of people can think for themselves, take responsibility for their actions, take the initiative, problem-solve with colleagues and come up with imaginative solutions. Where

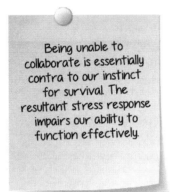

Being unable to collaborate is essentially contra to our instinct for survival. The resultant stress response impairs our ability to function effectively.

managers and leaders overlook this fundamental fact they ride roughshod over their subordinates' emotional needs. And this, as we have seen already in chapter 3, is likely to lead to some degree of stress arousal that in turn suppresses their subordinates' innate talents and faculties.

It is fair to point out that the command and control style of management can still be effective in the right circumstances. But only so long as long as the management also expresses a high level of emotional intelligence and a sufficient degree of creativity or competence that compensates for the infringement of emotional needs such as a loss of autonomy and control.

Thus competent but authoritarian management may set clear goals and clear boundaries of responsibilities, listen attentively to feedback and provide adequate training and support, etc. All of these standard management practices can lessen the stress response among the workforce that is otherwise generated by a top-down command and control style.

Impact of top-down command and control on the emotional needs

But we cannot escape from the fundamental problem of a top-down command and control regime. However much you dress it up to look different, almost by definition, top-down command and control leadership functions on a fear basis and excludes most people from making a useful contribution in managing their own activity.

Thus command and control is always liable to trigger a stress response among employees[2] due to the impact on the individual's emotional needs. Specifically the principal needs suppressed by top-down command and control leadership are:

- Employees' sense of any autonomy and control over their environment.
- Status and recognition.
- Attention: such regimes are largely indifferent or at least insensitive to emotional needs generally.
- Challenge and the opportunity to problem solve especially in pursuit of shared goals.
- Security and as a result this damages the feeling of being part of a community.

The pervading ethos is to keep your head down, don't rock the boat and mind your own business. This sort of attitude is not conducive to sparkling enthusiasm, commitment, creative thought or taking the initiative to problem solve.

Eight areas of weakness

The inherent threat of emotional arousal tends to exacerbate eight other weaknesses of top-down command and control leadership:

1. Stressed bosses can become tyrannical.
2. Top-down command and control management is highly fragile.
3. The problem of bounded rationality.
4. Prevalence of dysfunctional behaviour.
5. The wrong people tend to get to the top.
6. The crucial loss of organisational double-loop learning.
7. Authoritarian leaders are essentially self-selecting.
8. Power struggles.

1. Stressed bosses can become tyrannical

People occupying positions of power and responsibility are prone to becoming overburdened and stressed. This stress can result in impatience and anger towards subordinates and a tendency to interfere and assert even greater control over things.

Snapping at subordinates to get their own way in a hurry is an understandable stress response. However, the impact on those at the receiving end can linger on long after the actual episode and has the tendency to reinforce the habitual dumb subservience expected under the prevailing culture. These types of flare-ups further inhibit the proactive bottom-up presentation of new ideas, delivery of negative feedback or the initiative required for a vibrant, enterprising work culture.

A personal authoritarian style can sometimes indicate a personality disorder or, at any rate, a deeper insecurity. This subject is covered more fully in chapter 11.4 – "The 16% of managers to avoid". Tyrannical managers almost always harm the organisation they are supposed to be running.

2. Top-down command and control management is highly fragile

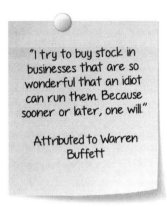

"I try to buy stock in businesses that are so wonderful that an idiot can run them. Because sooner or later, one will."

Attributed to Warren Buffett

The success or survival of a top down command and control regime rests heavily on the extreme ability and energy of those at the top. In other words, managers who adopt this style are required to perform at an exceptional level of competence in order for the whole system to work. Very often, this high degree of accomplishment is only achieved at great cost to the long-term health and personal lives of the leaders themselves. When they fail to maintain a level of excellence, the system begins to break down.

Although legend would have us believe otherwise, the evidence suggests that few people can sustain the required degree of consistent managerial excellence. There are without doubt some exceptional leaders out there, but they are few and far between. In addition to which it is very difficult to pick the right one.

The consequence of buying into the myth of heroic leadership is that most organisations are run by fairly able mediocrities struggling to excel under highly difficult circumstances. Where organisations have been lucky enough to be run by brilliant leaders, more often than not, those same organisations subsequently underperform when someone of more mediocre talent ultimately replaces them. This is perhaps the main reason why so many organisations suffer volatile track records over the medium to long term.

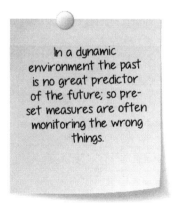

In a dynamic environment the past is no great predictor of the future; so pre-set measures are often monitoring the wrong things.

3. The problem of bounded rationality

Even the best managers have natural limits to their view on operations and events. As mortals, we live in a state of 'bounded rationality', that is, we are not 'all knowing and all seeing' and as such cannot hope to know everything that we need to know about our organisation's activity.

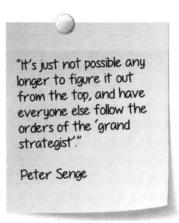

"It's just not possible any longer to figure it out from the top, and have everyone else follow the orders of the 'grand strategist'."

Peter Senge

The bigger the organisation the less we can really know about it. Consequently, we often have to make decisions on the basis of flawed or inadequate knowledge. Essentially the rationality of a decision is influenced by four factors:

1. The information available at the time,
2. The cognitive limitations of the minds of the decision-maker such as what they can actually see and hear
3. The state of mind that the decision-maker is in at the time of the decision – tired and stressed or relaxed and alert.
4. The amount of time available to make a decision.

"Bad news is unwelcome, people are often unwilling to accept new negative feedback that disrupts their settled opinion of the world."

The larger and more complex the organisation the more this limitation is present and the less likely it is for the people at the top to have a firm grasp on the running of complex functions and myriad interactions in the hierarchy beneath them. Command and control tends to reinforce bounded rationality as performance is supplied in pre-set measurements, KPIs and so forth. In other words managers try and predict what may go wrong from past experience and construct measurements to monitor these aspects. In a dynamic environment the past is no great predictor of the future and so pre-set measures are often monitoring the wrong things.

Command and control also inhibits or distorts information flow other ways. As we all know, bad news travels slowly up the hierarchy, if it travels at all. This occurs for three reasons.

Firstly, bad news is unwelcome on an emotional level and where bounded rationality is preventing people from knowing or discovering what they don't already know, they are often unwilling to accept new negative feedback that disrupts the settled opinion of the world that they already hold. It doesn't help that such settled opinions are often self-serving anyway. This is why shooting the messenger is a common fault of bureaucracies and other hierarchical organisations. (See chapter 11 section 7 for further details about how our beliefs and pre-conceptions can get in the way of learning and effective decision-making.)

Diagram 11

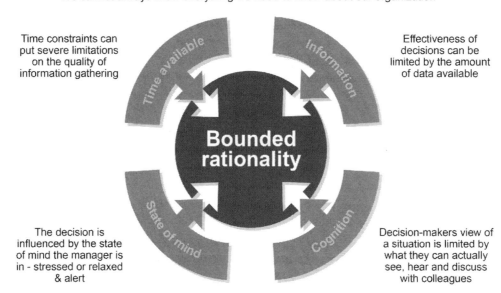

Secondly, from the subordinate's point of view fear of failure or retribution makes people unwilling to own up to mistakes and problems in their area of responsibility so they withhold information that may tarnish their image of competence.

Thirdly, in bureaucratic organisations reliance on predefined performance measures can easily overlook changes at operational level and new categories of activity that then go unrecorded and undetected.

These information flow-restricting factors often mean that managers are isolated from the reality of the situation. In addition to which, as we have seen earlier top down command and control managers are prone to stress and under these conditions their ability to identify and assimilate negative feedback is even further constrained.

4. Dysfunctional behaviour

Another risk with top-down command and control management is that it encourages a range of dysfunctional behaviours among subordinates, as depicted in diagram 12. Such dysfunctional behaviour adversely impacts the success and progress of the whole organisation by:

1. Constraining the flow of upward communication,
2. Blighting effective interaction and collaborative working,
3. Further limiting the leader's bounded rationality,
4. Hindering the organisation's ability to focus on relevant customer or client needs,
5. Inhibiting the organisation's learning capacity.

Diagram 12

Toxic impact of dysfunctional behaviour

Toxic impact

- Secrecy & lip biting self-censorship help isolate the boss from reality

- Hidden agendas and ideological fixations undermine organisational purpose

- Sycophancy further limits the leader's bounded rationality

- Impression management & covering up of mistakes promote incompetence & wrong information

- Blame games & witch hunts hamper fruitful collaborative working & group problem-solving

- Status & power struggles among subordinates jostling for position also wreck collaboration

5. The wrong people tend to get to the top

Where these toxic activities become prevalent, mature people tend to move on to healthier working environments elsewhere, whilst dysfunctional people tend to stay. Unfortunately, this type of work culture tends to attract further dysfunctional people. A large part of the reason for this damaging emigration of talent is that promotion seems to go to those adept at political manipulation or playing the system or to those who are nicely compliant. Real flair in this sort of environment seems to get overlooked, it can even be viewed as dangerous.

The direct consequence of this type of atmosphere is reduced creativity and productivity. The most creative and competent people will have either been subdued into unproductive inertia or will have left.

6. The crucial loss of organisational double-loop learning

Organisational double-loop learning is the organisational propensity to question the appropriateness of existing procedures and activity in the light of new evidence from the working environment. This is a vital faculty for an organisation, if it is to survive and prosper in an ever-changing economic climate[3]. Without this faculty we see organisations condemned to perpetuate the same mistakes over and over again that sooner or later become fatal.

"For successful double-loop learning to occur, organizations must develop cultures that support change and risk taking."

G Morgan - Images of organization

In a command and control system double-loop learning is the preserve of the senior management. Bearing in mind that senior managers operate under the conditions of stress and 'bounded rationality' then the ability of the whole organisation to learn lessons from operational experience is seriously inhibited and delayed

Double-loop learning illustration

A radiator thermostat will alter the heat output into a room when the heat breaches *predefined levels* – single-loop learning. However if the thermostat were able to determine what would be an appropriate temperature in the first place, that would be double-loop learning.

Basically in a command and control regime the majority of the workforce, even when engaged in some counterproductive or wasteful task are still unable to ask 'why are we doing this?' Even more importantly they are prohibited from coming up with some better way to do the job or perhaps do away with the job altogether.

Few people are in a position to initiate adaptation to changing circumstances except those at the top end of the hierarchy. This is a principle reason why bureaucratic organisations incur so much waste and are so slow to respond to change.

Diagram 13

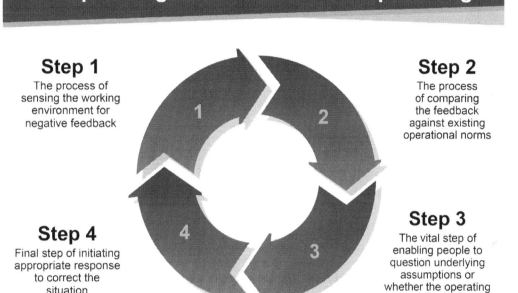

4 steps of organizational double loop learning

Step 1
The process of sensing the working environment for negative feedback

Step 2
The process of comparing the feedback against existing operational norms

Step 3
The vital step of enabling people to question underlying assumptions or whether the operating norms are still appropriate

Step 4
Final step of initiating appropriate response to correct the situation

7. Authoritarian leaders are essentially self-selecting

Effective leadership requires the cultivation and expression of a number of key qualities other than just the technical skills related to the job at hand (See box below). Although self-confidence is one of these qualities, all too often it is this one quality that makes people stand out as potential leaders.

In a very real sense those occupying leadership positions are often self-selecting in that candidates put themselves forward for leadership roles, in the fond belief that they are cut out for them, whereas other, less self-confident types, hold back. Research suggests that this overwhelming self-belief is rarely based on reality[4]. There is obviously an unnerving implication for organisational success here.

The reticence of the less self-confident candidates can be due to a more acute self-awareness that suggests to them that they might be lacking in some of the other necessary qualities. In the context of generating a truly collaborative working environment this humility and self-deprecation, far from disqualifying them for a leadership role would be a positive advantage.

Perhaps even more worryingly, the research suggests that the candidate's own self-confidence in their ability to lead convinces not just themselves, but those around them as well. In other words, the confidence that some people have that they can lead effectively is both convincing and infectious. The awful implication of this research is that the primary qualification for many, otherwise unsuitable, candidates wanting a top job is the vanity that they can do it[5].

8. Power struggles

It is not surprising that personal ambition and the desire for high status is invariably a key motivator for a leadership position. However, the problem with this type of motivation is that it can seduce such leaders into an authoritarian or autocratic style of leadership, a style that as we are discussing is not conducive to a coherent collaborative effort.

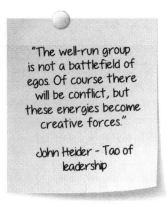

"The well-run group is not a battlefield of egos. Of course there will be conflict, but these energies become creative forces."

John Heider - Tao of leadership

There is a parallel from the animal world. Researchers have observed that the chimpanzees' status-obsessed hierarchies generate too much tension, conflict and aggressive political manoeuvring to allow for effective collaboration. The belligerent and aggressive drive for status and the resultant rivalry among the group means that chimps are unable to work as a team beyond a group size of about five individuals[6]. This is unlike _healthy_ humans who have evolved to collaborate naturally in groups of up to about 150 people[7].

In other words, as a species, the majority of us have inherited the ability to subordinate our own drive for status and power to the wider needs of the group and we have an enormous potential for self-management. But this fine balance can be upturned by the presence of individuals who crave the limelight, or the status and the authority that goes with the territory of a management title and who have the presumption that they can handle this level of status effectively. Such people risk damaging the ability of the group members to manage themselves and collaborate with one another.

Power struggles will always inhibit coherent, robust decision-making and problem solving among the group as a whole. The fear, resentment, anger and confusion invoked by such power struggles risks switching off the all-important individual self-regulating mechanisms needed for group survival. It is this particular insight that casts a large question mark over the desirability of promoting over-ambitious, unduly status conscious or authoritarian people to senior positions of leadership.

The remedy to stressful authoritarian management is collaborative leadership

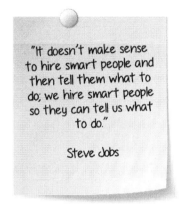

"It doesn't make sense to hire smart people and then tell them what to do; we hire smart people so they can tell us what to do."

Steve Jobs

Planning research at SRI (Stanford Research Institute) in California as far back as the 1960s demonstrated that it is always best if the people who do the work actually plan the work[8]. SRI found that organisational performance is up to 50% more effective where management enable employees to collaborate in the decision-making and planning process of their own work.

Later findings from neuroscience and psychological research support the earlier SRI findings. Essentially the research shows that group collaboration in the decision-making process is perhaps the most powerful organisational means to reduce stress and improve information flows and so dramatically raise both individual and group productivity and performance. In other words getting people more involved in the running of their organisations is the key to enhanced performance[9] and this means trusting your people with the necessary degree of authority to:

- Work together to achieve shared objectives
- Identify problems, waste and areas of weakness
- Question the appropriateness of theirs' and other people's actions,
- Solve problems on their own initiative
- Take the initiative to innovate and instigate their own ideas

Allow employees to do this and they will invariably take up the challenge and you will fire up their enthusiasm, loyalty, commitment and productivity.

Collaboration enhances organisational double-loop learning

> *"When ever men can be persuaded rather than ordered - when they can be made to feel that they have participated in developing the plan - they approach their tasks with understanding and enthusiasm."*
>
> Dwight D Eisenhower

Devolving authority and allowing people to take into account new situations as they arise, without constant referral to a third party or higher authority enables the crucial organisational double-loop learning capacity. Essentially in a collaborative environment the "thinking" part of the organisation is not just confined to the board of directors and/or corporate planning department. Intelligent action is dispersed right across every level of the organisation.

When you enable people to collaborate, they start to engage their brains and a myriad of problems start to be solved spontaneously and across the board. Remove pre-specification from above and along with it the apparatus for compliance and inspections and you will find that group problem solving becomes proactive. The organisation is then more able to adapt swiftly to changing circumstances.

Collaboration is a natural survival mechanism for human beings

The impetus behind this spontaneous release of energy and problem solving activity is that collaboration comes naturally to human beings. The instinctive inclination to problem solve and innovate on behalf of the 'host group' arises because it naturally satisfies a number of those emotional needs that are either threatened or neglected in the usual working environment constrained by top-down command and control principles.

Group collaboration in the decision-making process is perhaps the most powerful organisational means to reduce stress and improve information flows

The key point here is that human beings have largely survived as a species by learning how to collaborate. As individuals we are too weak to protect ourselves from predators. As solitary individuals we are too vulnerable to survive the vagaries and harshness of life in the wild. Individually we are pretty fair game and the odds of surviving in the wild on our own are small indeed. Our species has become one of the dominant ones on earth because we have learned to collaborate with one another[10].

104

Basically, those that tried the successful strategy of clubbing together in order to protect themselves, gather food, nurture children or share other survival activities survived better than those that did not. Every one of our ancestors survived long enough to pass on their genes to us here now. So, being able to collaborate is literally hardwired into our DNA.

The ability to collaborate is designed into our physiologies

There is a growing body of scientific evidence to support this idea that we are by instinct highly collaborative mammals. For instance scientists at the Donders Centre for Cognitive Neuroimaging in Nijmegen have discovered that the brain releases more of the dopamine hormone, a reward chemical, when we fall in with a group consensus[11].

According to Scott Wiltermouth of Stanford University in California, we can tune into group activities that are performed in unison in such a way that increases our group loyalty[12]. Perhaps this faculty helps to explain why extensive parade ground drill is still a significant activity in the armed services long after it has lost any practical use as a military tactic.

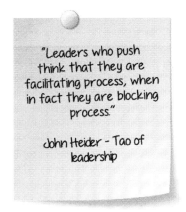

"Leaders who push think that they are facilitating process, when in fact they are blocking process."

John Heider - Tao of leadership

Psychologist Jonathan Haidt at the University of Virginia has been working on mirror neurons. These brain cells apparently fire-up not just when we perform an action but also when we watch someone else perform a similar action. Haidt is suggesting that our brains are literally geared to mimic our peers[13].

Some scientists now regard even the simple act of blushing as a natural means to help facilitate genuine teamwork. As Professor Frans de Waal says, blushing "interferes with the unscrupulous manipulation of others…We are the only primate that blushes in response to embarrassing situations, shame or when caught in a lie"[14].

The key lesson for leadership

These, and a range of other physiological features indicate that our brains and nervous systems are finely attuned to interacting with one another in the pursuit of shared goals. A variety of superb, natural and innate resources come into free play when we are operating in collaborative mode. Give people the opportunity and most of them will naturally resort to mutual collaboration in problem solving, creativity and other mutually advantageous endeavours.

On the other hand obstruct the collaborative mode of functioning and people become stressed. The unnaturalness of working in a top-down command and control hierarchy, whether it is a suffocating bureaucracy or repressive autocracy, triggers alarm bells deep within the human brain. Being unable to collaborate is essentially contra to our instinct for survival. The resultant stress response impairs the ability to function effectively.

Table 7:

	12 qualities that underpin successful leadership
1	An ability to empathise with colleagues and subordinates.
2	Self-awareness and an aptitude for self-analysis.
3	Social awareness – an awareness of the impact of one's behaviour on others.
4	The ability to handle uncertainty and ambiguity – patience and the ability to let progress and events unfold.
5	Self-confidence based on a rational and balanced self-assessment.
6	Honesty and integrity.
7	Field independence – ability to focus on the detail as well as retain a view of the big picture.
8	The subordination of self-interest to the interests of the group – humility.
9	Imagination in order to be able to conceptualise systems flow and the interconnectivity of the various elements of a system – Structure, interactions and function.
10	Positive outlook – optimism.
11	Low stress levels – equanimity in the face of both adversity and success.
12	Energy and stamina.

How to enable collaboration

Enabling effective, stimulating and productive collaboration is relatively easy as long as the leadership makes one all-important change of attitude. First and 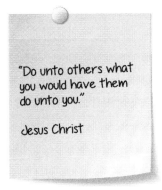 foremost collaborative leadership requires that you treat all members of your organisation like adult human beings. Adopt this approach and the rest falls rapidly into place. Unfortunately this first and simple step can go against some ingrained management attitudes.

"Do unto others what you would have them do unto you."

Jesus Christ

The truly frightening implication here for some managers is that collaboration means letting go of control and trusting that subordinates will behave responsibly and act intelligently. It especially means not treating them like irresponsible children or functional idiots that need to be kept on the tightest rein and have the simplest things explained to them. It also means not treating them as drones or even "assets" or "resources" or "human capital" to be exploited and then discarded as soon as they are no longer required.

The universal rule

The universal rule is just treat people the way you would like to be treated yourself; that way you cannot go far wrong. You enjoy being able to meet your needs and importantly so does everyone else.

To summarise then, a powerful way to improve productivity and performance is to enable employees to get their own needs met by enabling them to utilise their innate resources in collaborative problem solving and planning.

Structuring collaboration into the organisational design

Collaborative leadership does not necessarily emasculate the power of the senior management to generate ideas and develop strategic direction. It just shifts the emphasis away from telling and towards listening.

The focus becomes more on facilitating and managing the process of decision-making and less on controlling or directing the actual content of the decisions.

As an example, the team planning process I use called Team Business Development (TBD) revolves around a series of team-based planning workshops where the members jointly go through the logical sequence of planning events and activities. This process of mutual collaboration commences with the collection of views and comments from every member of the organisation and involves collaborative decision-making at management level. However, importantly the team leader still guides and controls the whole process from start to finish. Despite the appearance of a fairly relaxed decision-making process, such a collaborative planning approach is in effect driven by a set of formal and strict protocols and procedures. These provide the team leader with effective control and allow him or her to exert a strong and pervading influence throughout the process.

"Our brains and nervous systems are finely attuned to interacting with one another in the pusuit of shared goals."

But the influence of the team leader is more on the quality of the planning outcome and thoroughness of the process rather than the outcome's specific direction or details. In this way, the leader tends to act as a catalyst. With careful facilitation, policy direction or operational changes tend to emerge from the group as a whole in response to the apparent constraints and opportunities prevalent in the environment, as revealed by the bottom-up feedback.

Among other benefits, the leader's role as facilitator exploits TBD's team planning system to greatly expand the field of bounded rationality, stimulate double-loop learning and generate fresh ideas, solutions, enthusiasm, and initiative from the people who are involved in the day-to-day work. This in no way means that this sort of planning stifles a leader's own creativity and enthusiasm. You can read more about team planning in 7.1, 8.1 and 11.7.

Table 8: 10 ways neuroscience underpins collaborative leadership

Summary of brain research implications on leadership style, management function and organisational structure.
1   Challenges and problem solving stimulate the construction of new neural networks and connections in the brain. Enabling people to meet organisational challenges and problem solve in a collaborative working environment literally gets them functioning at a higher state of productivity. On the other hand when the management structure or function prevents people from active problem solving they become stressed. When people are stressed they begin to underperform in a variety of random ways.
2   In a low stress environment people can access the faculties of the limbic brain and neo-cortex and move away from the reptilian, black and white survival response to potential threats and challenges either real or imagined. This means an important leadership role is to work to remove active stressors in the working

environment.

3   The brain is hardwired to thrive off social interaction and collaborative problem solving. Working together in groups engages large areas of the brain and stimulates a range of positive responses in the limbic system that reduce stress and encourage use of the full range of mental faculties. The important implication here is that if you want to get people working in their natural brain state, just facilitate collaboration. Work with your group not over them.

4   The brain functions through neural networks, parallel processing and dynamic information exchange across all areas. This can be replicated in an organisation by widening responsibility for information exchange and information processing and shifting it downwards, freeing up the flow of cross information between individuals and departments. Freeing up the information flow results in a leap in positivity, problem solving and enthusiasm across the organisation.

5   Having some meaning to our lives is an emotional need. Brains find meaning through purposeful work. So enabling action based thinking and problem solving within the context of people's work is both motivating and exhilarating to them. Both personal and organisational performance improves as a result.

6   The brain utilises a system of negative feedback loops to generate 'double loop learning' that automatically engages in error detection and correction to refine and adjust a direction of activity. In a dynamically changing organisational environment, using negative feedback to create 'double loop learning' or the facility to question the appropriateness of an activity or response is of particular importance. This crucial faculty is inherently lacking in a bureaucracy but can be replicated in an organisation by devolving authority to question the status quo to the lowest possible level and especially at the interface with the customers. One significant advantage is that devolved authority enables a fluidly adaptive response to changing environmental and customer needs.

Achieving a fluid response to changing environmental circumstances means that the management emphasis changes from one of driving or pushing progress to *enabling* it by assimilating a continuous stream of negative feedback as a guide to removing obstacles and constraints to success. From a cybernetic point of view this faculty requires 'reference points' to avoid chaotic random activity and changes. In the organisational context these reference points are the shared vision, purpose and values of the organisation, that also evolve from feedback obtained from the customer interface.

7   The awesome self-regulating power of the brain provides it with almost infinite adaptability and creativity. This is facilitated by the dispersal of "intelligent activity" throughout the brain structure. This invaluable feature can be replicated in the organisation by enabling people to engage in 'intelligent action' through and across every level of the organisational structure rather than confining it to the higher reaches of the hierarchy.

8   Two incredible characteristics of the brain are its "neural plasticity" and the way it is designed to a "minimum critical specification". What this means is that it has the ability to reorganise and forge new patterns of neuronal activity when confronted with new tasks and new circumstances.

In the organisational context this means - drop rigid organisational structures such as organisational charts and detailed job descriptions and only define what is necessary to carry out the immediate task. In other words leave roles vague and even overlapping and rely on them being clarified at operational level by usage and collaborative questioning rather than any predetermination from above.

Crucially this facility allows different people to take the initiative on different occasions according to the contribution they are able to make at the time. They don't have to wait to be told what to do. The result is a great reduction in delays, waste and bottlenecks.

9   The colossal degree of interconnectivity in the brain and areas of excess capacity provide greater capacity in the system than is needed at any one time. For instance brain cells have multiple functions some of which are not always in use but can be used simultaneously with the other functions. This slack in the system is known as 'redundancy of function' and importantly allows for three powerful organising factors:

1. A 'sprint capacity' to be tapped into when needed
2. The ability of the system to cope with error
3. The facility to use the spare capacity to spontaneously evolve new structures and functions in response to external threats and opportunities.

It is possible to replicate this redundancy of function in the organisation by reducing specialisation and encouraging up-skilling and multi-skilling. This includes training everyone in a wider variety of operational skills but also skills that are usually the preserve of managers, such as analysis, problem solving and decision-making. These skills may not be required for traditional job roles but they enable people to take the initiative and implement new solutions straight away. All this saves time and avoids people passing the buck or remaining passively dependent on decisions being made further up the hierarchy.

10   In a group setting, individual brain states are highly contagious whether they are manifesting stress or happiness. With the right knowledge, leaders are in a powerful position to engineer a positive collective brain state in order to maximise coherent group activity and optimise individual creativity and productivity.

110

How collaboration meets a range of human needs

As the desire and ability to collaborate is in our very nature, so a truly collaborative style of leadership has a motivational impact on almost the complete range of our biological needs. This comprehensive impact brings down stress levels and boosts performance. In particular collaborative working addresses the needs for:

Fundamentally, people feel more secure when they have the power to fix things that they know are faulty.

Attention – Genuine involvement in the decision-making process requires a mutual transfer of attention between staff members and between staff and management. This reciprocal attention transfer enhances a greater depth of emotional connections.

Sense of security – People sense that their own survival is inextricably linked with the survival of their host group. They also sense when their host organisation is not running effectively. Being allowed input on relevant matters that then lead to improvements adds to the confidence they have in their own survival and the survival of their host organisation. Fundamentally, people feel more secure when they have the power to fix things that they know are faulty.

> *"Because people feel their ideas are being listened to I can see that they are much more motivated. People really feel the business is going places and want to be part of it."* Martin Daniel, Operations Director, SPS Group Ltd

A sense of autonomy and control over their lives – This need is closely linked to the need for security. It is successfully satisfied if people can make a genuine contribution to shape the necessary changes that impact their own lives. Not having control over our lives is a powerful stressor, as it creates uncertainty and doubt as to what is going to happen to us next. So achieving this need helps us feel more secure in the overall scheme of things and keeps us in our natural enthusiastic brain state.

"Our ability and need to collaborate is literally hard wired into our DNA.

Enjoyment, friendship and fun – Nature rewards us with a biological pay off when we can use our innate resources to meet our needs. Under these conditions

111

our physiology generates a flood of endorphins and neuro-peptides that make us feel good. This natural pay off means that genuine collaboration and teamwork in pursuit of a worthwhile group objective is highly enjoyable and truly exhilarating. Firm friendships are often formed in this sort of open working atmosphere.

Being part of a community – Healthy people are intrinsically loyal to their host group. People's survival instinct will drive them naturally to help solve the problems facing their host organisation[15] and participation in this process reduces stress levels by increasing their sense of belonging.

Table 9:

Emotional needs impacted by collaborative leadership	Positive impact	Negative impact
Security	✔	
Meaning	✔	
Emotional connection	✔	
Autonomy and control	✔	
Part of a wider community	✔	
Enjoyment, friendship, intimacy, fun	✔	
Status and recognition	✔	
Achievement and feeling of competence	✔	
Challenge – problems to solve	✔	
Privacy	✔	
Attention	✔	
Regular routine	✔	
Score	12	

A degree of status – Being asked to participate in a role otherwise regarded as the preserve of superiors provides welcoming recognition and respect.

Participants feel that they are being treated as mature, responsible adults with a valuable contribution to make to the overall effort.

Privacy and a balanced routine - Generally a collaborative work environment is naturally more amenable to respecting the individual physical needs of the participants including the need for privacy and a balanced routine. For instance, a collaborative planning structure provides a safe place in which individuals can come together and work in a less inhibited way. One characteristic of this is that team planning allows for specific thinking and learning time. This learning time allows individuals to ponder more than just the immediate concerns of a frenetic working day and among other aspects allows them to reflect on both their own learning needs and physiological needs.

Stretch, meaning and the need for a challenge – To remain healthy the human brain needs to problem solve. Problem solving is part of our very nature. The driving need to use this faculty both individually and with a group has been a powerful ingredient in the survival of our species. As such we find group problem solving truly satisfying and meaningful, especially if it is in pursuit of something worthwhile.

A feeling of competence – Being enabled to use innate problem-solving faculties that can otherwise lie dormant at work is satisfying and helps meet this need.

Meeting human needs fires up our innate resources

Satisfying all the above needs has the reciprocal effect of enlivening natural innate resources. When we are calm and relaxed through getting our needs met we have greater access to a variety of powerful innate resources.

A personal experience of running an upside down business

"As well as better service, I now also see better salesmanship and happier customers, and I'm happier too. Running the business has become much less stressful. We are attracting higher quality recruits and progress is no longer hampered by drongos (our name for useless underperformers). There is much more of a buzz about the business, with hardly a hint of 'them and us' between management and colleagues. I find that work is a lot more fun. It is definitely easier to run an upside-down business." John Timpson – "Upside-down management, A common sense guide to better business"[19]

113

Just as stress is contagious[16], group happiness is also infectious, only even more so than stress. In fact group happiness becomes greater than the sum of its parts. When there are clusters of happy people there is more than just an incremental effect on an individual's happiness[17]. Under such conditions, the whole group becomes more enlivened. Happy people at work tend to have an impact on the collective consciousness of the whole group; happy people reduce the stress levels of the people around them[18].

Being able to work with others to problem solve and innovate on behalf of the 'host group' satisfies just about all of our emotional needs.

So, meeting the above needs through mutually satisfying collaboration and problem solving automatically leads to an increase in people's natural enthusiasm to help their customers and colleagues. It also increases their feelings of loyalty to their organisation, their problem solving abilities, and their ability to empathise and support colleagues, clients and management.

An every day tale of top-down command and control management

Darren was a mortgage advisor at a high street branch of one of the leading UK mortgage lenders. He came for counselling in a stressed state due to the conditions he had to put up with at work.

At the time of our first discussion, Darren was in a quandary. He was being set a series of "priorities" by different central departments intent on imposing their various unilateral goals on the high street branch network.

In total, Darren was serving about seven different entities each of which seemed to have the right to dictate new terms or procedures on the sales force in the branches. These entities included the sales and marketing department at head office, the regional sales office (in the form of the regional sales manager), the IT department, the compliance department, the underwriters, a mortgage processing department and the HR department.

As though this wasn't difficult enough, each department appeared to have its own set of priorities and sought to impose these on Darren. Confusingly, individual priorities often seemed to work against the interests of other departments.

In addition Darren had another problem. Normally there was a branch manager to help him out, but at the time she was off on long-term sick leave, funnily enough due to stress.

As part of a preliminary investigation as to the cause of Darren's stress we looked at a normal day in his life at work. Although, perhaps normal is the wrong term here, Kafkaesque would be more appropriate.

First off, Darren had to attend a branch sales meeting from 9.00am to 9.30 am. The idea was to plan the proactive sales activity for the day. After which, the branch manager was required to telephone the regional sales manager and report the outcome of the meeting in a conference call with the other branches.

But remember, there was no branch manager.

Darren was actually the only sales person in the branch office. But under procedures set by the regional sales office he was still obliged to conduct a meeting on his own, then fax the minutes and report verbally on the proceedings to the regional sales manager. Part of the discussion with the regional sales manager was always to "agree" his sales action plan for the day. This pointless charade was played out every single day even though Darren never had any time available for proactive sales work at all and spent his days purely reacting to events as they cropped up.

That particular month the marketing department had decided that their priority was to target local estate agents. Their plan was for each mortgage advisor to canvass the local offices to build rapport and generate some mortgage leads. But, this campaign was in addition to continuing the previous month's initiative. The previous month the new plan had been for each mortgage advisor to make a minimum number of proactive telephone sales calls per day.

Darren was able to convey to me the content of that morning's conference call with his regional sales manager. The conversation went something like this:

Darren - "The estate agents aren't interested in us as they are already linked in with other mortgage lenders."

Regional Sales Manager - "Well the strategy here is to build rapport. Part of the strategy is to go in, have a cup of coffee and a chat with them and take along a tin of biscuits to share out. That should help get them feel more committed to helping you."

"Well I'm not really sure how that will work. There are other lenders who pay them 1% commission. That's got to be worth at least £500 every time they pass on a decent enquiry. Why would they want to give business to us in return for a biscuit?"

"Hey Darren, you are not being asked to develop marketing strategy that's the marketing department's job. They know more about this sort of thing than you do. I will be very interested to hear tomorrow how you get on today."

The other part of the telephone conversation is to explain why Darren didn't achieve yesterday's action plans.

"I'm the only person in the office".

"No you aren't, there is a branch manager and a cashier."

"The branch manager is still away on long term sick and I can't leave the cashier on her own in the office. Head office won't allow it for security reasons"

"Why haven't you contacted HR about that? This has been going on for a while now."

"I have, often. They say that the branch manager is still employed by the company, so we still have one and can't have another. I don't think they want to pay the extra overhead."

"Well in this climate, costs are a priority, you can still do the phone calls, why haven't you achieved your target here?"

"I can't make phone calls at the same time as handle mortgage enquiries over the desk and handle other enquiries. We were very busy yesterday."

"But you only handled one mortgage application yesterday, what was happening the rest of the day?"

"The mortgage application took me two and a half hours to complete. The marketing department have just started insisting that we offer critical illness insurance to every single new applicant without exception. The problem is that the forms take five minutes per page to answer and there are ten pages to cover."

"Did the client buy it?"

116

"Er .. no, she said at the outset she didn't want it, but I am told I have to run through the questions anyway. Otherwise I am not doing my due diligence in line with the compliance departments requirements."

"What did the client think of that?"

"She didn't, she left after quarter of an hour. She just wanted the mortgage arranged and had to pick her son up from school. I just had to make the answers up. As long as the form is filled in nobody is any the wiser, she isn't going to buy the cover anyway."

"What about the other ongoing mortgage applications?"

"They are still ongoing."

"Look Darren, they have been taking weeks, we offer a fast track mortgage service so the client can receive funding in less than a week. Why haven't you got this sorted already?"

"I know our sales literature and advertising offers a fast track mortgage process, but that isn't actually what we are able to do, is it? I have submitted the Ellis's application four times to the mortgage processing department and each time it comes back three or so days later rejected by compliance. Why does it take three days to read an application and reject it?

The rejection notice is almost completely undecipherable as they use codes instead of the English language. I don't have the authority to have a manual for the codes. So I have to email compliance just to find out what their other email was about. They don't handle these sorts of enquiries over the phone. Something to do with security I am told.

Then to get access to the mortgage processing on the computer I have got to have a daily password and this I can only get from head office. The whole procedure, just to read one of their emails, takes the best part of half an hour, and that's without any interruptions from customers over the counter.

Then I have to get back to the mortgage applicant and retrieve the necessary information, access the file on the computer and make the correction. It's a nightmare.

I must have spent three hours yesterday dealing with minor technicalities on different mortgage applications. None of them will make the slightest difference to the mortgage security risks. But they do tick all the boxes for compliance."

"Well compliance is a priority as you should know by now. But I really must emphasise the importance of prioritising mortgage applications, you are well behind your targets and you don't want to lose any deals here due to being too slow."

"Well I nearly squared off the Ellis's application yesterday afternoon. Unfortunately the IT department have decided to turn the computer system off dead on five o'clock these days. I was right in the middle of the amending process having had to wait for the password since three pm. I will have to start the whole process again today, but hopefully will have it completed by midday."

"Yes, well, security is a priority and we don't want people left in the building after hours with access to confidential client information. Anyway, you will have to delay doing the Ellis's application until after that I am afraid. I have to attend a sales and marketing meeting with the Group director at midday and you must collect the monthly statistics by then. This is a priority so please get on with it straight away."

Darren's predicament summarised

Please note the absence in this episode of any extreme control freak or dominating bully. What is evident though, is a high degree of insensitivity to Darren's needs and ignorance or denial of the reality of the situation in the high street offices. But this insensitivity probably derives from the overwhelming need by the various departments to meet the targets imposed on them rather than from any personal unkindness or indifference maintained by individual managers to their subordinates. Darren's senior managers are all under stress too.

Whatever the root cause of the inability to manage the situation effectively, it is obvious that the impact of this style of top down command and control leadership was de-motivating and stultifying of any enterprising initiative. Ultimately this method of running the organisation resulted in extra waste, paralysing chaos and failure.

Darren, and presumably every other mortgage advisor in the branch network, was placed in an impossible position.

In effect a variety of senior managers were imposing a stream of conflicting priorities upon the sales teams. Standardisation of everything from application procedures, to the approach made to prospects, meant that Darren and his colleagues had no discretion to avoid the imposed priorities. Just as hindering, he had no autonomy or control to find the means to fulfil them adequately.

There was a complete disregard to his objections and observations. Even though his observations were based on his close-up view of the practical realities of the situation. This simple discourtesy violated his need for attention and status as a valued member of a team. He was fully capable of making a significant contribution to improve things but was denied the opportunity to do so.

The impossibility of the targets threatened three needs:

Firstly, the unreachable targets threatened his security of employment as failure to perform invoked disciplinary procedures that would ultimately lead to dismissal.

Secondly, the impossibility of the targets overwhelmed any sense of them being a challenge.

Thirdly, the inevitable failure to perform at the required level provoked a feeling of incompetence, however much this failure was outside of his control.

In addition, the interdepartmental confusion as to the various priorities undermined Darren's need for meaning or purpose. At the same time, this level of bewildering chaos undermined his need to feel part of a coherent group effort.

Meaning and status were further undermined, as it was so clear to the sales staff that many of the different directives, instructions and initiatives were totally counterproductive to any effective sales effort. Many of these directives emanating from the senior hierarchy were quite frankly demeaning to the staff concerned. (For example not being trusted to use the computer server after 5.00 pm when they had been manning the office without a manager every day for several weeks.)

In essence Darren's entire working life, whether having a conversation with a prospect, managing his personal daily routine, arranging loans or developing sales contacts involved little more than pursuing compliance with other people's requirements and interests. Often these third party requirements were at the expense of his interests and the overall objective of his role.

Given the circumstances, I am surprised he managed to drag himself into work at all. Certainly the atmosphere created by the senior management was the exact opposite required to generate an enthusiastic and passionate sales effort. It is no wonder that he sought help for stress and low self esteem. What was required to untangle the mess was for the managers in the various departments to allow the sales staff to participate in the decision-making process. A key part of this would be to actively listen to their different objections and points of view. In this way, managers would then have learned about the problems arising from the numerous initiatives, procedures and directives and have had some chance to rectify the situation with the help and knowledge of the people on the ground.

The conclusion

I advised Darren to leave this company as soon as he could get another job.

Interestingly, the bank closed down the entire branch network about eighteen months afterwards. Predictably, the branches were losing money heavily, although of course this largely avoidable predicament was blamed on the recession. Unfortunately in the public sector, where top down command and control management is the preferred style, market forces can not be used to reward such low productivity and incompetence with closure.

6.2 How the power of trust forges a highly productive work culture

The problem defined: Stressor 2 - Institutionalised atmosphere of mistrust

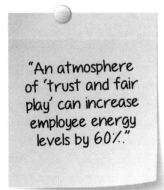

"An atmosphere of 'trust and fair play' can increase employee energy levels by 60%."

An institutionalised atmosphere of mistrust is a major stressor as it invokes fear and the usual stress driven survival reactions seen in the previous section. These have a corrosive effect on any working atmosphere, as enterprise, initiative, productivity and enjoyment all tend to evaporate. US research from the 1930s was perhaps the first to bear this point out. According to their findings at the time, the average employee performs at about 30% to 35% of available energy. However, where the situation is changed to an atmosphere of 'trust and fair play' employees were seen to input about 50% of their available energy. That equates to a 60% increase in input of energy[20].

It seems that the ability to cultivate an atmosphere of 'trust and fair play' is a powerful management tool for business and organisational improvement. There are a number of ways in which management tend to do the opposite and instead cultivate this type of unproductive working environment.

"Good leaders abhor wrongdoing of all kinds; sound leadership has a moral foundation."

Proverbs

Six reasons for mistrust

1. Unethical management behaviour

Unethical behaviour encompasses a whole range of possibilities but a common example arises when staff members are encouraged to lie to customers to cover up mistakes such as delayed delivery times, faulty quality, defective product features, restrictive terms and conditions and so on. People are not stupid. They know that if the management have no compunction about lying to customers then they will also easily lie to their staff. This understanding inevitably creates a backdrop of doubt and suspicion about management's true intentions.

2. Management deceitfulness

This category includes management lying or adopting a policy of secrecy (usually termed as confidentiality) to staff about their real intentions as to say prospective operational and structural changes, the viability of the organisation and the likelihood of redundancies. Another example is when leaders promulgate misinformation for some short-term gain such as hiding difficult issues or disagreements at senior level.

3. Authoritarian or severe behaviour

People feel insecure where there is an authoritarian or over-harsh imposition of the rules or where a management reaction unexpectedly and unfairly disadvantages someone for some minor misdemeanour or innocent error. Again, the result is a tendency to mistrust future management intentions.

The imposition or enforcement of politically correct views and opinions downgrades a person's status to that of being a mere mechanical functionary.

4. Political correctness

Political correctness or the imposition of ideological imperatives, i.e. telling people what they should believe, is a direct threat to people's ability to think for themselves. As such political correctness impinges on the emotional needs for autonomy and control and status and recognition (Being told how to think is essentially demeaning). As a result actions driven by political correctness are in danger of evoking a stress response. This sort of malignant subliminal pressure on the freedom of speech and freedom of action can also generate fear over one's personal security within the organisation.

The imposition or enforcement of politically correct views and opinions downgrades a person's status to that of being a mere mechanical functionary. Self-censorship is the immediate impact but a range of other factors also kicks in, as we shall see below in the section on the cost of mistrust.

5. Short-term or myopic thinking

Mistrust creeps in to working relationships when one party adopts short-term or myopic thinking and tries to get one over the other for a quick short-term gain. Good working relationships depend on the parties involved taking a long-term view that seeks to derive more than just a short-term advantage from the immediate transaction. In other words if you want to build a sustainable, high performance organisation, then your people need to trust that you and your organisation are looking to the long term and taking a generally holistic view of any given situation.

6. Blame games and witch-hunts

Under top-down command and control management, post-mortems into mistakes and problems frequently focus on identifying a culprit rather than on where the system broke down. Under these circumstances of endemic suspicion, mistrust among staff members and between staff and management inhibits the potential for drilling down to the root cause of the problem and arriving at a sustainable solution.

The cost of mistrust to an organisation

The real cost of unethical behaviour, lying or political correctness is out of all proportion to any gain. Apart from any other impact, mistrust usually aggravates the already corrosive "them and us" atmosphere common in any organisation where there is a top-down command and control hierarchical structure. Mistrust breeds a range of unwholesome consequences ranging from disloyalty, apathy towards the goals of the organisation, resistance to change, defensiveness, as well as turf wars and wasteful politics within the organisation. Crucially, people become wary of participating in any spontaneous collaboration in such an environment. The important follow-on of

"Unless conflict is eliminated, improved communication within a firm can hurt it, even destroy it."

RL Ackoff

this reluctance is that a lot of opportunities for improved working are missed out and hidden threats overlooked.

Mistrust breeds insecurity. Questions inevitably arise in people's minds as to a range of issues including the motives of the management, the safety of the organisation, the safety of their positions within the organisations, the likelihood of unwelcome changes being introduced and so on. Consequent rumour-mongering or simple overactive imagining can create sufficient emotional arousal to diminish employees' sense of control over their jobs, their ability to connect with those around them and their team spirit or sense of community. Nobody likes working in such an atmosphere, as it is generally repressive of the natural talents and attributes of normal rational human beings.

"The mark of a good leader is loyal followers."

Proverbs

Proponents of lean manufacturing already recognise trust as a core ingredient of participation. "Trust allows great swathes of bureaucracy and time to be removed, internally and externally … Building trust with suppliers gives them the confidence to make investments and share knowledge. Internally, trust allows a de-layered, streamlined and more creative organisation."[21] Toyota estimates that a culture of trust has enabled the slashing of as much as 30% costs in the supply chain[22].

Remedies

The simple remedy here is to be open and honest about the dealings of the organisation. This can be tricky if the organisation is operating in a way that will suffer from exposure to a wider audience. On the assumption that this factor is not an issue, then collaborative planning techniques excel in enabling openness and trust between management and staff.

Collaborative planning systems and much of lean management revolve around the full and frank dissemination of information to wherever it can be made use of and to whoever can make use of it. Decision-making is transparent and follows a clear and structured pattern that is understood and contributed to by all stakeholders. These sorts of methods tend to expose or neutralise secret agendas and also tend to nip disagreements in the bud.

"At heart we are group animals. Behaving responsibly is an instinctive survival mechanism for healthy adults."

123

Once you have openness and honesty and a fair and understood means of making decisions then you have the foundation for an atmosphere of trust. With trust prevailing in an open and collaborative working environment people's legitimate interests are far more easily catered for and this reduces stress levels further.

Give people information and they will feel more responsible

The concept of visual management, an integral part of lean manufacturing, is useful for enhancing more openness. Elements such as visual displays of simple performance measures (Key Performance Indicators - KPIs) and other information used in Kaizen and lean manufacturing, can have a powerfully motivating effect as they help transfer responsibility for higher performance down the line to those actually doing the work.

A warning here is that KPIs can have a de-motivating impact if they are imposed from above as targets (See Stressor 3 for more details of the impact of centrally imposed targets on motivation). The relevance of a KPI needs to be first agreed upon with those who have to use them. Otherwise, the more people are made aware of the true situation then the more they feel compelled to take responsibility for improving things and the more this awareness has a calming effect on stress levels. As a result trust stimulates a number of positive values including:

- A greater degree of loyalty and a much higher degree of commitment.
- People are more highly motivated to work on your behalf. There will be a greater "connectivity" within the organisation
- Improved upward flow of information particularly invaluable negative feedback
- A natural desire for collaboration
- People proactively look for solutions to problems rather than shrugging their shoulders and regarding a problem as someone else's concern

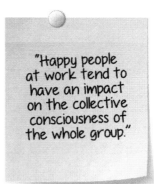

"Happy people at work tend to have an impact on the collective consciousness of the whole group."

Motivational impact on the human givens

At heart we are group animals and behaving responsibly is an instinctive survival mechanism for healthy adults. So, this is why when we are given the full information about the circumstances of the business or organisation we work for, we generally feel obligated to use this information in a responsible way.

"No one can expect the spirit of involvement and partnership to flourish without an abundance of information available even to the most humble employee…. The advantages of openness and truthfulness far outweigh the disadvantages. And a company that doesn't share information when times are good loses the right to request solidarity and concessions when they are not." Ricardo Semlar, CEO Semco.[23]

An atmosphere of trust has a cleansing effect on the whole organisation, as it impacts about nine biological needs. These include the need for security, attention, autonomy, emotional connection, friendship and fun, connection to a wider community, status and self-esteem, and sense of meaning. Different research studies show[24,25,26] that the resultant drop in stress whilst making people much happier enables them to:

- ❖ Listen to one another rather than just try and impose their own opinions.
- ❖ Reveal information and not hide it away as a potential source of more power or control or indispensability.
- ❖ Give non-judgemental negative feedback rather than blaming others to secure their own status.
- ❖ Accept constructive criticism, rather than be overly defensive.
- ❖ Learn from their mistakes rather than hide them.
- ❖ Risk incurring potential ridicule by suggesting something new that might be in danger of being inappropriate.
- ❖ Support other people so as to improve their own and the organisation's performance.
- ❖ Participate more enthusiastically in planning and management responsibilities.

In summary, once a feeling of trust is firmly established, it provokes a growing enthusiasm for collaboration that helps achieve group objectives. **This factor can be the core attribute that underpins the success of any group project**.

> Once a feeling of trust is firmly established, it provokes a growing enthusiasm for collaboration that helps achieve group objectives.

Chapter Seven

Types of management structure

Stressors reviewed in this chapter

Stressor 3   The imposition of goals or targets from a higher authority

Stressor 4   Unclear boundaries of functions and responsibilities

Stressor 5   Organisational units that are too large

7.1 Improving productivity without targets

The problem defined: Stressor 3 - The imposition of goals or targets from a higher authority

Managers tend to believe that to improve or even just maintain performance they need to get people motivated and engaged, tighten up on accountability, and induce them to work harder or smarter. Leadership is believed to be about doing things to help people improve personal efficiency and productivity. In this sense, the current management paradigm views personal productivity as one of the key factors in driving organisational performance improvements.

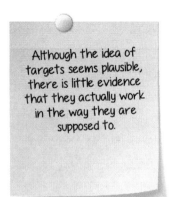

Although the idea of targets seems plausible, there is little evidence that they actually work in the way they are supposed to.

To improve personal productivity managers deploy an array of people management skills or techniques including coaching, training, mentoring, performance appraisals and supervision. These initiatives are all designed to maximise the effort contributed by the employee. A seemingly indispensible part of this array of personal productivity improvement activities is target setting. Targets are widely used as a means to monitor, motivate and control the activities of individual subordinates, work groups and even whole subsidiary organisations.

126

Widespread reliance on targets seems based on a near mystical belief, that somehow they have the power to transform management's ability to get results. It seems that, all that is required to 'make things happen' is to set a target and everything else will follow on from that.

A focus on targets ignores the constraints in the system that actually provide a rich vein of opportunities for massive improvements.

The almost universal popularity of target setting is further reinforced in the UK public sector by two other factors. The government has twin needs; first to ensure that the plethora of departments, agencies and quangos are pursuing their preferred policies. The second need is to ensure they are seen to be extracting value for money from tight budgets. In the fond hope of fulfilling these needs, central government departments, regulatory authorities and agencies set countless targets for a multitude of local operational units across the full landscape of government activities[1].

Targets are often counterproductive

In point of fact, although the idea of targets seems plausible, there is little evidence that they actually work in the way they are supposed to and a growing understanding, among people who study such things, that they are almost always counterproductive. In essence the whole concept is flawed as it is based on a misconception about how systems work and what keeps people motivated.

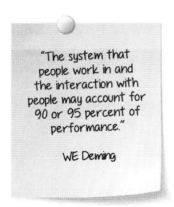

"The system that people work in and the interaction with people may account for 90 or 95 percent of performance."

WE Deming

From Edward Deming onwards, quality experts have recognised that 95% of performance variables are driven by the system's design, whereas only about 5% of these variables are driven by individual employee activity. In other words, it is not the people that are the key drivers to organisational performance problems or improvements but the organisational structures, management function and leadership styles, as these ultimately determine how individuals work.

It is the way management designs and runs the system that is the principle determinant of how well and smoothly the system runs, how good it is at doing what it is supposed to be doing and how efficiently people are working. So, when management and central government focus on targets as a means to improve performance they are unwittingly working with the residual 5%. As a consequence they ignore the constraints in the system that would otherwise provide a rich vein of opportunities for genuine improvement.

Why targets harm organisational performance

There are two generic reasons why targets, especially those imposed from outside the work unit, lead individuals and work groups to generally underperform:

1. Targets imposed from above or from outside the organisation distort operational focus away from customer needs and towards the meeting the needs of the hierarchy.
2. Arbitrarily imposed targets trigger the stress response because they undermine crucial emotional needs and suppress innate human resources. As soon as this happens, individual performance starts to wane.

The distinction between short term goals and targets

In any discussion about targets, we need to draw the clear distinction between targets imposed by a third party or higher authority such as senior management, a parent company, government department, regulatory authority and so on and those goals set by individuals for themselves or the sort of short-term goals set by managers during genuine consultation and collaboration with their teams and subordinates as a way to help clarify what a 'good' job looks like and how to make 'good' happen. Such short-term goals and perhaps more importantly, the process of setting them can be highly motivational as they provide:

- A meaningful aim for people to work towards,
- Clarity as to what exactly is supposed to be achieved (what 'good' looks like),
- Valuable guidance to assist productive or value added activity,
- Genuine input by the subordinate in the development of the goal. This includes attention being given to negative feedback about the constraints in the system preventing achievement of the goal.

Generic reason 1: Targets imposed from above or from outside the organisation distort operational focus

We can break the problem of distorted focus down into roughly four categories.

1. Targets shut down local improvement initiatives and provoke a static culture of dull conformism and compliance
2. Centrally imposed targets overlook local conditions and priorities

3. Targets induce 'failure demand'
4. Targets focus local ingenuity and creativity on compliance to the target, not on getting the job done right from the customer's point of view

Targets shut down local improvement initiatives and provoke a static culture of dull conformism and compliance

Senior management and government departments sometimes impose targets as part of the implementation of a 'best practice' regime. Unfortunately, 'best practice' is something of a misnomer as, from a practical point of view, there is no such thing as <u>best</u> practice only <u>better</u> practice.

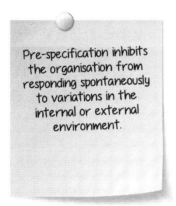

Pre-specification inhibits the organisation from responding spontaneously to variations in the internal or external environment.

It is an important fact of life, already well known in lean management circles, that nothing stays the same for very long. Change in organisational life, as in any organic system, is a constant; moreover although perfection in organisational terms is impossible things can always be improved.

In other words, if you make the assumption that you have realised some level of perfection and then compel everyone else to follow suit, you are likely to miss out on the need or opportunities for future innovations and improvement. Essentially you are using historic, not real-time data, to pre-specify what is needed. Pre-specification inhibits the organisation from responding spontaneously to any variations that occur either in the internal or external environment.

But that is the best-case scenario. At worst your assumption about what makes best practice may be wrong in the first place.

These problems are especially pertinent where people who are remote from the local operation have developed the best practice standard and who are therefore unaware of local conditions and other variable factors that prevail from time to time. These factors include the strengths and weaknesses of the individuals, systems and other resources at local level and the infinitely varied needs of local customers who stubbornly refuse to turn up in standard sizes.

Another danger arises in that sometimes during the formulation of best practice standards, the development process is hijacked by third party entities with a vested interest in instigating the standard. Examples of these interests include IT firms, management consultancies, training organisations and other suppliers, all of them lobbying to have their methods or technology adopted as the preferred solution. You can see the attraction; once they have their 'solution' built into the best practice standard, it becomes a licence for them to print money. The hapless user is locked in by compliance, whether or not this is what the customer needs.

Diagram 14

How targets distort operational focus

Conformance
Centralized targets prevent local improvement initiatives and provoke a static culture of conformism and compliance

Ignore local factors
Targets over look local conditions and priorities often relying on inappropriate or historic data. The result is unintended consequences

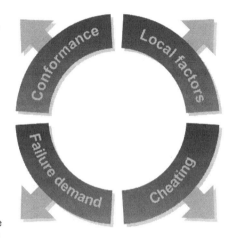

Failure demand
Targets typically apply superficial solutions that induce 'failure demand' that produces totally unnecessary waste elsewhere in the system

Cheating
Targets focus local energy & ingenuity on cheating the system to meet targets rather than focusing on customer needs & doing the job right.

Customers stubbornly refuse to turn up in standard sizes.

Wherever best practice is imposed from above, there is always a tendency to supress bottom-up innovation, independent enquiry, local and timely sensitivity to customer needs, creative enterprise and localised intelligent problem solving. In addition, such management condescension reduces everyone, subject to this regime, to feeling like they are non-entities with little contribution to make. Their skills, initiative, personal conscientiousness, professional experience and vocational calling are in effect ignored. As a result invaluable innate human resources start getting switched off and employees degenerate into 'jobsworth' mode.

In the unhealthiest cases, senior management views new ideas and practical objections as threatening the status quo and as evidence of a negative or insubordinate attitude. Such disdain further undermines local initiative and enterprise. This of course may be all well and good for a certain type of manager who has the impulsive need to feel 'in control' but is hardly conducive to meeting customer needs and fulfilling the purpose of the organisation.

In essence targets achieve a static culture characterised by dull conformism and compliance instead of a dynamic process of ongoing localised improvements and adaptation to client or customer needs. The stress generated means that people even lose the motivation required to fulfil the best practise criteria conscientiously (See generic reason 2 on stress below). The net result is that targets rarely facilitate even good practice, let alone best practice.

Targets overlook local conditions and priorities

A variation of the above problem is that invariably, targets set out to solve a problem recognised on the back of inaccurate or inappropriate data. Either the data is historic and obsolete or it is collected from a central location and well away from what is actually happening in different local areas.

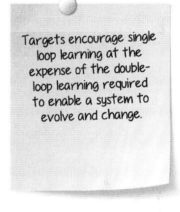

Targets encourage single loop learning at the expense of the double-loop learning required to enable a system to evolve and change.

Blanket targets, such as the government directive to limit hospital accident and emergency waiting times to four hours, are unable to take into account the almost infinite variation in local constraints, patient needs, opportunities and resources. It is these local variations that often invalidate the target objective. As in the point above, once the target is in place there is actually little or no opportunity for the local operation to develop an appropriate response to the local situation. The result is excessive waste and customer dissatisfaction.

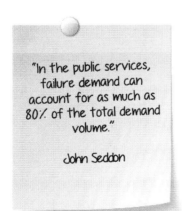

"In the public services, failure demand can account for as much as 80% of the total demand volume."

John Seddon

Targets induce 'failure demand'

Targets often lead to wide scale and totally unnecessary waste due to a concept coined by John Seddon as "failure demand" in his book 'Freedom from command and control'[2]. Failure demand is a highly useful term to describe situations where a failure to get something right in one area then leads directly to added and otherwise unnecessary demands on the organisation's resources elsewhere. In this respect targets, set by outsiders or third parties well removed from local conditions, are perennial culprits. The target setters typically apply 'solutions' to immediate or apparent problems without being able to drill down to find the local root cause in the system. As a result an inappropriate solution is imposed at the cost of not doing what needs to be done to solve the real and underlying problem. In this way, targets can be responsible for stifling improvements, actually lowering not increasing performance and generating waste and costs elsewhere in the system.

Failure demand case example

Incoming telephone calls were overwhelming a domestic-laundry customer-services department. Customers were complaining of constant engaged signals and were also irritated by having to leave recorded answer phone messages. To solve the problem the management were planning to hire an extra assistant and put in a new telephone line to handle the high volume of incoming calls. Fortunately a root cause analysis of the incoming calls revealed that a large number of customers were ringing-in simply to make the monthly phone payments; they were using the phone because they were unaware of the e-commerce and direct debit facilities. A good proportion of the other calls were enquiries about late deliveries and missing laundry items because customers had not been told of the direct line to the packing department. These latter calls took up telephone time while they were relayed to the packing department. Responding to answer phone messages took up a lot of telephone time further blocking the lines.

The next step down in the root cause analysis revealed that the reason customers were unaware of the alternative payment facilities and direct line was that the delivery drivers responsible for taking on new customers were not taking the time to provide them with the necessary information. The reason for this neglect was that the drivers all had to meet targets for so many deliveries and collections per hour. The targets didn't take into account the time required to handle new customer applications. Taking time to explain fiddly details therefore jeopardised the drivers' track records and they preferred instead to rush on to the next house.

The response from the company was to drop the targets, and inform all existing customers about both their e-commerce facility and the direct line to the packing department. Over a couple of weeks, incoming calls dramatically diminished, as did the need to return answerphone messages. This substantial reduction in demand on the system removed the need for new staff and an expensive new line.

132

Targets focus local ingenuity and creativity on compliance, not on getting the job done right

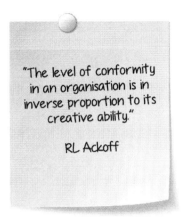

"The level of conformity in an organisation is in inverse proportion to its creative ability."

RL Ackoff

A key element of the target culture is the sanctions imposed to ensure compliance. Sanctions can easily provoke the law of unintended consequences. Instead of adhering to the spirit of the target there is a tendency that local management decisions, ingenuity and creativity revolve around achieving compliance to the targets by hook or by crook[3]. At this point the natural problem-solving skills nominally available to promote an organisation's goals and interest are turned against it and used to cheat the system.

In other words management time, effort and intelligence focuses on working out how they can satisfy remote third party requirements rather than focussing on the actual needs dictated by the local circumstances. As a result of distorting organisational focus, targets far from remedying situations, or improving performance, almost always make things worse.

With a target regime, underperformance is almost inevitable. Even where the targets are achieved it is almost always at the cost of other projects or other desirable outcomes such as customer satisfaction. The organisation's operations become distorted to meet the narrow imperatives dictated by the targets.

How targets distort priorities – case examples

Targets to reduce waiting times down to four hours in hospital A & E departments compelled managers in many units to act in entirely counter-productive ways so as to avoid sanctions. Ambulance patients were left waiting in their ambulances before being admitted to the A & E wards. At the other end of the process patients were discharged prematurely from A & E by being placed on trolleys in the main hospital corridors. All this was done to comply with what most people would agree was a laudable target.

At Epsom NHS Trust doctors reported that the pressure on managers to meet Whitehall's A & E four hour waiting time targets was relentless. For instance, one-hour meetings were held every morning to work out how to minimise any breaches of the waiting time target. These meetings involved at least ten managers and three doctors. As an estimate the costs of these meetings were a minimum of £400.00 per hour. That is an equivalent of £2,800 per week or £145,600 a year spent on meetings on target compliance not about patient care.

Generic reason 2: Externally imposed targets undermine crucial emotional needs and suppress innate human resources.

But warping operational focus is not the only unhappy consequence of a target culture; the stress generated by targets is another major factor in harming performance. In general terms, the effects of externally imposed targets on the human givens are much the same as for stressor number eleven – 'responsibility without the necessary authority to do the task'. Targets tend not so much to challenge and inspire people, but instead distract, shackle, overwhelm and frustrate. As such, externally imposed targets adversely impact seven emotional needs.

The need for some autonomy and control

Targets are arbitrary restraints on innate faculties and so act as a stress trigger.

Targets, almost by definition, diminish autonomy and control. Targets create a straightjacket that restricts the freedom and ability to problem-solve and innovate. Healthy people in a low-stressed state love innovating to improve things as they can make use of innate problem-solving abilities such as discretion, curiosity, judgement, rational analysis, long-term memory and imagination.

As such, targets are arbitrary restraints on these innate faculties and so act as a stress trigger. Under these constraints people feel frustrated or tend to lapse into safe compliance with the regime regardless of the impact this has on genuine customer or organisational needs.

The need for status and recognition

Targets tend not so much to challenge and inspire people, but instead distract, shackle, overwhelm and frustrate.

Being forced to comply with targets creates a feeling of subservience and so tends to violate the need for status and recognition. However senior management might like to dress up the situation; the blunt implications of imposed targets are that the authorities think one of two things about the subordinate management or worker. Either the people on the ground don't know what they are doing and need to be told, or they aren't motivated enough to improve things on their own initiative.

Whatever the approach, the management attitude that underlies target setting is demeaning to those who have to comply. It is especially demeaning to those who believe they are working in a vocational calling. For those holding significant responsibility, externally imposed targets provide them with no way to turn. Often, there is little credit for a successful outcome, as after all, compliance is expected, but they get all the blame when things go wrong.

Diagram 15

The impact of targets on emotional needs

Fun
Sense of fun needed for a satisfying career soon dissipates

Security
Fear of consequences to meet irrelevant goals that get in the way generate sense of insecurity

Meaning
The inability to achieve worthwhile goals & the time spent on worthless aims weakens the sense of meaning crucial in a vocation such as health or teaching

Autonomy
Almost by definition targets remove an important element of autonomy and control

Status
Status and recognition as a competent professional are undermined

Attention
Targets invalidate the attention factor as they are imposed regardless of local opinion and understanding

Achievement
Targets often obstruct the possibility to achieve something worthwhile

The need for attention

The need for attention is another casualty. Where authorities impose targets wholesale and regardless of the individual needs and competence of the stakeholders they are implicitly being insensitive to the feelings, opinions and concerns of those subjected to them. This insensitivity is a potent stress trigger.

The need for achievement and a feeling of competence

Employees know when they fail to meet customer needs. They are the ones having to deal with the disappointment, dissatisfaction, frustration and even rage when things go wrong. So, where targets contribute to this failure by restricting the organisations response to varying customer needs there is an inevitable feeling of non-achievement and incompetence. Frustration at the

135

ensuing confusion and the non-achievement of relevant objectives is stress inducing.

Over the long term, employees can suffer low morale leading to apathy, absenteeism, and even depression. Conscientious high performing employees tend to leave to protect their own health, sanity and self-esteem.

The need for meaning

A genuine sense of meaning is lost, as so much time, energy and resources are wasted having to meet the target terms and conditions. This extra work and cost also involves handling the inevitable compliance culture of auditing, seemingly endless and pointless reporting, controls, inspections and so on. All this activity is engaged in at the expense of not focusing on the real needs of the moment, as perceived by the customers and relevant stakeholders on the ground. All this provokes the sentiment "What is the point?"

Furthermore those involved at the sharp end can see for themselves that the operation may not be improving even when the targets are met. Further demoralisation is then produced when the authorities use the fulfilment of their targets as a basis for pronouncing that all is well when it is apparent to everyone concerned at ground level that it is not.

The need for physical security

A further knock-on effect is that the failure to meet the targets or at least the very real risk of failure to meet them tends to engender a fear for job security. This, in turn of course, generates individual blame avoidance tactics, box ticking, "impression management" and other time-wasting ruses to deflect blame and maintain an image of competence. Again energy and focus is pulled away from the customer's needs and towards self-preservation.

The need for a sense of fun and friendship

The struggle to comply with nonsensical, irrelevant or unobtainable targets that get in the way of real work soon diminishes the sense of fun needed for a satisfying and rewarding career and low stressed high performance. Similarly, friendships at work can become frayed when the stress of responsibility to conform to performance targets without the necessary means of achievement creates a competitive internal environment, strained communications and a blame culture when things inevitably go wrong.

136

The overall impact on stress

Imposing targets is one of the surest routes to suck the intelligence out of a system.

Being prevented from exercising real autonomy and innate problem-solving skills, being denied genuine attention, failing to achieve anything worthwhile or pursue activity with any real meaning slowly but surely undermines self-esteem. Employee self-esteem is important for an organisation. Under these depressing circumstances highly competent, well-balanced and enterprising people tend to leave to take up more worthwhile careers elsewhere. The organisation experiences a spiral of decline.

Operationally, the overall impact of a target culture is that the thinking capacity of the organisation is increasingly shut down, as people tend to develop a 'jobsworth' attitude. In fact imposing targets is one of the surest routes to suck the intelligence out of a system. Managers go into personal survival mode and become too keen to create audit trails that offload responsibility down the line and 'prove' their compliance to the target regime. Such a culture is the very antithesis of an intelligent organisation focussed on excellence and with everyone inspired by the desire to satisfy customers' needs.

Of importance to care-organisations such as the NHS and social services is that stressed employees can very soon lose the natural empathy and sense of conscientiousness needed for compassionate caring. Perhaps the use of targets as a means to drive policy initiatives helps to explain why an estimated 910,000 'patient safety incidents' occur every year in NHS hospitals. Out of this figure 91,030 are fatal[4]. Targets are a large part of the reason why, generally, low performance in the public sector has become almost legendary, at least among the hapless users if not recognised by politicians and senior civil servants.

Targets generate box ticking, 'impression management' and other time-wasting ruses to deflect blame and maintain an image of competence.

The impact of targets on such a wide set of biological needs also explains why staff turnaround, sickness, absenteeism and early retirement are so rife in the public sector. Vocational professions such as teaching and the police are especially badly effected in this respect.

An example from the social services

A nationally imposed target set for the social services is meant to speed-up the time taken for a new referral to be assessed and allocated to a caseworker. As is often the case, the objective behind the target appears practical, as it is designed to reduce the waiting lists of clients actually being helped by a social worker. However the intention and the reality on the ground are two very different things.

Managers go into personal survival mode keen to create audit trails that offload responsibility down the line and 'prove' compliance to the target regime.

Prior to the new target, social service teams would work progressively through their waiting lists. As new applicants arrived they would be put on the list and then take their turn waiting for somebody to be freed up to give them due attention. Their allocated caseworker would then carry out an assessment of their case and at that point instigate some action.

Essentially what happens now is that a caseworker is allocated to a new applicant straight away. In order to fulfil the target the caseworker then carries out an assessment immediately. So, that particular box is ticked to the satisfaction of department heads and Whitehall civil servants. All well and good except for two factors.

Firstly the allocated social worker is dragged away from dealing with someone else. This means disruption at the very least and inconvenience to other clients. But it often means duplication of effort, as the threads of the case have to be picked up again later on after an awkward lapse of time.

Secondly, more duplication of effort is required as the immediate assessment is usually now only an 'initial assessment'. This means that the assessment has to be carried out again at a later date in greater depth when there is more time available.

"Don't push growth; remove the factors limiting growth."

Peter Senge

Of course, once the initial assessment has been carried out, the client is no longer on the waiting list. But they still have to wait for any genuine attention and help. In fact the wait is usually longer than before. The reason being is that the limited resources in manpower now have to cope with two assessments not one, as well as the disruption to existing schedules and planning. Apart from impairing the service to the client, the targets have the effect of rendering the social workers' lives more difficult, more frustrating and less fulfilling. This in turn makes them less effective at work and less committed to the overall objectives of their departments.

Remedies

Get the people who do the work to plan the work!

The remedy to this unproductive way of functioning is to avoid setting targets and instead adopt two key principles of collaborative leadership. These are the continuous improvement concept and the principle 'Get the people who do the work to plan the work'.

As an example, TBD's collaborative planning system develops continuous improvement initiatives driven by "bottom-up" organisational-wide feedback. The outcome from the initial comprehensive feedback is a wealth of written real-time data generated from all interested stakeholders, especially those at operational level and at the customer coalface.

During the first multidisciplinary planning workshop, the management team reads every item of stakeholder feedback to acquire a more holistic view of the situation. The team then sets about responding to the feedback by developing remedies and action plans. The idea is to achieve agreed improvements wherever the people involved consider them necessary. Essentially, the bottom-up feedback and collaborative planning enable the teams to build on the perceived **Strengths** of the organisation, compensate for or remedy **Weaknesses** or constraints in the system, investigate and exploit **Opportunities** and avoid or confront any **Threats**.

These responsive action plans are regularly updated and adapted **not** in response to directives and new policy initiatives from higher authority but in response to ongoing feedback from customers and local stakeholders. In this way, the people that really know what is going on drive the improvements.

Realistic goals that are then achieved confer feelings of status or recognition, security, self-esteem, a feeling of competence and a sense of belonging.

One crucial difference of collaborative planning to top-down targets or "blue sky thinking" is

139

that long-term policy and strategy is allowed to EVOLVE or emerge from the constraints and opportunities within both the inner and outer environments. (This factor produces certain key advantages for strategy formulation that are discussed in 8.1 on major strategic change.)

An added advantage is that these action plans have the benefit of enthusiastic support from all the relevant stakeholders. Resistance to change tends to evaporate. There are a number of very good reasons for this invaluable buy-in.

Motivational impact on the human givens

The employees have shared in a meaningful way in the development of the improvement projects. Being allowed to apply their own direct experience, training, skills and enthusiasm is emotionally satisfying and tends to ensure a high degree of commitment and enthusiasm to following through with the implementation.

Removing targets and enabling groups to "self-regulate" and improve things for themselves, raises the whole tone of the organisation.

New tasks generated by the collaborative planning process satisfy the need for a real challenge. As such they tend to be more enjoyable as well. Realistic goals that are then achieved confer feelings of status or recognition, security within the group, self-esteem, a feeling of competence and a sense of belonging. The planning and implementation of goals that are perceived to be worthwhile provide meaning and purposefulness as well as giving a real degree of autonomy.

This type of team planning process is often described as invigorating by the participants. It empowers people to utilise a range of inner resources that typically lie dormant in top-down management command and control structures.

Removing externally imposed targets and enabling work groups to "self-regulate" and improve things for themselves, raises the whole tone of the organisation. The raised energy levels and competence transform the organisation's ability to deliver excellence to its customers, provide job satisfaction to its employees and fulfil its core objectives.

7.2 The vital role of defining clear boundaries for functions and responsibilities

The problem defined: Stressor 4 - Unclear boundaries of functions and responsibilities

This stressor typically involves people constantly tripping over each other and having their work outcomes threatened by outside interference to their area of responsibility. Both confusion and conflict can quickly arise as a result. The effect is similar to two other stressors – 'unclear goals' and 'responsibility without authority'. All of these lead to a dispersed effort and a waste of time and resources.

> Human beings need space within which to live, grow and prosper. Where there are unclear boundaries, this personal space is impinged.

Human beings need space within which to live, grow and prosper. At work, where there are unclear boundaries, this personal space is impinged. This stressor also impacts the autonomy and control required to do a worthwhile job and so, in turn, impacts self-esteem and the need to be able to meet a challenge. This stressor risks provoking political rivalries and turf wars as those affected struggle to make sense of the confusion. Such conflicts soon sour personal relationships. So when this stressor is present friendship and fun suffers. A sense of status and meaning can also be diminished if responsibilities or functions are undermined or removed. You will not get the best out of people under these circumstances and both individual and group productivity will inevitably suffer.

Remedies

To overcome this stressor, ensure that operational planning involves mutually agreed and clear demarcation of responsibilities. Collaborative planning and decision making involving all the significant stakeholders helps here. In a group planning environment the whole team is kept informed and consulted over new initiatives as and when those initiatives are conceived and developed.

This means there is ample time and opportunity for feedback so that vague boundary lines, ambiguities in function, responsibility and authority can be sorted and agreed at the planning stage by the people actually doing the work. The outcome of a well-structured team planning process is that people know exactly:

- What they have to do
- Who they have to answer to
- Whose support they can expect to rely on
- Exactly why the project or job they are doing is important in the context of the overall purpose of the organisation

Motivational impact on the human givens

Clear and unambiguous boundary lines created by mutual agreement mean that team members, feel a strong sense of personal autonomy within a secure territory. The harmony created by clear and agreed boundaries helps make for a strong sense of team spirit. Self-esteem and a feeling of achievement are enhanced, as team members are able to fulfil their functions and responsibilities sufficiently.

7.3 Getting the size right

The problem defined: Stressor 5 - Organisational units that are too large

"Large, centralised organisations foster alienation like stagnant ponds breed algae. In massive corporations, an employee will know few of his colleagues. Everyone is part of a gigantic, impersonal machine, and it is impossible to feel motivated when you feel you are just another cog. Human nature demands recognition. Without it, people lose their sense of purpose and become dissatisfied, restless and unproductive. Stalin understood this. Prisoners in his gulags were obliged to dig enormous holes in the snow, then fill them in again. It broke their spirits." R. Semlar, CEO, Semco.[5]

200 years since the industrial revolution is hardly enough time for our genetic make-up to adjust to the colossal size of organisations today.

Human beings have been functioning and working together in small groups for tens of thousands of years mostly in small farming or tribal communities. Only very recently, in evolutionary terms, have we migrated to working in large highly-structured organisations. Any sort of drastic change like this takes our genetic make-up some time to get used to and the 200 years or so since the advent of the industrial revolution is hardly

142

enough time for the human genetic make-up to adjust.

The author Anthony Jay in 'Corporation Man'[6] reckons the ideal group size that people are really efficient and effective in is only about ten individuals. Other researchers have concluded that the human psychophysiology responds and functions much better in units of less than 150 people[7]. Importantly for organisational effectiveness beyond this significant size of 150 people, employees start to get stressed and the organisation suffers from increased sickness and absenteeism. Essentially we start losing that close emotional connection and interchange of attention between people that helps to maintain low stress levels.

Small groups, where everyone has a possibility of knowing everyone else, have the advantage of being more cohesive – everyone can share the same goals and values. Such a size also allows for closer community support, and co-operation. So the key human givens impacted in large organisations are:

- Attention
- Safe territory to work in
- Emotional connection to co-workers
- Some degree of status and recognition
- A close connection to a wider community

The limiting factor of 150 people obviously has significant implications for large companies and organisations such as schools, hospitals, prisons and so on.

In many areas of working life, particularly in the public sector, there is still an accountancy-led drive for efficiency through specialisation and the economies of scale. The result is the generation of larger and larger operational units, the very opposite of what is required for both individual and group efficiency and effectiveness. Successful experiments to limit organisational size to 150 people have been carried out.

One such company is Gore Associates. Perhaps best known for their Goretex brand of outdoor clothing, Gore, set up in 1958, is now a $1.6 billion company and is regularly included in Fortune's annual list of top companies with world-class new product development across a range of innovative markets. Gore constantly maintains their divisions at about 150 people by splitting off and re-dividing as them as they grow. They find this tactic helps retain

> Large organisations lose that close emotional connection and interchange of attention between people that helps to maintain low stress levels.

143

innovation, peer pressure and interconnectedness.

This entrepreneurial culture is enhanced by a lattice organisation with no traditional hierarchy, no predetermined channels of communication and no lines of control. Instead, communication with one another is direct. Accountability is towards the fellow members of the multidisciplinary teams[8].

The amoeba approach

Semco is a family-run Brazilian manufacturer of a range of products from industrial pumps to dishwashers. Their owner, Ricardo Semlar has pioneered what they call 'running a natural business' and it is now one of Brazil's fastest growing companies. The key to their outstanding business success has been to establish genuine and comprehensive worker participation in small units of production that never grow beyond 150 – 200 people.

As factory sizes grow so units are split off like an amoeba. Each new unit is fully autonomous with managers using their own discretion, independent of head office interference but always using full worker involvement in the local decision-making processes. Head office is there to support but only at the request of the local manager.

Semco's first experiment with the amoeba approach eliminated bottlenecks in production allowing production to meet sales demand. Faulty product was reduced from 10% to 1%, inventory reduced by 40% and productivity doubled. Semco finds that the smaller plants, despite the loss of economies of scale, are far more innovative than their larger ones, make more money during the good times and bounce back quicker during recessions[9].

Chapter Eight

Strategic and operational issues

Stressors reviewed in this chapter

Stressor 6   Major strategic change

Stressor 7   Onerous externally imposed deadlines

Stressor 8   Boredom and monotony

Stressor 9   Low quality work

8.1 Achieving buy-in for strategic change

The problem defined: Stressor 6 - Major strategic change

The ability to adapt and cope with changes in the environment is a prerequisite of life for any organism. Change is written into the natural order of things and what goes for the organism goes for the organisation. Seismic or step change however can bring acute challenges that threaten to overwhelm the natural ability to adapt. Dramatic changes in the external environment, such as the sudden arrival of a dominant new competitor or an innovative competing technology, need a matching strategic response from within the organisation. Such a response means structural, operational, technological, employment and relationship changes, the bigger the changes the greater the turbulence within the organisation.

Impact on human givens

This type of major strategic upheaval can easily undermine an employee's feeling of physical security and threaten long-standing working relationships and routines, all potent stressors. However the impact on the human givens can be significantly influenced by the style with which the management conduct the change programme.

When senior management impose their own response to change from above they adversely impact other biological needs as well. Insensitive or authoritarian imposition particularly undermines the needs for:

- Some level of autonomy and control
- Connection to a wider community
- Status
- Attention
- Intrinsic meaning and purpose

This is why strategic change invoked by top-down command and control can work directly against the change objectives. The accompanying stress response stimulates dread and resistance among stakeholders. Apart from hampering the change process the stress also undermines productivity and performance for the duration of the change and often for sometime after as well.

Thus, adept handling of the stress related to a change process has to be a strategic priority and has to be an integral part of the strategic planning process. If you fail to jump this hurdle, the very people who are supposed to be implementing your new strategy will be trying to thwart it, or at the very least they will be implementing it half-heartedly and less effectively.

Remedy

The easiest way to avoid this debilitating impact of stress is to get all the stakeholders on board at the very inception of any major strategic change initiative. Getting early buy-in also happens to be a great way to develop robust and successful plans.

This means getting people to accept the idea of change even <u>before</u> senior management have come up with their strategic plan. In other words, do not fall into the trap of announcing some grand new vision and then expect everyone else to fall meekly into line with it. Accepting such proposals doesn't come naturally to most people and you are simply taking on the onerous burden of a hard sales challenge for your ideas.

Don't impose a vision, facilitate its emergence from the group

The conventional approach is that the leadership presents the new vision as the starting gun to the change journey. This is a popular strategy, as unfortunately it appeals to the vanity of would-be visionaries and egocentric bosses firmly wedded to the top-down command and control style of leadership or who are dedicated to being seen to 'make a difference'. Unfortunately the truth about visionary leadership is more prosaic.

Apart from successful private enterprises, most people in leadership positions are not, by any stretch of the imagination, entrepreneurial geniuses or pioneering founders. Unless they have owned and successfully run their own business they can rarely claim to have reached the rarefied heights of leadership responsibility through boundary-breaking or paradigm-shifting ideas that have launched their organisations into world-beating enterprises. The reverse is usually the case. Many leaders are corporate or public sector functionaries promoted into their jobs through diligent and orderly career progression. At best this promotion has come about through their prudence, competence, hard work and a passive acceptance of the prescribed norms. At worst, as we have seen already, a major contribution to achieving high rank is often docile compliance with the ascendant hierarchy and/or skilled political manoeuvring.

> Rarely do bureaucracies rear the free spirits with the original imagination and daring needed for a powerful and inspiring paradigm shift in vision.

How often in today's organisational life do we find the indomitable vision of a Martin Luther King, the missionary zeal of a William Wilberforce, the tactical resourcefulness of a Field Marshall Montgomery, or the teckie genius of a Steve Jobs? In fact rarely, if ever, do bureaucratic organisations rear the sort of mavericks and free spirits who have the style of original thought and daring imagination required for a powerful and inspiring paradigm shift in vision.

So, humility is essential here. Genuine respect for the total brainpower of all their employees would help corporate and public sector leaders recognise that their personal vision does not carry a fraction of the weight of the collective vision that can emerge from the group they lead, that is, once they choose to facilitate it.

In addition to this salient weakness, adopting the vision-first tactic puts the cart before the horse in terms of planning a coherent strategy.

Where are we now?

The best place to embark on any significant journey is to find out exactly where your starting place is.

The best place to embark on any significant journey is to find out exactly where your starting place is. In the organisational context one of the most effective ways to orientate yourself accurately is to ask all your employees for their viewpoints on the situation, especially those people engaged in some way with direct interaction with the customers. There are three good reasons for this.

Firstly, collecting everyone's views provides invaluable data on the true situation, such as the constraints or those hidden weaknesses that are holding you back, the strengths to build on, the threats to avoid and the genuine opportunities available. Digging up this data invariably uncovers buried obstacles that would otherwise have harmed the successful implementation of a new strategy.

Secondly, inviting participation from all employees, at the very start of the strategic change process, and then making participation an ever-present feature of on-going change will also engage them emotionally. People feel they are being taken into account, that their views, beliefs and values are recognised. They are more inclined to believe that the whole process is being undertaken as much for their benefit as for the management and owners. As fear is reduced and feelings of security enhanced so you instil the necessary commitment and motivation to implement a rapid and successful new direction in strategy.

Thirdly, deriving everybody's viewpoints at the start of the process and then being sensitive to the revealed facts on the ground enables a genuine consensus to emerge with all those involved as to the new direction of the organisation. This saves time and energy that can otherwise be wasted in tough negotiation, fruitless argument, turf wars and political manoeuvring.

Making the change journey smooth

As a cautionary note, the wealth of data collected and the involvement of a wide body of stakeholders can, unless handled correctly, lead to delays, mistakes, chaos and confusion in the decision-making process. The immediate challenge is to reconcile four seemingly conflicting factors:

1. The need to generate widespread participation from all levels and across all disciplines and functions whilst at the same time …
2. The minimisation of operational disruption
3. The need to stimulate new learning as well as creative and boundary-breaking thinking and ideas
4. At the same time as maintain cohesiveness, consensus and a firm control of events and finances

Researchers at SRI back in the 1960s developed a structured approach to this multidimensional problem based on emerging ideas about how the brain processes information and reaches decisions. The solution they came up with was an integrated team-based planning system pivoted around a sequence of planning workshops. The SRI system forms the core of TBD's integrated planning process and takes just a few days to convert the organisation-wide feedback into a robust and comprehensive 'Management Action Plan'.

Team planning is based on emerging ideas about how the brain processes information and reaches decisions.

In essence the system involves a multidisciplinary management team working in a series of planning workshops through a step-by-step planning process that often includes rapid improvement events, and accelerated learning sessions. This type of collaborative planning speeds up implementation dramatically. Even major change initiatives tend to take weeks not months to instigate. The accumulative effect, of all the various improvement projects being planned and initiated together in an integrated way, combined with the emotional engagement of a wide group of stakeholders creates a wave of transformation right across the organisation.

An evolutionary change occurs

"TBD has achieved more in three weeks than I normally achieve in six months".

Jeff Heyes,
veteran print industry
turnaround specialist

Two important advantages accrue from this collaborative planning process. Not only do the various short-term plans improve operational productivity and performance, they also redirect organisational initiatives towards the new change requirements. In this way the organisation functions more like a human brain, in that the vision and strategy EVOLVES step by step and in line with the bottom-up sensing of the reality of the organisation's circumstances.

This evolutionary change has important implications for the role of leadership. The process of leadership in this context is one of facilitating the emergence of a group vision that everyone can buy into easily and wholeheartedly. In other words, instead of driving change and depending on leaps of faith and blue sky thinking the new direction evolves from a process of refinement and adjustment in line with ongoing live feedback from the working environment.

Motivational impact on the human givens

In terms of the human givens' perspective, this type of collaborative approach makes employees and managers feel more in control of their working lives. Instead of feeling swamped, managers feel more like they are surfing the waves of change.

> The process of leadership is one of facilitating the emergence of a group vision that everyone can buy into easily and wholeheartedly.

Collaboration transforms the change experience from one of anxiety or fear to something more like exhilaration. Participating actively in making decisions enhances a sense of security. People feel that they are being taken into account, that they matter and that they are not going to be left behind or washed up. If the major strategic change can accommodate a series of small step changes rather than giant leaps so much the better, as the challenges set feel that much less overwhelming.

Case example – A formal team planning process driving a rapid turnaround at a failing pharmaceutical factory

> Instead of feeling swamped, managers feel more like they are surfing the waves of change.

A Swiss multinational pharmaceutical company was forcing one of its subsidiaries to close down. The factory, based in Scotland, had been floundering under the weight of a number of intractable problems that had eroded gross profit margins. Ageing machinery was delivering an unacceptably high rejection rate and suffering a growing amount of downtime. Low staff morale and poor labour relations not only generated low productivity but also provoked dogged obstruction to technical innovations and automation. This obstruction prevented the company installing the modern equipment

150

required to stay competitive and maintain profitability. The upshot was that the Swiss parent had had enough. The multinational decided to cut its losses and sell the plant.

The impending shut down at last galvanised the local management into energetic action. Determined to avoid closure they called in a team-planning specialist to facilitate a rapid turnaround. They had absolutely no time to lose. As a first step the specialist recommended the appointment of a planning team headed by the local MD and comprising the heads of all the company's various functions and departments.

The next step was to gather written feedback from a wide body of staff members. Everyone from every level of the organisation was asked to participate in the writing up of "planning issues". Literally hundreds of written planning issues provided an in-depth and multi-pointed view of the company's real circumstances. The planning team then took 3 days out from their everyday activities to translate the stakeholder feedback into a range of different improvement projects.

This collaborative exercise generated a widespread sense of urgency. It also attracted the necessary buy-in from the staff and generated many fresh ideas. These ideas ironed out a lot of snags and bottlenecks, speeded up workflow and instigated a number of other immediate improvements to efficiency.

The early momentum on improvements alone began to turn the existing operational situation around, but this was only the start of the turnaround. The team consolidated the various improvement projects into a comprehensive business plan that justified the investment of £140 million to fully re-equip the factory (1980 prices). Within a matter of three weeks, the whole planning team presented their new business plan to the parent company in Switzerland.

As a direct result of this concerted team planning effort the parent company consented to the proposed regeneration plan. The money was raised and the factory went on to become one of the largest vitamin C manufacturing facilities in the world.

Importantly, a number of factors had combined to convince the parent company of the factory's future prospects. Specifically they were impressed with the:

1. Dramatic turnaround in productivity on the shop-floor.
2. Planning team's obvious in-depth knowledge of the factory's problems and their ability to correct them.
3. Apparent thoroughness of their research and analysis.

4. Robust and detailed action plans to improve the business at every level and in every area.

5. Team's evident renewed enthusiasm and commitment to driving through the immediate improvements and restoring the company back to full health.

8.2 Making deadlines work for you

The problem defined: Stressor 7 - Onerous externally imposed deadlines with insufficient time to do the task

The pressure to meet regular overambitious deadlines can create imbalances to lifestyle, and a healthy routine. In turn these imbalances risk creating trait anxiety, exhaustion, and ultimately burnout. The resultant mistakes and degradation of relationships created under these conditions leads to customer dissatisfaction, waste and rework. There is also a danger of a high turnaround of the affected staff with the consequent danger of losing valuable experience in those areas most under pressure.

On the psychological level, onerous deadlines can impinge upon any feelings of autonomy. As with chaotic routines, (See chapter 9 section 5) life feels out of control and physical and mental exhaustion can soon set in. Such exhaustion not only impairs judgement and a sense of fun but, crucially for those in a caring profession, also harms our ability to empathise and give effective personal attention. This applies to people both at work and at home. As the weight of work crowds in and crushes the sense of awareness the observant self becomes clouded bringing a sense of disorientation and loss of self-awareness.

Another problem to look out for is that if the pressure includes late working to catch-up then sleep disturbance impinges on the dreaming state. This interference further undermines the individual's capacity to alleviate the stress of the working day and assimilate the daily burden of events. Lack of sleep also impacts our inherent problem-solving ability and our capacity to have innovative ideas[2]. As a result, unremitting pressure of deadlines can develop a spiralling of lower productivity.

Remedies

The remedies available for this stressor occur on two levels – the group level and the personal level.

On the group level, a powerful remedy is for the management to adopt a collaborative leadership style and team planning structure as advocated for the previous stressors. The creation of a strong team spirit engendered through genuine collaboration and planning helps to induce a feeling of "ownership" over fast moving events. Adequate training and the adequate provision of the necessary equipment are, of course, also vital. These factors go some way to alleviate the feeling of loss of control over personal destiny that can occur when there is such a rush to meet deadlines.

Collaboration in short-term planning and the pursuit of a continuous improvement culture makes it easier for people to do their work, smoothes out the obstacles to successful achievement of tight deadlines and so helps create short-term 'wins'. Successful achievement of deadlines helps restore confidence, a feeling of competence and self-esteem.

Unfortunately working to onerous deadlines or at any rate having to submit to tight time constraints is an inherent feature of many jobs. Urgent medical intervention, whether A & E, surgery, or intensive care nursing, journalism, printing, air traffic control and many other professions are all characterised by the need to perform consistently and professionally under extreme pressure of time. In these instances the deadlines are outside the direct control of either the management or the organisation. When this is the case then of paramount importance is the availability or encouragement of an effective personal stress management regime.

"A relaxed individual, free from the distractions of anxiety and worry, can more easily and more completely apply his creative potential".

Maharishi Mahesh Yogi[14]

There are available today a wide assortment of stress management aids ranging from aerobic exercise, yoga, meditation, guided visualisation, breathing techniques, lifestyle advice, to name a few. It is, however, not the purpose of this book to discuss remedies to individual stress. The purpose here is to identify organisational means to remove or at least alleviate stress from the work environment. Having said that, research shows that the most powerful stress management method is a meditation technique known as Transcendental Meditation or TM as it is usually referred to. Plus-points for this technique, as opposed to say mindfulness meditation, are that it is very easy to learn, enjoyable to do and does not intrude into the work environment, as it is integrated easily into a daily personal routine. TM is also validated by a mass of research published in peer-reviewed journals.

The benefits of TM arise from the concentrated rest attained during the twice-daily practise of twenty-minutes of deep meditation. These brief periods, when the metabolism settles down to profound levels of rest, have a powerful restorative effect on the nervous system and enable a rapid recovery from stress. As a result of this stress reduction, regular practitioners of TM report improvements to a wide range of performance factors and these improvements seem to accumulate over time.

As examples, the research indicates reduced stress[3] and anxiety[4], improvements to IQ[5], optimized brain function[6], increased creativity[7], improved productivity at work[8], reduced insomnia[9], improved creativity[10], enhanced field independence[11] as well as other important factors such as better health[12], and a reduction in cardiovascular disease[13].

Motivational impact on the human givens

Galvanising team support and developing a greater capacity for individuals to cope with stress, precipitates a dynamic change in the ability to meet biological needs despite a difficult environment.

Firstly, employees begin to feel more in control of events.

Secondly, they can experience real highs when achieving tasks successfully, despite the odds and the onerous time constraints.

Thirdly, the process of group work and subsequent achievement often leads to strong bonding and friendship in the workplace. In a genuine team atmosphere there is an improved ability to give and receive attention and connect emotionally with peers and work colleagues.

Fourthly, low-stressed individuals enjoy the benefit of greater access to their rational mind, their imagination and other faculties required for effective problem solving.

8.3 Stimulating enthusiasm for boring work

Stressor 8: Functional specialisation - boredom and monotony

For a large section of the working population, the daily reality of job specialisation and the division of labour is boredom and monotony. Automation and deskilling down to a minimalist level starves employees of the opportunity to utilise inherent resources and is therefore prone to inducing stress.

We have within us an almost infinite capacity for creativity and the use of our intelligence. But boring, restrictive and tedious jobs cramp the opportunity to express this creativity. It is the friction between our inner potential and the reality of everyday existence that stimulates the stress response[15].

So, although we have reaped extensive economic benefits from the division of labour there is a downside. Endless repetitive tasks and high degrees of automation may exploit the best from capital equipment but are hardly conducive to instilling motivation, commitment and conscientiousness among employees.

As a result, individual productivity suffers in a boring and monotonous working environment. Ironically, managers often reward slow working with time-based incentives such as overtime payments. But other problems occur including careless production of excess waste and scrap through inattention. In extreme cases of boredom and frustration people are known to commit minor acts of disruption, obstruction and even sabotage.

Service employment fairs little better with tedium and monotony fraying tempers and inhibiting genuine teamwork. Positivity and enthusiasm towards hard-won customers and service users also suffer.

In these sort of low-paid environments, there is a tendency for a high level of staff turnover. This adds significant cost in terms of recruitment, induction and expensive learning curves for new staff.

The underlying problem is that under normal healthy circumstances, boredom and monotony are unnatural. If such a mental state is continued over a prolonged period, it will trigger a stress response by impacting a number of the human givens. The likely impact on the human needs include:

- First and foremost the need for attention; by implication, managers who create such a repressive work environment display a significant lack of interest for the concerns and welfare of their staff.
- A direct loss of autonomy, as people feel trapped by standard operating procedures, rules and regulations that tie them down to the seemingly endless repetition of closely prescribed tasks.
- Almost by definition, there is a lack of fun, achievement and challenge in such a humdrum existence.
- Minimal status and sense of meaning in these sort of monotonous jobs resulting in loss of self-esteem.

- Any real security is somewhat diminished; people know that they are being treated like drones and so recognise that they are entirely dispensable. A drop in sales, a sudden focus on cost cutting and they know they are out.

As you can probably imagine this is all rather depressing. Perhaps this is why high alcohol consumption, smoking, ill health, obesity and absenteeism are more prevalent among people employed in these sorts of low-paid jobs.

Remedies

"If you want people to do a good job, give them a good job to do."

Frederick Herzberg

A number of remedies for stress-induced boredom and monotony help improve motivation and productivity. Initiatives such as training employees in multiple skills and organising job rotation provide employees with crucial variety and greater and more rewarding responsibility[16].

Do a cost benefit analysis into replacing the dumbed down jobs altogether and creating work that requires a mix of skills that adds up to a reasonable level of expertise and variety. A current state cost exercise should take into account the indirect costs to the organisation including items such as high staff turnover, excessive recruitment and induction costs and the real impact of errors, scrap and dissatisfied customers due to interaction with disengaged staff.

Ergonomic layouts can help too as they can include opportunities for social interaction. Adequate breaks and rest periods can be provided that help to maintain attention and focus.

Different approaches to collaborative working all help inspire greater interest and enthusiasm in what are otherwise extremely tedious jobs. Team working, self-directed teams[17], lean management and Kaizen all help alleviate the problems associated with dull and boring work. This is especially the case as these approaches combine with principles of continuous improvement or total quality that offer a greater degree of meaning to those involved.

Motivational impact on the human givens

These types of collaborative initiatives all help people on the factory floor or working in routine administrative tasks feel they and their needs are being taken more into account. Even this modicum of attention and involvement has a marked effect on stress levels with a knock-on impact on work performance. A degree of self-management of mundane tasks invariably results in innovative ways of relieving the tedium. People feel more in control, become more emotionally connected with their colleagues, feel part of a team (wider community) and have the need for attention alleviated to some degree.

Management strategies such as lean management and the pursuit of continuous improvement provide a greater degree of accomplishment and purpose to people's working lives that would otherwise seem pointless and soul destroying. Participation in such methods allows for the use of mental faculties and problem-solving capacities, as people are confronted with the challenge of finding ways to improve productivity. Work actually becomes a lot more enjoyable. As a direct result productivity goes up and sometimes quite dramatically.

Case example of self-directed teams creating massive productivity gains

Wesley Jessen, a contact lens manufacturer, was experiencing low productivity. Issues included:

- 84% scrap rate, as scrap accumulated at each stage during the multistage production process.
- Six-week average production time per lens.
- Manufacturing costs of £5.00 per lens.
- Waste and delays at each stage of production.

The fundamental cause of low productivity was that the factory was run on strict hierarchical lines. The six separate stages of production were carried out in fragmented departments almost completely isolated from one another. Division of labour was high and demarcation even within the departments was strong. The three hundred, mostly female, workforce spent their days carrying out the most routine, repetitive and boring of tasks usually with no clue how their tasks fitted into the overall picture or even how their own work fitted into the next stage of production.

The catalyst for change was a shift in the market place towards disposable lenses. Therefore there was a need for cheaper lenses and this was placing a growing pressure on production costs.

Demarcation of roles into de-skilled and monotonous tasks had encouraged a mercenary attitude by the staff towards any performance improvements. Existing work practices had become deeply entrenched even though they were pitifully inadequate for the required productivity in terms of both speed and quality.

The change process started with a number of highly successful initiatives.

- Staff members were encouraged to change places with other employees at different stages of the production line and in different departments. In this way they experienced a welcome change from the tedium of doing the same job. Significantly they also experienced what other departments' problems were and could see how their own activity contributed to both other department's problems and the end product.

- Operators were trained to handle a variety of different processes. This multi-skilling enabled flexibility of deployment as well as a greater understanding of production issues. The multi-skilling included training the machine minders in cleaning, basic machine maintenance and simple repairs. This initiative reduced machine downtime that was previously wasted while waiting for maintenance staff to turn up and do routine maintenance work.

- Group problem solving was introduced with cross-functional team discussions. This further enhanced the more holistic view of the whole production process, and empowered the operators to solve problems for themselves and implement ideas for improvements. Teamwork encouraged social interaction between the staff in different departments creating a greater community atmosphere and a feeling of mutual support.

- Operators were tasked to carry out their own quality control extending their skill set and responsibility. This new responsibility further underlined their status as valuable members of a team.

- A process of regular and frequent communication between staff and management provided two-way feedback about overall factory performance, individual performance and technical issues. The feedback included keeping staff informed on a daily basis what the yields were and what the scrap rate was.

These combined initiatives enabled the operators to think for themselves and participate in the problem-solving and decision-making process. The mercenary culture diminished and demarcation issues dissolved. Greatly improved productivity generated dramatic savings.

The outcome from this string of operational improvements was that the cost per lens shrunk by a massive 80% from £5.00 to £1.00. Production time halved to three weeks, scrap rate dropped from 84% to 20% and plant capacity improved incredibly from 500,000 units to 8 million. No new equipment or machinery had been required to instigate this dramatic improvement in productivity[18].

8.4 How aiming for quality motivates

The problem defined: Stressor 9 - Low quality work

Dr W. Edwards Deming, the guru of the post-war Japanese industrial revival and one of the originators of Total Quality Management (TQM), was perhaps the first management thinker to recognise that poor quality and poor decision-making creates frustration, conflict and confusion and, as such, is a major source of stress for workers[19]. Low quality performance can generate a wide range of negative reactions among staff whether the poor quality results in a defective product or a slack and inefficient service that is incongruent with client or patient needs.

"Quality is everyone's responsibility."

W. E. Deming

Any normal person would become demoralised if part of their everyday job were to constantly compensate for deficient quality by frantic fire fighting, covering up about defective features or lying to customers. Apart from the usual 'conflict and confusion' element any sense of meaning is lost. It is very difficult to believe that you are doing anything truly purposeful if you are stuck in such a demoralising environment. In the long run the consequent nagging sense of inadequacy and pointlessness will also tend to undermine self-esteem.

The fundamental point to remember here is that healthy unstressed people are naturally conscientious and enjoy feeling they are making a valued contribution to a wider community. Thus, being forced by the system to deliver poor quality is inherently dissatisfying. This factor is of paramount importance in parts of the public sector where a sense of vocation is a main driver for the compassionate delivery of healthcare or social services and the conscientious delivery of professional services such as teaching or policing.

Under the circumstances of poor service delivery, feelings of status are also hit. Few employees relish being known to be working for an outfit that is considered useless or inferior. And this would apply as much to an incompetent government bureaucracy as to a cowboy business.

Remedies

The obvious remedy is to aim for high quality whether you are providing a service or manufacturing a product. The emergence in recent years of lean manufacturing has demonstrated that employees find that the striving for and accomplishment of world-class excellence is hugely motivational. One of the underlying reasons for this motivation is that lean management has as core principles the concepts of *collaborative problem solving* within a continuous improvement process.

Quality improvement initiatives involving the whole organisations and based on adequate training, good teamwork, the devolvement of authority and mutual problem solving to the lowest possible level are exhilarating to those involved. These sorts of dynamic approaches imbue a real sense of purpose and achievement into the participants. Operational team-based planning workshops result in far greater enthusiasm, clearer thinking, better problem solving, greater motivation and conscientiousness.

With collaborative problem-solving people can actually have fun at work, fulfil their need to be stretched and add some meaning to their working existence. Collaborative problem solving also enhances self-esteem and status. People respond to a genuine drive for excellence with greater loyalty, competence and commitment, as a range of inherent problem-solving skills are put into action. Stress levels fall commensurately. The direct result of such initiatives is a dramatic increase in overall productivity.

Chapter Nine

Elements of the management function

Stressors reviewed in this chapter

Stressor 10   No clear short-term goals to work towards

Stressor 11   Responsibility without the authority to do the task

Stressor 12   Career uncertainty often a result of short-termism

Stressor 13   Insufficient or inappropriate support from management or colleagues

Stressor 14   Loss of a natural routine

Stressor 15   New functions being allotted without adequate training and guidance

Stressor 16   Disagreement with organisational values or philosophy

Stressor 17   The unequal treatment of equals or the equal treatment of "unequals"

Stressor 18   Fast track career paths

9.1 The function of clear goals as a key motivator

The problem defined: Stressor 10 - Short-term goals

Getting employees to work towards clear short-term goals is already recognised as good management practice. Where this is overlooked, the absence of coherent goals can lead to a degree of uncertainty, doubt and confusion. These feelings are all fairly potent stress triggers that reduce mental and emotional performance to whatever degree the stress response kicks in, including a reduction in empathy with work colleagues and reduced access to rational thinking and creativity.

> "So much of what we call management consists in making it difficult for people to work."
>
> Peter Drucke

At the organisational level, lack of clear goals leads to incoherent operational planning unnecessary overwork and the overuse of other resources. The lack of a clear direction also tends to increase interpersonal and relationship conflicts.

Political rivalry is also inclined to increase the more people feel they have to compete for limited resources without the guidance of clear organisational priorities. This competition produces tension and conflict that further exacerbate the stress response.

Lack of clear goals impinges on people's feelings of security, as there is no perceived scope to unfold well. Typically in a working environment where there are no clear goals, there are likely to be no clear performance criteria either. When this happens employees' self-esteem can become impacted, as can feelings of competence. Ironically, lack of clear goals can also reduce a person's sense of autonomy or control, as he or she does not know what they have to do to succeed. Employees stuck in these sorts of situations tend to lose a sense of purpose or meaning with their work.

Remedies

The simple remedy to this stressor is to instigate collaborative short-term planning that sets clear goals for people to work towards. In this respect, a short-term goal is very distinct from targets set by third parties or higher authority (See stressor 3). There are four factors that clearly differentiate short-term goals from these sorts of demotivating targets:

> Lack of clear goals impinges on people's feelings of security, as there is no perceived scope to unfold well.

1. The goal setting is part of a collaborative planning effort involving all the relevant stakeholders.
2. The process ensures that each individual knows his or her exact purpose and

function within the context of the organisation's objectives and why this purpose is important to the organisation.

3. Thorough planning makes sure the goals are clearly defined. The well-known SMART acronym is a useful tool (SMART goals are Specific, Measurable, Actionable, Realistic, Timed).

4. Collaborative planning enables individuals to change their goals immediately the circumstances dictate it, preventing them from wasting their time pursuing redundant or meaningless goals.

Effective short-term goals - case example

The introduction of clear and mutually agreed goals can be transformational. At a small engineering works, unambiguous goals set during a team-planning workshop galvanised a credit control clerk into action. Fully understanding the importance to the company of what she had to do, she cleared her desk of low priority work and focussed on her core role of reducing the company debt. With the full understanding of what was at stake, she saved the £2 million pa company from bankruptcy by removing £300,000 from the debtors list within an amazingly short four-month period. This was accomplished mainly by doggedly chasing late payers, halving the average time it took customers to pay from 143 days to 75 days.

Motivational impact on the human givens

The motivational benefits of producing realistic and clear short-term goals derive from their impact on at least six of the human givens. In this context, agreed, clear, measurable and realistic goals:

- Give people a means to judge how well they are doing. This enables them to sense how safe their position is within the organisation and they can gauge and enjoy their own success.

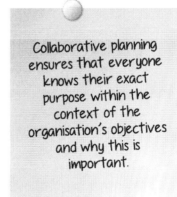

Collaborative planning ensures that everyone knows their exact purpose within the context of the organisation's objectives and why this is important.

- Provide stretch and some degree of purpose or meaning to their working life.

- Develop a real sense of autonomy over their work.

- Are also more enjoyable to work towards and

- Promote self-esteem and a feeling of competence once they have been achieved.

163

If employees have participated in the setting of the goals, they can see why they are doing a particular task and the importance its contribution has to the whole effort. In this way they feel more connected to the group and this reinforces a sense of status or value.

9.2 Delegating authority correctly

The problem defined: Stressor 11 - Responsibility without the authority or means to do the task

A typical symptom of poor, or at least inconsistent, management is the expectation that staff or managers have to achieve what is required of them without the necessary authority or other means that enables them to actually do the job in question. This can be a serious stressor for any individual. If it persists over the long term this stressor can provoke ill health, but in the meantime it will inevitably generate both individual under-performance and an incoherent group effort.

Part of the stress arises because the affected manager is in a lose-lose situation. Just as in a target culture, usually there is little credit for a successful outcome but plenty of blame when things go wrong.

Impact on human givens

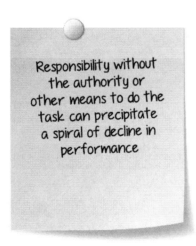

Responsibility without the authority or other means to do the task can precipitate a spiral of decline in performance

In terms of the impact on the human givens, this unfair situation can certainly ruin any sense of fun that a manager might have with his or her work. Perhaps more importantly, there is also fear for his/her own job security and, of course, almost by definition a lack of any sense of real autonomy[1]. Coupled with these three factors is probable damage to status, and lack of achievement. A feeling of incompetence arises, as it can be so difficult to actually achieve results. This, in turn, hits self-esteem over the long term.

In other words this stressor has a direct harmful impact on quite a handful of our human needs. But there are indirect implications as well. Managers who experience this type of unfair management control often end up over-working to try to compensate for the twin worries about their own incompetence and their own security within the organisation. What then typically happens is that

164

overwork destroys a balanced and healthy routine and impinges on their domestic and family life. The ensuing tiredness further impairs their ability to think rationally, empathize and connect with others and retain the observant self.

Diagram 16: lack of authority perpetuates overwork

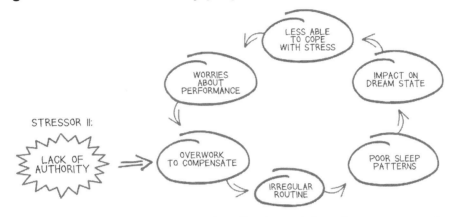

Sleep patterns can become disturbed easily through long hours, overwork and mental strain. In turn disturbed sleep impacts the dreaming brain and this further impairs the individual's capacity to cope with stress at work.

Remedies

Sometimes it is enough to bring to the awareness of the offending management that what they are doing is putting their subordinate in an impossible predicament. This allows the senior management to set clear boundaries and define the extent of the necessary authority to mutual advantage.

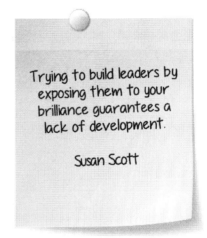

Trying to build leaders by exposing them to your brilliance guarantees a lack of development.

Susan Scott

Where the problem arises because the senior management have a fear of letting go of their own authority, or are driven by their own inner insecurities to interfere, then the situation tends to become perpetuated. If this is the case then probably the victim's only resort is to leave.

A collaborative leadership style and collaborative management techniques such as team-based planning of operational improvements tend to neutralize this problem naturally. Genuine participative decision-making provides both the opportunity and approval for two-way feedback. This two-way flow of information about how and why to do a task tends to result in the assignee negotiating the required levels of authority needed to fulfil it. The transparency within a team-planning decision-making process can also engender sufficient confidence to enable the senior party to trust the outcome to the junior manager or staff member and so let go of the necessary authority.

Motivational impact on the human givens

Once in place, the required authority to actually do the task effectively enables the manager to embark upon any new project or area of responsibility with confidence of a successful outcome. Instead of an overwhelming chore, the task is more likely to appear as an interesting challenge capable of providing enjoyment, and a sense of meaning within the context of the overall objectives.

Clear authority to fulfil a meaningful task helps confer or confirm a degree of status within the work group. Being able to rely on his or her own resources to achieve success, the individual will also experience a greater feeling of security and ultimately when the task is fulfilled there will be a gratifying sense of achievement.

9.3 Clarity of career paths

The problem defined: Stressor 12 - Career uncertainty often a result of short-termism

Career uncertainty impacts the individual's needs for security and attention and as such tends to lead to anxiety. Depending on the circumstances this has been seen to provoke sloppy or irresponsible behaviour and other symptoms of low motivation. One knock-on effect is that underperformance, low self-esteem and anxiety can all develop into depression over the long term.

> Prolonged uncertainty about career progression can develop into depression, further reducing the subjects ability to cope

In addition, the resultant feeling of unease or anxiety impacts the individual's capacity to think clearly, problem solve, utilize sound judgement and express positivity towards colleagues and customers. Anxiety tends to constrain enthusiasm as well. Obviously these states of mind do not help the organisation.

166

Career uncertainty also impinges the need for status and the need to feel part of a community. After all how can you feel part of a team if you do not know whether you are even going to be around next week or as soon as there is a drop in sales or new cost-cutting initiative? Under these regimes the more self-assertive and talented staff tend to pursue opportunities elsewhere where they can feel more secure and more able to progress their careers. So any short-term objectives or strategy that do not take employees' long-term career needs into account can easily damage the organisation's interests as much as the staff members.

Remedies

Management can remove this problem, quite cost-effectively, by simply giving some time and attention to the affected parties. Taking time out to alleviate someone's worries and fears over their place in the future of the company generates a highly disproportionate payback in terms of re-energising commitment and enthusiasm. It is especially important in this respect to offer clear and ongoing performance feedback, both positive and negative. The operative word here is ongoing. Waiting until the six monthly or annual performance appraisal is insufficient attention to be motivating. An important element of any manager's toolkit is the ability to deliver immediate, pertinent and motivating feedback. Ongoing feedback is known to be the most effective method to maintain enthusiasm and commitment.

Where career uncertainty is due to external factors such as a deteriorating market condition, the remedy is still to a great extent in the hands of senior management. As we have seen in 8.1, management can alleviate worries concerning a deteriorating market by instigating a dynamic, focused turnaround driven by the participation of as many stakeholders as possible in the improvement planning process. This kills two birds with one stone.

Reassuring someone over their place in the future of the company generates a highly disproportionate payback in terms of re-energising commitment

Firstly it alleviates the sense of insecurity attached to the perception of the company's destiny.

Secondly, the participative nature of the planning ensures that the individual feels they are making a valuable contribution to the future of the organisation - they feel more part of the team.

Motivational impact on the human givens

Participation in the improvement planning process and the receipt of ongoing feedback from managers caters for people's biological need to be involved in and useful to a wider team or community.

Ongoing and clear performance feedback together with the provision of resources for adequate training and self-development assists and confirms career development or career security.

Task planning is far more robust, thorough and effective where there is collaboration with all involved with the work. Such collaboration leads to more successful outcomes and this, therefore, underpins the security and growth of the business. People tend to feel they are genuinely part of a vibrant, healthy and useful concern.

Group problem-solving, team-planning workshops, collaborative decision-making of one sort or another all help create far better rapport between the levels of managers and staff. This rapport provides greater opportunity for ongoing career feedback and meaningful discussions on long-term career aims and requirements.

Case study

As with short-term goal setting, fixing this stressor can transform individual performance out of all proportion to the cost involved. A clear example of this arose at a diamond drill-bit manufacturer where the sales manager was nominally in line for a directorship. Some while after the promotion had been mooted, however, the manager's enthusiasm and confidence seemed to have waned. The MD was also beginning to have his doubts as to the pending career move.

The cause of the decline turned out to be due to a lack of follow-up discussions regarding the manager's career progression. As time past, the manager had begun to doubt the sincerity of the proposal and began to lose heart. Sales suffered and this only reinforced the MD's doubts as to the wisdom of the promotion. The situation changed both rapidly and dramatically when the MD was persuaded to take his original offer of promotion seriously and re-enter discussions with the sales manager.

An initial meeting was held between the two and each side was able to discuss their concerns. At the same time, the MD was able to confirm to the sales manager that if he improved the company's sales performance he was still in

168

line for a directorship. The manager became far more focussed in his role as sales manager. His personal enthusiasm and growing confidence in sales management skills motivated his sales team. The team's new energy and direction lifted sales by about 10% in six months without any extra expense on advertising or other promotion.

9.4 The pivotal role of emotional support and encouragement

The problem defined: Stressor 13 - Insufficient or inappropriate support from management and other colleagues

This stressor is demotivating, provokes anxiety and represses the creative capacity and people's commitment to the goals of the company. Lack of emotional support violates a whole range of emotional needs (see table 9), especially the crucial need for attention from other human beings.

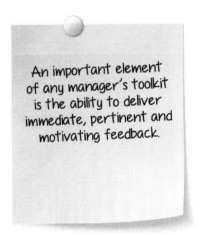

An important element of any manager's toolkit is the ability to deliver immediate, pertinent and motivating feedback.

According to David Sirota of Sirota Survey Intelligence, employees generally receive inadequate recognition and reward:

"About half of the workers in our surveys report receiving little or no credit, and almost two-thirds say management is much more likely to criticize them for poor performance than praise them for good work." As a result he says that "management unwittingly demotivates employees and diminishes, if not outright destroys, their enthusiasm"[2].

Zero feedback is the most harmful in the context of relationship-building

The importance of the emotional need to receive 'attention' means that lack of any signs of appreciation or 'zero feedback' can be more demotivating than criticism or negative feedback. Giving 'zero' feedback through neglectful management is liable to provoke a whole range of negative symptoms including irresponsibility, resentfulness, anxiety, depression, anger, disloyalty, lack of cooperation and so on. The impact on productivity and profitability is

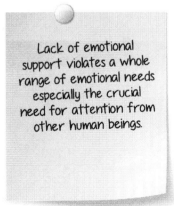

Lack of emotional support violates a whole range of emotional needs especially the crucial need for attention from other human beings.

commensurate. Interestingly, negative feedback is less demotivating than zero feedback. Negative feedback at least provides an element of attention and in addition it gives someone with something useful to work with to improve his or her performance. A cautionary note here is that regular negative feedback can sometimes satisfy the subject's deficit in their emotional need for attention. Whatever we put our attention on grows. So relying solely on negative feedback to motivate improvements in performance in our employees can have the opposite effect. Believe it or not, the subject may well start to underperform as a means to obtain feedback and so satisfy their need for attention.

Table 10:

Emotional needs impacted by 'zero' feedback	Positive impact	Negative impact
Security		X
Meaning		X
Emotional connection		X
Autonomy and control		
Part of a wider community		X
Enjoyment, friendship, intimacy and fun		X
Status and recognition		X
Achievement and feeling of competence		X
Challenge – problems to solve		
Privacy		
Attention		X
Regular routine		
Score		8

Positive feedback creates a positive emotional state in the listener

"Whatever we put our attention on grows."

Maharishi

In terms of motivating higher performance, the most effective feedback is positive feedback. Unlike either zero or negative feedback, positive feedback creates a positive emotional state in the subject[3]. And this is actually measurable in the psychophysiology. Neuroscience now recognises that both *giving* and receiving positive feedback stimulates the production of positive bio-chemicals in the brain physiology.

This factor is significant in terms of inspiring productivity as certain types of bio-chemicals actually improve our ability to utilise significant attributes and skills needed for high performance. These skills include our ability to focus, problem solve, access our imagination and long-term memory, empathise with colleagues, customers and subordinates, listen attentively and learn.

Remedies

So the remedy is easy, straightforward and cost-free to the organisation – simply ensure that you give people attention and provide regular positive feedback. By regular does not mean once every year at the annual performance review.

Too often, the annual performance review is a stale, formalised tick box ritual and is hardly sufficient as a forum to transfer spontaneous empathy and enthusiasm to your work colleagues. In motivational terms, annual reviews are often counterproductive. Genuine emotional support only comes from giving honest, positive feedback generously, copiously and fervently as part of an ongoing relationship-building exercise with whoever it is you are working with.

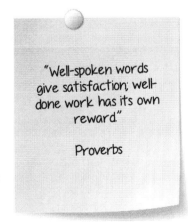

"Well-spoken words give satisfaction; well-done work has its own reward"

Proverbs

Show interest and support in this way and you will go a long way to meet the all-important emotional need for attention. You will help shift your colleagues into a dynamic and positive brain state and it will make you feel a whole lot better as well. You will feel liberated as a result.

Take a minute out of your time to praise people

What do we mean by positive feedback? Ken Blanchard, of "The one minute manager" fame,[4] recommends that you go out of your way to catch people doing something right and when you do instigate his "one-minute praising" procedure.

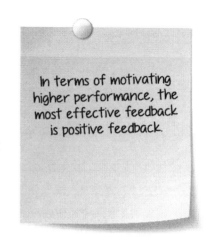

In terms of motivating higher performance, the most effective feedback is positive feedback.

1. Express thanks and appreciation for what they have done.
2. Clearly confirm that their actions are exactly in line with what is wanted.
3. Tell them why this is so important to the firm.
4. Tell them *how you feel about it*.

Blanchard recommends not taking longer than about a minute with it. If you have never done this before you may find it difficult to do. You might feel awkward and even embarrassed. (Incidentally so might the subject of your newfound attention.) That is no reason to stop trying. Practice makes perfect. Keep trying until it comes effortless and natural to you. In effect what you are doing is dropping an old habit and cultivating a new one by developing new neuronal pathways in the brain; old habits die-hard as they say. By practicing you are literally rewiring the brain circuitry to be more positive and emotionally connected.

Praising them in front of someone else has a powerful effect

"Everything each of us says leaves an emotional wake ... For a leader, there is no trivial comment."

Susan Scott

Another very powerful method of praising people is to let them overhear you praise them to a third party. Doing it this way can help overcome the embarrassment and can have a more telling effect on the person concerned.

An important tip here is that you must *make sure that you are praising them for something worthwhile*. (Hence the importance of an initial goal-setting exercise) The key action point is for you to **recognize** those aspects of their work that have been done well – NOT JUST TAKE THEM FOR GRANTED. People don't like being taken for granted and can become

172

surprisingly stressed as a result.

By the way, if you belong to that category of manager that believes nobody else around you seems to be doing anything right then, reflect on this. If your company or organisation is functioning in any way that is generating sales, and income and some form of successful operational results (however unsatisfactorily in your view,) then an awful lot of things must be going right *all the time*. In the whirl and flow of events these "right actions" may be largely hidden, but in reality each individual in the organization must be doing a whole series of things right, minute by minute, day by day, week by week. If this weren't the case then your operation would have ground to a halt ages ago.

Table 11:

Emotional needs impacted by 'positive' feedback	Positive impact	Negative impact
Security	✔	
Meaning	✔	
Emotional connection	✔	
Autonomy and control		
Part of a wider community	✔	
Enjoyment, friendship, intimacy and fun	✔	
Status and recognition	✔	
Achievement and feeling of competence	✔	
Challenge – problems to solve		
Privacy		
Attention	✔	
Regular routine		
Score	8	

Effective negative feedback

But, of course, there are those occasions when you may find employees doing something that you are not happy about. When these situations occur then make sure that any corrective feedback is supportive, non-judgemental and skilfully applied. Wherever possible treat honest mistakes as learning experiences to be built on rather than as an excuse for retribution. Criticism applied ineptly and perhaps in the heat of the moment can easily provoke the exact opposite reaction to the one you require for productive performance.[5] When you give employees personal or inept criticism, they can become defensive or start making excuses. They can even develop a tendency to avoid responsibility altogether. Another defensive tactic is to stonewall and avoid contact with the critic or, of course, blame someone else.

Such attitudes can develop into a vicious spiral of non-communication and non-cooperation that ultimately leads to the employee parting company with the firm. This is why surveys report that incompetent criticism is the most important reason for conflict at work; over and above issues like pay, mistrust, personality and power struggles.[6]

Seven guidelines for productive negative feedback

Firstly and perhaps the most important aspect of negative feedback is to make the criticism about their behaviour not about them. Personal criticism challenges their self-belief, quickly sets off a defensive reaction and will usually be self-defeating.

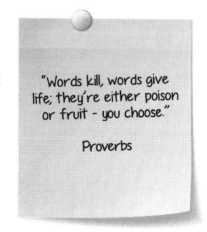

"Words kill, words give life; they're either poison or fruit - you choose."

Proverbs

Secondly, carry out the negative feedback promptly. You will do more damage avoiding the issue, as you are likely to become more and more heated by the employee's performance over time. Eventually you risk blowing up and saying something from an emotional level rather than from a rational point of view.

Thirdly, be specific. Don't just blast away at their overall performance or use vague generalisations. If you do they are less likely to believe you anyway and it will feel more like a personal criticism. You will not be providing anything useful for them to focus on or that they can work with to improve. It is much more easy to be specific with your feedback if you have already set measurable goals for the individual to work with.

Fourthly, it really helps to work with the subject to find a solution. Ask them how they think they can resolve the issue rather than offering an immediate solution yourself. Asking them for a way forward reinforces the learning experience and helps meet their needs for problem solving and for autonomy and control. Only offer a suggestion as to a possible way forward if you fail to get a satisfactory response. Whatever you do don't just leave them floundering.

> Often, the annual performance review is a stale, formalised tick box ritual, hardly sufficient as a forum to transfer spontaneous empathy and enthusiasm.

Fifthly and very importantly it is best to carry out the criticism face-to-face. Trying to avoid the pain of confrontation by pinging them an email is likely to make things worse by inflaming feelings especially if they are aroused anyway. Remote criticism leaves less scope for the subject to respond and enter into a fruitful dialogue with you. Face-to-face, you can both read each other's body language and so be more able to deal with any negative emotions as they arise. Remote criticism is far more likely to set off a stress response as you are undermining their autonomy to do something about it. You are also denying them that essential level of attention that helps bring stress levels down during moments of potential crisis.

Sixthly and overall, be sensitive to the impact the criticism is having on the person at the receiving end. Empathising with the person softens the blow and indicates that this is a problem that can be worked out together in collaboration rather than just an unequivocal condemnation. This is another reason why empathy is such an important quality for good leadership. Lack of empathy during negative feedback can easily make it destructive. Instead of motivating people to improve, hurtful criticism can quickly lead to resentfulness, bitterness and hostility.[7]

Seventhly use the reprimand as an opportunity to reinforce their feeling of value to you and the rest of the team. The reprimand is about some specific problem which can be solved not a general condemnation of their status. We want an adjustment to their behaviour not an assassination of their personality. For this reason, Ken Blanchard recommends starting and finishing a reprimand with a positive affirmation of the person's worth both to you as their manager and to the organisation[8].

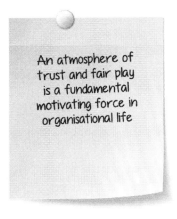

> An atmosphere of trust and fair play is a fundamental motivating force in organisational life

The power of timely, competent and ongoing feedback is yet another reason why a collaborative style of leadership can be so motivating. A collaborative style provides ample opportunity for honest and neutral forums for non-judgemental correction and performance feedback and where both leader and peer group have a chance to give input, be heard by others and so receive positive and morale-boosting support.

Early researchers into team planning at SRI back in the 1960s noticed this particular benefit of collaborative decision-making, referring to the resultant culture as an atmosphere of "trust and fair play"[9]. They recognised that this atmosphere was potentially a fundamental motivating force in organisational life.

Motivational impact on the human givens

Positive attention and support from both superiors and peers has a whole range of benefits to an organisation[10]. First and foremost, of course, is that the whole climate of work is more enjoyable. On an individual level research demonstrates giving adequate emotional support helps:

- Lubricate mental efficiency
- Ease intellectual understanding
- Enhance decision-making
- Improve ability to make complex judgements
- Fewer mistakes and so less wasteful rework
- Greater positivity towards customers
- Enhance creativity
- Improve disposition to collaborate
- Improve willingness to satisfy customer needs

Case example

Sheila's subordinates had grown to dislike her. There was a worrying degree of hostility and resentment towards her. The team members had reached the point where they wouldn't lift a finger to help out unless they absolutely had to. Instead they often engaged in petty resistance and obstruction to the flow of work.

The reason for this growing bloody-mindedness was that Sheila never had a good word to say to anyone. She never gave any recognition for a job well done, and was nearly always critical. She constantly complained about staff members behind their backs to other employees. A coaching session revealed that Sheila had a phobia about being in front of a group. She was fine with one-to-one discussions but with two or more people the stress response kicked in and she became negative.

The root cause turned out to be an upsetting public speaking experience when she was at school. This incident was now stored as a self-limiting emotional memory. This memory stored as a rough-and-ready pattern kept matching with current group involvement, triggering a stress response and making her bad tempered and hostile. After a session of guided visualisation this pattern matching was switched off and the subliminal fear evaporated.

Sheila was then able to lead and handle group discussions and meetings without experiencing a stress response and with growing ease, fluency and confidence. Quite quickly she became able to offer praise and positive support and just as importantly was able to restrain her criticism. Where negative feedback was genuinely necessary Sheila became proficient in providing constructive reprimands rather than her previous wounding personal criticism.

Bit by bit the team began to trust her more and responded positively to Sheila's lightened demeanour. In only a few weeks this personal change transformed the working environment. The atmosphere lightened and as time went on genuine collaboration and cooperation between Sheila and her staff developed. Productivity rose accordingly.

9.5 A natural daily routine - the backdrop to productive organisational activity

The problem defined: Stressor 14 - Loss of natural daily routine

"Personally I think stress is overrated."

How many times have I heard managers make this or similar comments. This exact comment was made to me by Peter, a senior manager who had recently experienced a serious glitch in the installation of a new IT system in his department. The cost to sort the mess out amounted to an eye watering £600,000 that he now had to find from other seriously tight budgets.

As it turned out this loss was a self-inflicted wound, as it was more or less predicted in an organisational stress audit carried out on his senior management team. But at the time he took no notice of it, after all he thought "stress was overrated". The stress audit picked up that Steve, an interim IT project manager was experiencing a seriously stressful lifestyle. The main reason for the stress was the 100-mile distance he was commuting to work that wrecked any chance of a healthy routine.

After several months the commute taken from the West Country soon began to take its toll. To try and alleviate the problem, Steve had chosen to work a four-day week and stay in a bed and breakfast during the week. He tried to compensate for his absence on Monday mornings and Friday afternoons by working twelve-hour shifts. This presented him with three problems. First it limited his physical interaction with his office colleagues and other departmental partners to the midweek period. Second of course the twelve-hour shifts were too long and he suffered from fatigue and loss of focus. Third, the situation damaged his home life and this exhausted him emotionally. After nine months, Steve signed off sick with depression never to return, leaving the project with a difficult void to fill.

"When we are tired we invite disaster."

Maharishi

But Steve's exhaustion and burnout had become evident a lot earlier. He often lost concentration during meetings and there had been complaints from colleagues about his lack of focus and disorganisation. There had been episodes of brittle emotions that led to strained working relationships with other key members of the installation team. Disturbingly, he had recently been involved in two serious car accidents and had also been diagnosed with diabetes at the age of forty-two. Crucially, Steve's lack of drive and focus meant that the momentum needed to get the project back on track never materialised. He simply did not have the energy and focus left to carry out the necessarily exhaustive analysis and come up with creative solutions. A number of hidden technical problems began to arise that were not exposed until after his departure.

This totally avoidable mishap only occurred because the phenomenon of poor routine and its consequential stress was just too intangible to be plausible to the departmental management.

The long-hours culture is an important contributor to high stress and low performance

A long-hours culture is now prevalent in many parts of the public sector and many UK firms. This culture with its rushed or absent meal times, back-to-back meetings, multitasking, late working hours and weekend working is an important contributor to stress and low performance[11]. The problem of lack of sleep deserves a special focus. Inadequate sleep[12], rest and recreation sooner or later leads to psycho-physiological imbalances occurring, leading in turn to fatigue, burnout, demotivation, low creativity, mistakes and increased time off due to sickness.

If you are overworking your people there may well be a short-term advantage in getting urgent things done when you want them. Working like this may be OK as a one-off or when a special effort is required to rescue a situation or grab an opportunity. But no one can persist with this type of lifestyle indefinitely or even for very long without some degradation on their performance.

> "If you work consistently long hours, over 45 a week every week, it will damage your health, physically and psychologically."
>
> Professor Cary Cooper

Any short-term advantages gained will be more than offset by disadvantages accruing later on. But even these short-term benefits are questionable depending, of course, on the circumstances. For instance, recent research on students shows a massive drop of 40% in learning aptitude during periods of sleep deprivation when they stay up all night to cram for exams[13]. A study on healthcare workers found that increased workloads, stress and fatigue are a major contributing factor to medication errors at the drug administration stage and are a serious safety problem in intensive care units. Over a 100-day period 861 errors affecting 441 patients were reported out of a total of only 1,328 adult patients in intensive care. Staff members reckoned subjectively that tiredness and fatigue were behind 33% of errors[14]. In a different published study, the contribution of stress and fatigue was reckoned to be even higher at 37%[15]. Another study indicates that there is an almost exponential increase in accidents after a night shift worker has done eight hours of work[16].

The human psychophysiology works best if synchronised to its innate natural rhythms. Essentially we are attuned to a cycle of rest and activity. These rhythms or cycles such as the daily (circadian) and ultradian cycles (ninety minutes cycles of more intense and less intense alertness) and even weekly and seasonal cycles influence almost every aspect of bodily function. As a result the simple timing of our everyday activity can impact the quality of sleep we experience, the effectiveness of our digestive system, our peak activity, our vulnerability to disease and our response to its treatment. As an example, numerous studies[17] show that lack of synchronization between shift workers' rest and activity and night-time and daytime patterns leads to greater risks of cardiovascular disease, diabetes, seasonal depression and even cancer[18] over a long period of time. It is now clear that it is better for night shift workers to maintain a regular routine rather than keep changing shift patterns.

Another example of our sensitivity to natural cycles is that exposure to natural daylight in the morning is a significant pre-requisite to getting a good night's sleep. Exposure to daylight in the morning helps the body release melatonin later on in the day when it is time to feel sleepy[19]. Miss out on this exposure and you feel less sleepy. As a result you stay up later and begin to deprive yourself of the level of sleep required for a healthy and active working life.

The cultural orthodoxy for long working hours and extended periods of concentration means that we tend to override our body's natural inclination to take a rest every ninety minutes or so. Manually overriding this ultradian cycle leads to the activation of the stress response in the form of the release of stress hormones such as adrenalin and cortisol. There is a consequent impairment of performance typical of stressed behaviour, which includes impaired judgement, loss of any sense of fun, and an inability to empathise and give good personal attention to others. The antidote is simple and yields a return far in excess of the cost of taking time out. Simply break off from meetings and other work activities every ninety minutes or so to indulge in some sort of relaxation including sitting quietly, undertaking some aerobic physical exercise or social activity.

Employees working to exhausting, unnatural or chaotic routines, experience weakened immune systems and poorer general performance.

On the psychological level unhealthy irregular routines can easily impinge upon any feelings of autonomy as life feels out of control. Once physical exhaustion sets in the observant self is clouded, as the workload crowds in and crushes the sense of self-awareness.

Regularity of routine is an important ingredient for maintaining peak performance over the long term

The human physiology performs better when you live and work in alignment with these important biological cycles and rhythms. This means following a natural routine that respects the natural cycles and comprises a healthy balance of rest and activity, regularity of physical exercise, regular mealtimes and adequate sleep times[20]. The implication for organisational effectiveness is clear. Where employees work to long working hours, exhausting, unnatural or chaotic routines then you can expect them to experience weakened immune systems, more accidents[21] and poorer general performance.

Diagram 17

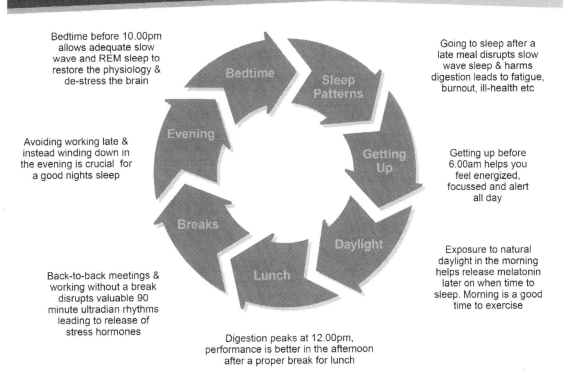

Elements of a healthy daily routine

Bedtime before 10.00pm allows adequate slow wave and REM sleep to restore the physiology & de-stress the brain

Going to sleep after a late meal disrupts slow wave sleep & harms digestion leads to fatigue, burnout, ill-health etc

Avoiding working late & instead winding down in the evening is crucial for a good nights sleep

Getting up before 6.00am helps you feel energized, focussed and alert all day

Back-to-back meetings & working without a break disrupts valuable 90 minute ultradian rhythms leading to release of stress hormones

Exposure to natural daylight in the morning helps release melatonin later on when time to sleep. Morning is a good time to exercise

Digestion peaks at 12.00pm, performance is better in the afternoon after a proper break for lunch

Sleep deprivation harms health and performance

Sleep deprivation is particularly harmful for good health and high performance. Even missing as little as one hour's sleep at night on a regular basis is known to treble the likelihood of catching a cold[22].

Where an exhausting or stressful daytime activity disturbs sleep patterns, this disturbance will also add to the existing mental exhaustion by impacting the important dreaming state. As we have seen earlier in 4.3.9, adequate dreaming defuses the stress arousal experienced during the day.

Without adequate dreaming we gradually become more and more stressed.

Workaholics are more than likely costing the organisation money.

Skipping lunch, or perhaps making do with a sandwich whilst working through our lunch breaks impacts our sleep patterns. Missing lunch usually means having to eat a heavy meal at night. Going to

181

bed with undigested food in the stomach tends to prevent settled sleep and this in turn impinges the important night-time sequence of alternating slow-wave sleep followed by dreaming or rapid eye movement (REM) sleep. This sequence of different sleep states is a key mechanism for both enjoying sufficient restorative rest and alleviating the daily accumulation of stress.

The net result of regular unsettled sleep, due to skipped lunches, is the gradual accumulation of stress levels in our physiology leading to minor ailments taking their toll in increased absenteeism or days off for sickness. In addition we experience progressively lower enthusiasm and lowered mental performance.

Diagram 18: Skipping lunch creates a spiral of decline

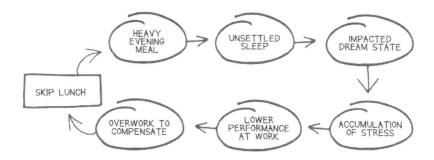

"The human body is hard-wired to pulse, and requires renewal at regular intervals not just physically, but also mentally and emotionally. Unfortunately, rest and renewal get no respect in the organizational world. Instead most managers instinctively view those who seem to need time for rest and renewal as slackers." Tony Schwartz, author of "The way we're working isn't working: the four forgotten needs that energise great performance"[23].

Lack of sleep increases levels of cortisol and adrenalin, making us tetchy. Lack of sleep also tends to impair our working memory. Moderate to severe insomnia is now linked to paranoid delusions[24] and lack of sleep generally has severe results for health and social wellbeing[25].

According to Russell Foster, Professor of circadian neuroscience at Oxford University, lack of sleep directly impairs the brain mechanisms that allow us to innovate, problem solve and organise others. He is currently concerned that the average sleep time is now only six hours a night down from eight hours in

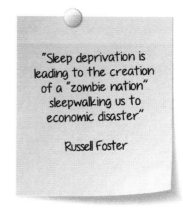

"Sleep deprivation is leading to the creation of a "zombie nation" sleepwalking us to economic disaster"

Russell Foster

the 1960s. He is quoted as saying that this sleep deprivation is leading to the creation of a "zombie nation" sleepwalking us to economic disaster[26].

Electronic overload

Professor Cary Cooper of Lancaster University Management School reckons that the downsides of social media and e-mails now outweigh the benefits. Cooper believes unmanageable workloads including the "unending electronic overload experienced by many of us, day in, day out," the loss of face-to-face relationships with colleagues and the misuse of emails to avoid having difficult face-to-face discussions are all having their toll. In particular, the intrusion of email exchanges after work-hours and even during weekends and holiday periods is likely to be having a "hugely negative impact on the quality of home life" and this is likely to spill-over into the quality of performance at work[27].

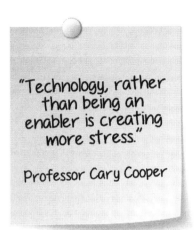

"Technology, rather than being an enabler is creating more stress."

Professor Cary Cooper

Remedies

The consequences to the organisation of unnatural routines indicate that it is essential to employ well-trained managers with both an orderly personal routine and with an understanding of the importance of enabling healthy routines for their staff members. In this context it is important not to tolerate workaholics, as they are more than likely to be costing the organisation money.

Good management means taking a more holistic view of life. This means anticipating the long-term needs of employees' health and wellbeing not just immediate short-term operational objectives. Continuity of managers and long-term career planning for employees helps in this respect. If managers know that they are going to be around for a while, they know they will have to live with the consequences of driving themselves or other people too hard or creating quick fixes in preference to long-term solutions.

The need is to change the culture of the workplace to one that supports natural routines. Insist on people stopping work completely for a proper lunch, going home on time, and maintaining natural breaks during the day. It would really help if employees weren't expected to handle emails after working hours. How can you switch-off and recuperate from the day's hassle and stress if your line manager or other colleagues send you messages that expect an immediate response? We all work with a human physiology that has constraints and limitations. Working beyond those constraints for any length of time will inevitably develop lowered performance.

Team planning tends to take into account human constraints

Team planning tends to enhance orderly scheduling and realistic workloads. The reason is that the participants are usually more likely to take into account their own personal physical limitations than some remote planner would.

"Rest and activity are the steps of progress."

Maharishi

Typically with a collaborative effort, goals and deadlines tend to be more realistic; worries are shared and more quickly dealt with. When this happens the overwork, to compensate for operational problems and management oversights, tends to be reduced as well.

Meditation as an antidote to stress

As referred to in chapter 8.2, a good personal antidote to an unnatural routine and unsympathetic workload is Transcendental Meditation (TM)[28]. The recommendation for this simple, easy to learn twenty-minute mental exercise is based on the third party endorsement of a wide body of research. There are many other techniques of meditation and methods for relaxation, but the research shows that TM, used as part of a daily routine, outperforms other techniques at promoting good mental health[29].

TM also enhances a number of qualities useful to management. The evidence suggests that the regular daily practice enhances sleep patterns[30], improves overall health[31], develops more orderly and creative thinking [32], improves memory [33], and generates quicker recovery time from stressful stimuli[34]. Psychologists have also observed that TM seems to enhance field independence - the ability to focus attention on details without being distracted by the environment around[35]. Psychologists associate such field independence with good mental health, reduced anxiety and stability of the autonomic nervous system.

Motivational impact on the human givens

Employees who are free to enjoy the benefits of a natural routine tend to be a lot less stressed as they are satisfying a number of crucial needs. Feeling fresh and energetic instead of jaded and worn out enhances a feeling of security.

184

When energised you feel more in control of events and you enjoy more fun from your work and activities as well.

Management sensitivity to people's essential physical needs helps to satisfy their need for an appropriate degree of attention. In turn this attention helps reinforce a sense of belonging and a sense of loyalty and commitment. In total this is a wide range of benefits for not falling into the trap of pushing people too hard and too fast in order to capture short term gains.

9.6 Giving the right training for the job

The problem defined: Stressor 15 - New functions being allotted without adequate training and guidance

Poor or inadequate training costs money. Save pennies on training costs and you lose pounds perpetuating low productivity. You get unhappy clients and customers, simply because employees cannot undertake their work competently. Although this fact is pretty well known, many organisations still yield to the easy temptation of saving immediate costs on relevant training programmes.

> Trying to make progress in an environment where people are incompetent and inadequately skilled is like wading through treacle.

Never is this temptation more beguiling than during a recession. Panic sets in and training programmes get slashed to cut overheads and reduce the break-even point. Typically, this policy is counterproductive. Holding back on training is costly for more than the obvious reasons to do with poor quality, mistakes, rework and missed deadlines.

Letting people loose onto the shop floor, or in front of customers or, for that matter, in the management suite without ensuring that they can actually do the job properly is also a significant stressor. As such, inadequate training generates a range of indirect costs that can destroy cohesive working and hammer the bottom line. Poor or inadequate training breeds confusion, demotivation and frustration amongst managers and employees alike. Trying to make progress in an environment where people are incompetent and inadequately skilled is like wading through treacle.

The impact on the human needs where people are forced to work without the necessary skills is much the same as for 'responsibility without the necessary authority to do the task' (See stressor 11, chapter 9 section 2). Lack of adequate training often changes the nature of a new task from being a challenge and can instead simply overwhelm the employee. As a consequence, lack of training impacts several human givens including generating a fear about job security, and a feeling of encroachment on any real autonomy, probable damage to a feeling of status within the work group, and a feeling of lack of competence with an accompanying feeling of non-achievement.

The knock on effect of this is that people under this sort of stressor tend to do one or more of the following:

- Develop low self-esteem, at least if the stressor continues over the long term
- Over-work to try to compensate for feelings of (or the reality of) incompetence
- Learn impression management and political skills to hide their incompetence
- Leave to get more satisfying work elsewhere

Save pennies on training costs and you lose pounds perpetuating low productivity.

Remedies

The remedy is to build training costs and a learning curve in at the planning stage of any new function, task or project. Avoid falling into the tempting illusion that you can cut corners by the expedient of ignoring training needs. Typically, management assumptions as to the amount of training and the length of learning curve required to make a new operation run smoothly are months and sometimes even years too short. A number of factors can contribute to this misconception. One such is the usual 'bounded rationality' that conceals so much organisational reality from management. Another common factor is the perennial priority to get things done immediately often driven by 'wishful thinking' (see chapter 11 section 7) or the stress-driven, quick-fix mentality already discussed in chapter 1.

As with other stressors, a collaborative style of management can alleviate this problem. This is partly because participants in a collaborative process are more likely to be aware of what they lack in the way of skills and so are more qualified to provide a realistic estimate of training needs and the anticipated length of any learning curves. After all, they are the ones that are going to have to implement the plan and naturally want to avoid being unable to cope and feeling inadequate. In addition to this natural tendency for the participants to want to feel competent however, a formal team planning process also makes use of a concept known as the 'study phase'. The assumption at the start of any business improvement process is that to avoid repeating the same mistakes over and over again some new learning is required[36]. This learning is facilitated by inserting into the sequence of planning a formal pause for study, training, reflection and research. Certain key questions help provoke the necessary reflection in this respect:

- ➤ Do I know exactly how to solve the problem or achieve the aim of the project?
- ➤ Are there any skills that I lack to accomplish the project?
- ➤ What don't I know about the project?
- ➤ Who else on the team or elsewhere in the organisation can help me?

Insisting on your team members taking time to go through this study phase for each of their improvement projects will help ensure that when a new function or responsibility is being created the relevant parties will acquire the competency to get on and actually achieve an optimum result. There is more about the study phase in chapter 11.7 table 13 – Eight ways team planning reduces confirmation bias

The reluctance by many managers to invest in training is understandable when, so often, training programmes prove to be expensive, dull, wasteful and disruptive of operational schedules and activity. Traditional corporate training is often a turn-off to participants with the average person retaining about 10% of what the training delivers.

To avoid this problem ensure that training follows 'accelerated learning' principles[37]. Concepts such as total learner involvement, activity-centred learning and group problem-solving are based on the same brain research that is behind the collaborative leadership concept and often results in twice the amount being learned in half the time.

Motivational impact on the human givens

Equipping people with adequate training and guidance goes a long way to help meet the need for attention. People feel that you are taking their needs into the account. This aspect alone enhances self-esteem and this quality is inevitably reinforced when their improved competence results in the achievement of a job well done.

Adequate training for the task in hand also improves a sense of belonging and meaning. People feel they are part of something that is growing and worthwhile. It also enhances a feeling of personal security within the organisation as the training given is taken as indicative of their value and worth to the organisation.

Collaborative decision-making requires training too

Although collaborative working comes naturally to people, like other innate talents it still requires nurturing and developing. Researchers at SRI found that planning outcomes improved immeasurably when the planning team were trained up in core elements of decision-making and planning skills[36]. Ensure training improves any weaknesses in:

Root cause and impact analysis	Financial appreciation
Cost benefit analysis and estimating	Collaborative problem-solving
Strategic analysis	Team planning
Project management	Decision-making techniques

9.7 Alignment with values – the foundation for high performance

The problem defined: Stressor 16 - Disagreement with organisational values or philosophy

Disagreement with organisational values can be demoralising for the individual and potentially damaging for the organisation if the conflict is intense. Value conflicts can precipitate harmful behaviour ranging from dull compliance, passive resistance, a lack of collaboration or ultimately in extreme cases to sabotage.

Clearly if we find ourselves working in conflict with our own values this can impact our sense of meaning in the work we are doing. Not everyone is looking for any great meaning from their working life, often it is enough to have several of the other needs met at work such as getting paid in a steady job with a fair degree of intrinsic enjoyment, social interaction, responsibility and a degree of worthwhile challenge and sense of achievement. Even so, on a subtle level, conflict with the group's core values will at the very least lead to a shrug of the shoulders and a "who cares?" attitude that is hardly conducive to a wholehearted focus on excellence and world class customer service. Where there is significant conflict with deeply held values however, it can impact self-esteem if the conflict induces questioning or doubt over an individual's personal core values. This in turn will affect the sense of being part of a wider community and a sense of security. Hence conflicting values can be a potent and corrosive stressor.

Remedies

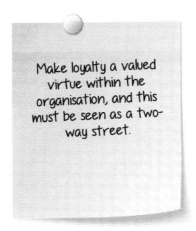

Make loyalty a valued virtue within the organisation, and this must be seen as a two-way street.

Ultimately if the conflict in values is irreconcilable the two parties should part company. However a lot can be done to alleviate this schism in the meantime by working towards meeting other emotional needs such as a feeling of achievement, competence, attention and so on.

A collaborative style of management, utilising bottom-up feedback as a basis for developing improvement plans, tends to imbue the goals and projects with the values and ethics held by the participants. This tends to resolve this type of conflict harmoniously at the same time as enhancing stakeholder 'buy-in' into the organisation's strategy.

Motivational impact on the human givens

People operating within a mutually-held value system tend to be more enthusiastic about their tasks. There will be a greater connection with other members of the team and a stronger sense of identity with the group. This affects self-esteem and their feeling of status within the wider community too. Work becomes more meaningful and the outcome, whether product or service, becomes that much more valuable to the employee with the result that more care is taken with customers and tasks and in supporting other colleagues.

Case example

A team-planning initiative at a mental health charity provides a good example of the transformation that can take place when values are aligned. The charity runs a carer support service; sheltered housing accommodation; substance abuse recovery services and self-help groups.

The problem arose because two rival factions had been fighting it out over policy direction. The disagreements over fundamental issues about client care had developed to a point where the CEO felt much of her work was being sabotaged. The activities of several of the antagonists were nearing the stage of disciplinary and grievance procedures. The CEO was literally at her wits end and "stressed to high heaven". The bitterness and hostility that had developed between the two factions meant that day-to-day work at the charity was deeply unpleasant with tensions breaking out into arguments. This sort of conflict periodically disrupted workflow and client focus.

A team-planning exercise starting with bottom-up feedback from all stakeholders reduced the temperature immediately as the antagonists began to understand the other side's point of view in a more objective way. The planning workshop structure and the written nature of much of the work enabled the planning team to work together in a calm and reflective atmosphere. Team members began to empathise more with each other's problems, views became less entrenched and research into the facts of the situation began to reframe the participants' ideas on policy.

The planning workshop concluded with the instigation of a range of agreed improvement projects delegated to relevant members who then were able to implement their projects with the full support of their colleagues.

9.8 The positive role of inequality in the workplace

The problem defined: Stressor 17 - The unequal treatment of equals or the equal treatment of 'unequals'

An example of the unequal treatment of equals would be a situation where most team members are working conscientiously and quietly alongside one another with no thought of an extra reward for doing so. Whilst on the other hand, a troublemaker manages to acquire unequal treatment from the management. He or she attracts the most attention from management and even elicits appeasement through pay-offs or other special conditions. This is a case of the squeaking joint getting the most oil and such situations can breed a variety of negative emotions such as resentment to the co-worker or antagonism to the organisation.

Similarly, favouritism can be galling for those excluded and this can give rise to anger where the exclusion creates a real disadvantage. Nepotism can be an example of this, where family members are given preference in salaries or in promotion. Although it has to be said that the adverse impact here can be reduced where there is already an expectation of such a practice in an openly family-run business. The unequal treatment of equals often arises by default due to neglectful or haphazard management. Essentially management is giving insufficient attention to the individual needs of their group members.

Perhaps the most prevalent experience of this stressor is of the equal treatment of 'unequals'[38]. An example of this is where there is a one-size-fits-all reward system despite there being a very real discrepancy between the best performers and the worst. The whole effect of this standardisation is de-motivating and apathy-inducing, as the more productive workers perceive that their contribution is just getting lost amid the general scrum.

Remedy

To avoid both categories of this stressor what is required is a more consistent focus on providing effective accountability that takes into account individual competence and diligence. To avoid creating stress and instead motivate high performance requires that there are consequences for each individual arising directly out of the quality of the work they are doing. Effective accountability fulfils five criteria:

1. Prompt

When things go wrong, prompt accountability signals that you are giving a high priority to the standard of work required and this on its own helps motivate better performance. For as long as you delay you have to put up with the poor behaviour in the interim and this also upsets conscientious co-workers. If you delay unduly then when you finally get around to giving negative feedback you are implicitly failing to recognise all their good behaviour in the intervening period.

2. Frequent

Keep in touch; don't leave people hanging and wondering what they should be doing. Similarly, frequent feedback prevents them thinking that they have wriggle room to shift priorities without you really knowing. Regular reporting by subordinates helps you monitor whether things are on track and enables you to take swift action when they are not. Reward good work with recognition on an ongoing basis, not just as a one-off (See 9.4 about emotional support). Don't take routinely good work for granted; you will miss it when it's gone. Frequency of feedback helps to satisfy people's need for attention; a powerfully motivating human need.

3. Specific

Whether the situation is negative or positive ensure employees know exactly which aspect of their behaviour is being addressed. They are then able to rectify poor work or reinforce good work.

4. Clear

Set out unambiguous guidelines as to expected outcomes and the consequences of both meeting them and failing to deliver them. Ensure that subordinates are in no doubt as to what is required of them and why and how and when they should be reporting back to you.

5. Direct

People need to be clear to whom they are answerable. Without this clarity subordinates can easily stray from the required direction as third party pressures make them shift priorities. Indirect feedback delivered through a third party prevents the subject discussing the situation openly and interactively and so prevents valuable two-way feedback.

Diagram 19

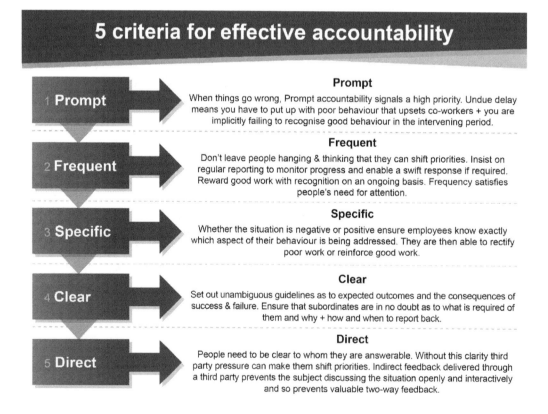

Motivational impact on human givens

Effective accountability helps meet the need for a challenge and reinforces the needs for status, recognition and meaning. Direct, clear and frequent accountability also goes some way to meet the psychological need for an appropriate level of attention. Accountability makes people confident that their work is making a valued contribution to the overall effort and this engenders pride in their work and greater commitment to the overall communal effort.

9.9 Aligning individual career paths with organisational needs

The problem defined: Stressor 18 - Fast track career paths

A fast track career path is one of the routes to get promoted to the very top. The term implies job-hopping to collect credits for the CV, always moving from one job to a bigger, better job elsewhere. Such behaviour has several disadvantages for the host organisation, not least of which is a tendency for short-term thinking.

> "It usually takes great skill for people to disguise that they are smarter than their bosses. However, this ability is essential for survival in most organisations."
>
> RL Ackoff

The pressure to achieve quick results mean that this type of ambitious individual wants to be seen to make an impact, as a launch pad for moving on to greater things. Unfortunately quick results are often achieved at the expense of more long-term but sustainable improvements. Such managers are not around to pick up the longer-term consequences of short-term policy decisions that looked good at the time but perhaps fall apart later. For instance short-term thinking managers tend to hire and fire in a panic reaction to the immediate economic climate; a whiff of a downturn and heads begin to roll.

Maintaining a loyal, experienced and highly productive team for the long-term takes a low priority compared to this quarter's profits. This attitude undermines loyalty within an organisation as it threatens employees' needs for security, status, and the sense of belonging to a wider community.

High ambition can be a dangerous expression of vanity

As discussed under stressor one (chapter 6 section 1), overweening ambition, far from being a positive for organisational effectiveness, is very often the reverse, as it reflects a strong 'me-first' attitude. High ambition is dangerous for an organisation where instead of being an expression of real competence it is merely one of vanity or a compensatory impulse to satisfy unmet personal needs. Another problem is that whatever the underlying motivation, ambitious people tend to have a preference for a top-down command and control style of management that is so harmful to stress levels at work.

Remedy

Avoid recruiting candidates on fast track career paths and instead focus on developing talent in-house. Develop a greater organisational awareness of the problem of fast track career paths by undertaking a long-term cost benefit analysis on hiring and retaining senior staff and management, including taking into account an extensive learning curve that can be measured in years not months. The tendency is that the longer people have stayed with an organisation the more valuable their knowledge and experience becomes and the more you can rely on their inherent loyalty.

Drawbacks of fast track career paths to the organisation

Recruiting people on fast track career paths tends to:

1. Encourage short-term decision-making.

2. Expose the organisation to the risk of a strong 'Me First' attitude from those in positions of responsibility.

3. Attract managers who adopt top-down command and control leadership tactics.

4. Lead to a faster turnaround of managers with all the attendant costs that this incurs in terms of learning curves and loss of organisational knowledge.

5. Undermine other people's loyalty to the organisation.

194

Loyalty needs to become a valued virtue within the organisation, and this must be seen as a two-way street. Creating an ongoing loyal and committed team is one of the surest routes to long-term success. Loyalty among all stakeholders promotes continuity of excellence and experience in terms of both the organisation's output and customer relations.

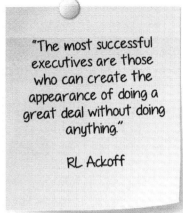

"The most successful executives are those who can create the appearance of doing a great deal without doing anything."

RL Ackoff

You enhance loyalty and commitment by giving it

As mentioned in chapter four, loyalty as a primeval survival strategy is an innate resource. We need our group to survive in order for us to survive. However, loyal and dedicated employees don't just grow like mushrooms in the dark. Leadership can nurture and nourish loyalty over the long-term by focussing on several key factors:

- Provide a high degree of job security for those who are competent at their jobs
- Keep channels of communication open and clear so that people know in which direction the organisation is moving
- Provide training and development opportunities within a coherent career path so that when senior positions become available internal candidates are equipped to handle them and can be offered the job
- Make sure that pay and benefits are perceived as fair within the industry relative to what employees can achieve elsewhere
- Treat people the way you would like to be treated and enable them to participate in management decisions

Motivational impact on the human givens

Employees feel more part of a community if there is continuity of employment at every level, including among senior managers. The more coherent pattern of decision-making and long-term thinking will provide a feeling of greater security.

Relationships are likely to be more productive where there is real continuity of service and the various parties have a greater depth of knowledge about each other. As a result there is likely to be a greater amount of enthusiasm, commitment and focus by staff towards the organisation's goals with a commensurate increase in productivity and performance.

Chapter Ten

Physical factors in the working environment

<table>
<tr><td colspan="2">Stressors reviewed in this chapter</td></tr>
<tr><td>Stressor 19</td><td>Environmental factors</td></tr>
<tr><td>Stressor 20</td><td>Stale air, electromagnetic fields and artificial day lighting</td></tr>
</table>

10.1 Getting the space right

The problem defined: Stressor 19 Environmental factors such as excessive noise, poor surroundings and inadequate equipment

A hazardous environment threatens the most immediate human need - security. Apart from the risks of ill health and a fear of accidents due to either inappropriate or defective equipment, negative environmental factors impact other human needs. Lack of care about the working environment is often indicative of a lack of attention by management towards their staff. Employees do not feel part of a supportive community. There can also be resentment, and frustration at being obstructed from doing a good job.

Such resentment can be expressed as apathy towards work, and other forms of sub-optimum performance. The attitude "If the management doesn't care, why should I?" can easily develop.

On a purely financial level, ill health and accidents due to faulty or inadequate equipment lead to compensation claims for negligence at a current rate of about £200,000.

Being unable to control even simple aspects of life such as room temperature or ventilation can have a disproportionately high impact on the emotional need for autonomy and attention.

The impact on productivity can be in terms of people's loyalty, positivity, willingness to co-operate, ability to think straight, attitude towards co-workers, management and customers and the desire to take responsibility. Basically, saving money on maintenance and repairs can yield a disproportionate cost in lower performance.

Remedies

As a minimum, when undertaking planning and cash flow projections, take into account replacement and maintenance of ageing equipment. Here again a collaborative management approach helps. Participative planning involving the processing of views and input from all relevant stakeholders tends to ensure that employees have at least the basics to do the job. Apart from any other factor, this helps the participants feel more appreciated and this alone has been shown to significantly improve productivity and performance[1]. Even something as simple as attending to the amenity of the working environment can have disproportionate pay-offs in terms of motivation. For example, recent research shows that organisations can improve the quality of working life to the advantage of both mental concentration and measurable productivity by the simple expedient of introducing plants into the office environment[2].

Motivational impact on the human givens

It is certainly more fun working in a healthy environment. Active and prompt responses to staff requirements for physical wellbeing and the necessary physical resources to do the job help satisfy a basic need for attention. People don't feel they are being taken for granted, their self-esteem is lifted, and they feel a valued member of a wider community.

10.2 Letting people breathe - literally

The problem defined: Stressor 20: Stale air, electromagnetic fields and artificial day lighting

Strange as though it may seem, one of the most direct ways in which an organisation can improve all round performance and productivity is to improve the quality of the air. Focussing only on temperature, humidity and recirculation rates overlooks two key elements of air quality - air-ions and airborne particulates.

The importance of this was initially highlighted by a 1933 study. Rats were kept in a cage which, although well ventilated, had all air-ions removed. All the rats died within two weeks. The study has been replicated several times since then[3] but the findings are still largely ignored.

As mammals we have evolved over millions of years in an ion-rich atmosphere. The ion component of fresh outdoor air is reckoned to be about 1,500 negative ions per millilitre. At high altitudes the ion content is particularly rich with alpine air containing as many as 10,000 negative ions per millilitre. This is in stark contrast to a negative ion content of only 50 ions/ml in a typical mechanically-ventilated office. Naturally ventilated rooms do not fair much better with a content of 250 ions/ml.

Restoring natural levels of negative ions and reducing particulate levels reduced headaches by 78%

Modern commercial and industrial buildings contain a complex variety of materials that either earth electrically charged ions or give off a positive static charge. Earthed metal ducting, heat exchangers, metal ventilation grilles, artificial fibre in carpets, ceiling tiles and furnishing fabrics all help deplete the negative ion content. This depleted level of ion content is comparable to the thick and enervating atmosphere we experience just before a thunderstorm.

Where we are placed in sealed "artificial" environments depleted of negative ions we gradually experience symptoms of ill health and stress similar to those defined as "Sick Building Syndrome". Reported problems include breathing difficulties, sore throats, cold or flulike symptoms, tiredness or fatigue, headaches and other stress symptoms such as lack of focus, irritability, sleeping difficulties during the night, depression, pessimistic outlook and short-term memory deterioration. There is also the extra problem that stale air with a high level of particulates helps foster cross infection of airborne viruses.

Artificial lighting is also depressing on both energy levels and the immune system. Working in an artificially lit environment has an adverse impact on the quality of sleep[4] with implications that we have already outlined for stressor 14.

Electromagnetic fields provide a wide range of problems to do with suppression of the immune system and upsetting hormone balances. This is a particular problem for modern offices stacked with electronic equipment.

Remedies

The remedy for stale air is to install air processors that use a high voltage corona discharge technique to generate negative ions to a more natural level.

Research carried out by Dr Hawkins of Surrey University demonstrated that restoring natural levels of negative ions and reducing particulate levels reduced levels of stress and ill health complaints significantly. Headaches were reduced by 78%[5]. A more recent study carried out in conjunction with a manufacturer of air ionisers at BT call centre sites broadly confirmed Hawkins's findings, showing a comprehensive range of improvements[6]. Of 1,159 subjects, 57% reported reduced environmental stress symptoms at work, 59% reduced respiratory stress symptoms, and 71% reduced headaches. There was a reduction in sickness absence of 35%. Overall productivity improvements measured in terms of call handling times and calls answered, ranged between 5 – 15%.

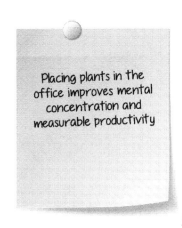

Placing plants in the office improves mental concentration and measurable productivity

Using these air processors also helps prevent the spread of viruses and dust particles with an overall reduction of over 90% in respiratory particulates both organic and inorganic.

Work carried out by Leeds and Southampton Universities in the UK even indicate that there is a lethal effect of negative ionisation on micro-organisms. Importantly, for our annual flu epidemics, this could mean viruses are not just being cleared from the atmosphere but actually being killed as well[7]. The impact would be a significant reduction in days off for sickness among the effected work force.

Motivational impact on the human givens

The impact is similar to the remedy for stressor number nineteen above, in that it is certainly more fun working in a healthy environment. Protecting people from the very real risk of virus infections and irritating or uncomfortable stress symptoms enhances their feelings of security and a sense that the management is attending to their needs. A greater sense of commitment and enthusiasm are more likely to be maintained in this healthier environment.

Chapter Eleven

Psychological or personal and relationship factors

+---+
| ### Stressors reviewed in this chapter |
| |
| Stressor 21   Negative relationships |
| |
| Stressor 22   High internal competitiveness in the work culture |
| |
| Stressor 23   Incompatibilities |
| |
| Stressor 24   The presence of a socialised psychopath |
| |
| Stressor 25   Organisational straight-line thinking |
| |
| Stressor 26   Performance enhancing drugs |
| |
| Stressor 27   Botched decisions due to managers' subconscious insecurities |
| |
| Stressor 28   People bringing their own stresses to work |
+---+

11.1 Relationships - the glue that sticks organisations together

The problem defined: Stressor 21: Negative relationships

Group leaders can exert significant influence on working relationships. Where a leader introduces stressors such as inadequate training, poor demarcation of responsibility and so on these can harm employee interaction. As we have seen, such stressors provoke an emotional stress response, and so can lead to the growth of misunderstandings, conflict and hostility.

But leaders also set the tone of the workplace culture both by example and by applying some element of control over social interaction. Thus, simple acts of incivility and rudeness help to tarnish the working atmosphere, hampering smooth and efficient communication and interaction. Rudeness can have an impact on cognitive skills and so cause staff to make mistakes. Studies show that such mistakes can arise even if the individuals are only observing the incident rather than being subjected to the rudeness themselves[1]. Likewise arguments between co-workers can also lead to errors and mistakes[2].

Negative relationships breed a negative atmosphere

Essentially negative relationships breed a negative atmosphere and this can breed mistrust throughout the workplace.

As seen in stressor 2, mistrust will evoke all kinds of behaviour that is unhelpful to the fulfilment of the organisation's purpose. Such behaviour includes:

- Withholding of collaborative support and information
- Dissipation of energy on wasteful turf wars and politics
- Impression management to hide incompetence
- Obstruction to changes in order to undermine rival positions or bolster prestige

Remedies

Harmonious relationships are the glue that sticks organisations together.

Where you see other stressors generating negative relationships then follow the advice laid out in the various remedy sections. Otherwise, the general rule is to lead by example and take a proactive role in setting a positive tone by adopting, and insisting that others adopt, civility among the group. Extending simple old-fashioned everyday courtesies and politeness to everyone around you goes a long way to lubricate human interaction and lift the emotional atmosphere.

However, just saying 'good morning' every day, 'please' and 'thank you' when required is hardly sufficient to establish good working relationships. In addition it is essential to maintain a positive outlook yourself and prevent other people's negativity poisoning the working atmosphere. This means always being alert to and discouraging a range of negativity such as rumour-mongering, malicious gossip, emotional criticism, sarcasm, complaining, attribution of negative motives where things have gone wrong and backbiting.

Human nature being what it is, banning such activities is counterproductive and risks creating an even more oppressive environment. Never the less it is important to tackle such negativity resolutely and this has to be done by example.

> "The fundamental outcome of most communication is misunderstanding."
>
> Susan Scott

For instance if you hear a colleague disparaging a third party behind their back, avoid indulging the critic. Instead ask them directly whether they have confronted the other person with the issue. If the answer is no, inform them that you will be happy to discuss the issue with them only when they have first addressed the issue with the other person and so have given them an opportunity to respond. If the problem they are complaining about still exists after that, suggest that then is the time for the three of you to get together to chat about it.

Reframing negativity

Similarly, when you are confronted with a stream of negativity from someone about a situation simply ask a question that reframes the situation in the speaker's mind. In other words encourage them to stop dwelling on the problem and focus instead on the solution.

A question such as "What do you propose we should do to resolve the situation?" can interrupt the flow of negativity and make them stop and think in a more positive frame. Show genuine concern for their feelings and suggest that when they have had a chance to think up a real solution they come back and talk to you then. Essentially, when someone is in a stress-driven negative frame of mind they are in a trance state as mentioned earlier in 2.5. Challenge them to take responsibility for a solution and you can help them snap out of the trance and get them back onto a positive and rational track. However be prepared to ask the question more than once to get the desired result.

Failed relationships take up more time than cultivating good relationships

In general terms to achieve greater harmony at work take the time and trouble to cultivate sound and meaningful relationships with colleagues and subordinates. The problem with today's rushed work culture is that so often, busy managers feel that there is no time for this perceived luxury. The irony is that <u>failed relationships take up a lot more time than the cultivation of good relationships</u>. Think from your own experience about some awful row or conflict that has blown up at work. Then think back how much time, effort and emotional energy was involved in putting things back together again. Harmonious relationships are the glue that sticks organisations together. Leaders who appreciate this fact ultimately enhance the smooth function of any work group. This is why a good degree of emotional self-awareness, empathy and emotional self-control are all-important faculties for a leader and why active listening skills and conflict resolution skills are vital leadership tools.

11.2 The role of competition in the work culture

The problem defined: Stressor 22 - Internal competitiveness in the work culture

Internal competitiveness within the organisation can lead to unnecessary tension, conflict, hostility and obstructiveness. Unfortunately, many managers actively encourage competitiveness in an attempt to drive up individual performance.

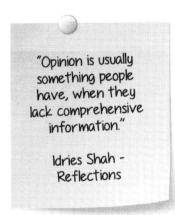

"Opinion is usually something people have, when they lack comprehensive information."

Idries Shah - Reflections

Competitiveness is a particularly common malaise at board level, where powerful ambition and strong egos combine to create a highly competitive environment that is not conducive to calm reflection, rational thinking and coherent group decision-making.

An over-competitive environment is also unpleasant for most people to work in. Although it has to be said some highly ambitious people appear to like this atmosphere. Meanwhile, in general terms, where competition is intense, the essential emotional connection is missing and staff miss-out on the opportunity to form true friendships with work colleagues.

They also miss out on a sense of community spirit and fun and, almost by definition, the feeling of security has to be undermined. There is also a possible loss of self-esteem over the long term for those who feel they are losing out. For every winner in this type of environment there has to be, by definition, a number of losers and nobody enjoys being a perpetual loser.

With internal competitiveness, there can only be a very fragile team spirit and this is usually reflected in team members receiving no meaningful attention from work colleagues. Basically under such management conditions the staff member knows that he or she is on her own. Over time the relative isolation and onerous workload will lead to burn out and nervous exhaustion. Under these conditions staff turnover can be high with the consequential costs that frequent departures, recruitment and induction of new recruits incur.

The insecure existence endured in a highly competitive workplace may also be one of the reasons why the alcohol and performance drug intake is so excessive among such occupations such as city traders. The tension created in such an environment has to induce high emotional arousal and so, although possibly helpful in a sales or dealing environment, is not conducive to creative, settled, analytical or even ethical thought.

Remedies

A major part of any remedy here is for leaders to be sensitive to personality issues. This means intervening in a positive way to resolve or avoid serious differences between competing individuals. This is another reason why it is useful for managers to have some basic training in active listening, mediation and conflict resolution. Another important element is to remove any extrinsic incentives such as sales commissions, that are encouraging individual competition as opposed to encouraging a group effort

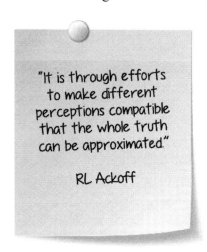

"It is through efforts to make different perceptions compatible that the whole truth can be approximated."

RL Ackoff

Where an organisation adopts collaborative planning and decision-making, the openness and transparency of the procedures provide a structured forum that enhances trust and a feeling of fairness among the team participants. Potential work-related conflicts arising from internal competition therefore tend to get resolved amicably at the planning stage. It is an obvious fact that arriving at a consensus eliminates the wasted energy spent on arguing and political manoeuvring. Arriving at a consensus enhances mutual collaboration, eases decision-making and channels everyone's energy and focus on achieving the shared goals; everyone benefits.

Interestingly, one of the greatest obstacles to consensus is, almost by definition, people's opinion. It is people's opinions or *the lack of fully comprehensive information* on a subject that is so often the root cause of disagreements, arguments and conflicts. Opinions can therefore fuel negative internal rivalry and competition.

An important way that you can avoid this type of head-to-head arguments is by taking the time and trouble to establish and agree the true facts about a problem as a starting point to any significant decision-making process. The means to avoid argument-creating opinions at the planning stage is by rigorously measuring four factors:

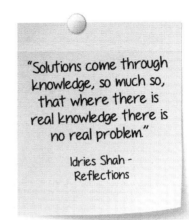

"Solutions come through knowledge, so much so, that where there is real knowledge there is no real problem."

Idries Shah - Reflections

- Ultimate cause of the problem (root cause analysis)
- Exact cost of it and its consequences (current state cost and impact analysis)
- Exact cost of solving it (Brain storming alternative ideas in a group and doing future state cost analysis on the most feasible options)
- Precise benefits of solving it (Future impact analysis and cost benefit analysis of alternative solutions)

Thoroughness in establishing the real and pertinent facts takes time but pays dividends. Getting the facts right at the start helps you avoid the easy trap of adopting an opinion as to what is best in any given situation and thereby walking slap into a head-to-head argument with someone who has adopted a conflicting opinion.

However, the problem can sometimes arise that any estimates of the prospective benefits of a solution to a problem can be very subjective. For instance a project to improve staff morale or to reduce stress or even develop a new market for your products can be influenced by a number of variable and potentially unknown factors. The creation of an estimate in these circumstances will typically involve the use of some imagination to identify and provide measurable outcomes. This subjectivity is why it is best to discuss rough estimates and draft ideas openly amongst a planning team at the very outset of project planning. In an open team forum, the group can challenge the originator's ideas and estimates, and subject them to negotiation and further targeted fact-finding. This way a consensus gradually evolves through a dynamic group dialogue.

Getting people to present their ideas and estimates publicly at the conceptual stage of a project has the further advantage that at that early stage they have not invested any strong emotional capital into their ideas. As a result they are less apt to defend their views from an emotional standpoint and are far more open to challenges and practical input from colleagues. You can read more details about the problem with opinions and beliefs and how to deal with them using Team Planning and other methods in 11.7 specifically Table 13.

> "No problem can really be solved merely by assuming that it can be solved and or that its solution lies in hard work – anymore than its solution lies in inaction."
>
> Idries Shah – Reflections

Where you have not established the concrete facts, you are simply presenting *an opinion* to the team as to what you think should be done and what the likely costs and benefits are. In this sense you are inviting an argument, as *you are inviting everyone else to have an opinion as well*. So a powerful deterrent to wasteful argument and counterproductive competitive rivalry is the preparation of a project case with irrefutable facts. This tactic really helps arrive at an early and harmonious agreement.

There is another important point here. Bad feelings generated from serious arguments also debilitate group effectiveness in other ways. Arguments based on differing opinions easily sour relationships and diminish collaboration and mutual respect. So, rigorous fact-finding is important for good teamwork as well as just effective problem solving. In the instances where we see that an argument persists despite the facts, this usually reveals a conflict of fundamental values. The exposure of this at the team planning stage enables the ironing out of these fundamental differences at a relatively lower cost to the organisation than if the conflict surfaces at a later stage in a project.

Essentially, collaboration is the antithesis of competitiveness. The emphasis is on everyone working harmoniously together to achieve a unified purpose rather than fighting amongst each other for the spoils of commission, bonuses, promotion, status, glory or whatever.

Motivational impact on the human givens

Leaders, who advocate a highly competitive working environment, often overlook the potential for high achievers to perform even better in a collaborative, supportive environment. Low-stressed, fun situations free the mind to be more creative and dynamic. There are also long-term benefits to be had for the organisation as turnover of staff is reduced through less burnout and the sharing of a greater sense of team spirit or being part of a wider community. There is a greater opportunity for giving and receiving attention and to be more emotionally connected to colleagues.

11.3 Balancing team attributes

The problem defined: Stressor 23 - Incompatibilities

Incompatibilities between team members can also lead to negativity and stress. Incompatibilities within the team tend to disrupt the flow of creativity if, for instance, two "shapers"[3] are constantly going head-to-head both trying to push events their own way. This sort of argument can waste a lot of time and energy and arouse hostility. Where arguments become heated, personal relationships and collaboration suffer.

Conflict arising from incompatibilities will restrict fun, friendship and, depending on the nature of the conflict, a whole range of other human givens. If there are "winners" and "losers" in the situation there is a risk that several of the losers' needs will be unfulfilled, such as the need to be connected to a wider group, the need for recognition and status and a sense of control over their affairs at work. The situation may also impact the loser's self-esteem.

Remedies

Techniques such as Dr Meredith Belbin's team role analysis can assist a good mix of temperaments[4]. But here again a collaborative leadership style helps as well. The openness and consensus-building procedures of a collaborative planning process tend to help directly by alleviating incompatibilities and also by exposing the problem at an early stage of a project allowing the team leader to take some remedial action.

A well-structured collaborative planning system allows people a large degree of autonomy within their own field of responsibility albeit with input and direction from the rest of the team. This high degree of autonomy within a supportive and collaborative working environment relieves a degree of stress and this relief helps smooth out those incompatibilities that can otherwise lead to tension and conflict arising in a pressure cooker atmosphere.

Motivational impact on the human givens

One feature of collaborative planning and decision-making is that "incompatible" people find that they are working in a less highly-charged atmosphere. Friendships and fun can flourish even within a dynamic operational environment where creative tensions are being generated. Genuine participative planning thrives on and caters for diversity so everyone's contribution is valued.

11.4 The 16% of managers to avoid

The problem defined: Stressor 24 - The presence of a socialised psychopath

Two men from a local village were making their way through the jungle when suddenly they came across a large and hungry tiger. "Quick!" said one. "We had better run away." "What's the point?" said the other man. "The tiger can run faster than us." "Yes." said the first. "But I can run faster than you."

The psychopathy personality disorder afflicts 16% of UK managers compared with an average of 2% of the total population.

You might ask why the subject of psychopathy is in a book about leadership.

The unpalatable truth is, that a worryingly large proportion of managers fall into this category of personality disorder. According to one survey this disorder afflicts 1 in 6 (16%) of UK managers[5] as compared with an average occurrence of 2% of the total population. It might be that this statistic is an exaggeration, for reasons mentioned later. Even so there are still a lot of ruinous bosses out there damaging their organisations and making life miserable for hundreds of thousands or even millions of employees. Elsewhere in the world and throughout history we have seen and experienced what happens when someone with this type of personality disorder gets into a position of leadership. So it makes sense to be equipped with the knowledge and understanding to prevent such a calamity occurring in your own organisation.

In brief a socialised psychopath is an extreme and pathological example of the "Me First" attitude and is a huge five star stressor for any team or organization. Although psychopathy is a spectrum disorder and can therefore occur in mild as well as extreme and criminal forms, the pattern in the leadership context is typified by the obsessive pursuit of self-interest either at the expense of, or at least with reckless disregard of the wider group interests. Ambition is not necessarily a characteristic of the psychopath and such people can be found holding lowly positions as well as high ones. The focus here is more on those with the drive to play out their pathology in a position of power.

208

Almost by definition, socialised psychopaths can conceal their pathology effectively unless exposed by someone with experience. Nevertheless despite their ability to function almost unseen, socialised psychopaths are extremely destructive within a team and organisational context.

Characteristics of a socialised psychopath

Socialised psychopaths often have a ceaseless need for stimulation and change and have a craving to be at the centre of things. Unfortunately, these attributes are usually accompanied by an impulsive attitude towards their responsibilities. They are often recklessly driven towards the rewards associated with "success"[6] and can quickly display bullying aggressiveness and become manipulative when things are not going their way. This dangerous mix is centred around an inability to genuinely empathise with other people and their problems[7]. Unnervingly, this lack of empathy can be concealed behind a facade of easy charm.

The need for constant excitement often translates, in the organizational arena, into an obsession with organisational change or success. This can quickly undermine the foundation of an organization in terms of its key relationships, operational procedures, organisational knowledge and structures.

Psychopaths stir up constant turbulence, manipulation and power struggles around them and this sows exhaustion and de-motivation in the minds of subordinates and co-workers. Those impacted by a psychopath, often experience corrosive doubt, as to their own mental stability. In this high-stress atmosphere, projects can be unwittingly destroyed. However, psychopaths are past masters at deflecting blame and actually prosper in a secretive blame culture. Under these unpleasant conditions, good people tend to leave as they feel they don't have to put up with the stress. On the other hand, less self-assured or less stable people tend to stay and often react in a number of bizarre ways, as the stress in the environment triggers their own emotional arousal. This side effect often means that the real victims become the apparent cause of the problems at work further concealing the pernicious influence of the psychopath.

People under stress can sometimes appear psychopathic

It is important to observe caution in arriving at a "diagnosis" as a number of the above characteristics can sometimes apply to anyone under stress. Manifesting some of these characteristics does not make someone a psychopath. This feature may account for the high statistic that one in six UK managers is a socialised psychopath. During stressful episodes it is possible to manifest some of these symptoms that may then diminish after the stress subsides. For instance a stress episode can easily make someone more tyrannical, reckless, unethical or unable to empathise about other people's problems. A psychopath, on the other hand, will exhibit more than a majority of these characteristics pretty consistently over a long period of time and regardless of the different circumstances they are in. So, if you ever have to consider whether or not you are dealing with a socialised psychopath, examine the subject's good or natural behaviour along with the unnatural to arrive at a balanced view.

Using the socialised psychopath checklist

The checklist (See table 11) is based on observation and experience of socialised psychopaths. Where you see more than about sixteen symptoms occurring you are probably dealing with a socialised psychopath, the higher the score, the stronger the indication. Psychopathy is a spectrum disorder. This checklist is not meant to be an infallible diagnostic test but just a rough and ready guide to help you gain a rational insight in a stressed situation.

If you fail to take a balanced view then you run the risk of developing a witch-hunt that can lead to all kinds of complications and can also quickly be exploited by genuinely antisocial elements wanting to disrupt your existing arrangements. In this context, it is important to remember that if you are in a stressed relationship one common stress response is to 'pathologize' i.e. view the other person's behaviour as manifestations of a pathology. The reality may be that they are also suffering from stress and are manifesting typical stress symptoms, which will pass under calmer conditions. The checklist can, if honestly and objectively used, provide you with a fair indication of whether further investigation and help is necessary.

This feeling of "Am I going mad?" is a common occurrence for people involved with socialised psychopaths.

Using this checklist will certainly help relieve the tension from a relationship when the stress has reached a level where you are beginning to doubt your own sanity. This feeling of "Am I going mad?" or "Am I in the wrong?" is a common occurrence for people involved with socialised psychopaths. Hopefully, if you have been honest and objective, a high score will indicate it is more likely to be "them" that's mad not "you". You can then take steps to do something about the problem.

Table 12: Checklist of socialised psychopath characteristics

	Socialised psychopaths have a tendency to:
1	Be attracted to the centre of things
2	Manipulate others to achieve self-centred goals, with no consideration of the effects on those being manipulated
3	Tell bare faced lies to your face without compunction, are cavalier with the truth
4	Be incapable of productive self-criticism and self-analysis; they have to be right
5	Have no apparent sense of remorse, shame or guilt when they have done wrong
6	Exude superficial charm that can be switched on to suit immediate ends
7	Experience episodes of self-importance, or self-righteousness
8	Get bored easily and need persistent stimulation and change
9	Display apparent human emotion despite a real callousness or lack of empathy
10	Blame others for their mistakes and put enormous energy into protecting themselves
11	Provoke instability in relationships; tendency for short term relationships.
12	Speak in mainly broad generalities and often uses nominalisations that invoke emotional arousal
13	Trade in bad news, critical or hostile remarks that invalidate and suppress others, rarely passing on good news or complimentary remarks but embellishing bad
14	Have had episodes of juvenile delinquency, rebelliousness, truancy or crime
15	Often exhibit parasitic behaviour such as scrounging off others or milking the system
16	Tendency for impulsive and reckless behaviour and decision-making
17	Indulge in promiscuous sexual behaviour
18	Be belligerent and have a bullying manner especially when threatened
19	Lose their temper quickly
20	Set unrealistic goals and long term aims
21	Act irresponsibly and have a bad sense of ownership, especially with other people's property
22	Lack any real ability to empathise with other people's problems
23	Inherent incompetence, inability to complete a full cycle of action successfully.
24	Surrounded by cowed or sick associates and colleagues who often behave in bizarre ways themselves and whose own lives seem to be troubled and falling
25	Tyrannical and controlling behaviour over subordinates and colleagues alike

Do not try and tackle the situation on your own. Share the problem with your team and if necessary call in an expert to get an objective view.

The socialised psychopath's frequent habitats

Generally this type of personality disorder can be found in positions of leadership or authority where there is either one of, or a combination of the following factors:

1. Top-down command and control management with a strong authoritarian culture.
2. An autocracy where the leader is hardly accountable or effectively unaccountable to other stakeholders either below or in authority above them.
3. Where there is a fair degree of imperviousness to pressure or influence from outside factors such as competition or market forces or, in the case of political organisations, an active and alert electorate.
4. Where there has been a loose or absent organisational structure that provides a power vacuum for a psychopath to exploit in a bid for power and control.
5. Organisations or institutions which are essentially destructive in nature even though they may pose as working towards the common good; for example extreme Political parties such as the Communist, far left or National Socialist Parties. Tragically, care institutions and public social services can come into this category where in the name of altruism and kindness much cruelty and oppression can be inflicted on the hapless victims.

The socialised psychopath's overweening compulsion to "be in control" and "in the centre of things" added to the superhuman energy they are prepared to expend to achieve this status, means that such personalities can be found in senior positions within the following types of working environments:

➢ Public sector services, academia and the political arena
➢ Charities with a low level of accountability to outside influence or perhaps with passive trustees
➢ Large corporations with fairly passive shareholders
➢ Owner-managed businesses that have acquired relatively secure niches in the market place
➢ Religious or quasi-spiritual organisations.

In healthier environments where there is a satisfactory level of accountability, the psychopath's behaviour gets challenged at an earlier stage and their inherent incompetence is exposed. As a result they tend to move on or are moved on very quickly. Hence one bit of evidence to look for is a track record of job changes.

Impact on the human givens

When this type of dysfunctional personality is in a position of power and authority within an organisation he or she will impact just about all of the human givens. The psychopath's obsessive drive to control things will diminish everyone else's autonomy. Incessant change, intrigue and politicising will damage personal relationships within the group as openness, honesty and trust deteriorates. The sense of community and enjoyment experienced in a healthy team evaporates.

Other people's self-esteem is threatened, as sometimes is physical security, when the psychopath also feels threatened. People's ability to use their rational mental faculties is impaired as there is usually a high level of emotional arousal through fear of failure, fear of threats, fear of being ostracised and so on.

The constant tension, worry and anxiety among subordinates and peers leads to a range of stress symptoms including lack of sleep, exhaustion, irrational or negative personal responses to situations and depression to name a few.

As if this wasn't bad enough, the inherent incompetence of psychopaths tends to mean the workgroup experiences a number of the other major organisational stressors as a matter of course. Thus:

- There is always an unpleasant atmosphere of mistrust (Stressor 2) the pervasiveness of a blame culture and witch hunts are both unnerving and intrude into people's privacy
- In the reckless pursuit of success, the psychopath may well set onerous unilaterally imposed goals or "targets" on subordinates (Stressor 3) leading to timewasting overwork and morale sapping meaninglessness
- The psychopath may demand responsibility of subordinates but withhold the necessary means or authority for tasks to be accomplished (Stressor 11)
- There is increasing career uncertainty (Stressor 12)
- Personal criticism and lack of support are typical and undermine people's sense of wellbeing (Stressor 13)
- Chaotic routines and procedures become prevalent in an ever-changing environment (Stressor 14)

- Generally people working in such conditions experience a growing disillusionment with the organisation's values and purpose (Stressor 16)
- A classic psychopathic tactic is the unfair treatment of equals as they pay off favourites and allies at the expense of others (Stressor 17)

Remedies

The best remedy is prevention. If you are involved in the selection process of candidates for senior or managerial positions it is best to vet them for their level of emotional intelligence as well as for technical skills and business track record. In this context, suitable candidates for a leadership role should display, among other qualities, high degrees of self-awareness, loyalty, emotional self-control, transparency, integrity and adaptability.

Table 13:

Emotional needs impacted by the presence of a socialized psychopath	Positive impact	Negative impact
Security		X
Meaning		X
Emotional connection		X
Autonomy and control		X
Part of a wider community		X
Enjoyment, friendship, intimacy and fun		X
Status and recognition		X
Achievement and feeling of competence		X
Challenge – problems to solve		
Privacy		X
Attention		X
Regular routine		X
Score		11

As regards identifying the appropriate level of social competence, look for candidates that are able to empathise well, have a proven capacity for collaborating with others and have an inherent attitude of service towards their colleagues and subordinates[8].

What this means in practise is that the selection procedure for senior positions has to probe a lot deeper than simply relying on recruitment agency screening, CV appraisals, one or two interviews and psychometric tests. These standard methods are hardly sufficient to filter out problem cases as they are vulnerable to the psychopath's innate ability to lie effortlessly[9], turn on the charm to deceive and recruit compliant referees who then provide glowing testimonials.

Include in the selection process, in-depth investigations with past employers and other former colleagues as to the true character and track record of a candidate. The point to remember is that psychopaths don't just grow overnight. If the candidate under examination falls into this category then there will be a history of psychopathic behaviour that other people will be able to tell you about.

Clear accountability can expose a psychopath at work

If you are already in the unfortunate situation where a psychopath is working for your organisation then the remedy lies in clear and firm accountability. Follow the five criteria of effective accountability, covered in 9.8 (making accountability current, frequent, specific, clear and direct) and you will prevent a serious problem arising either by exposing the problem of this personality disorder or making the psychopath feel uncomfortable enough to precipitate their early departure.

A warning here, if you find yourself dealing with this type of personality disorder, you may find the process of imposing accountability and feedback deeply challenging. Typically the psychopath will try to manipulate or bully you into submission. They will enlist allies to support them and deflect blame from themselves. They will lie, withhold information or provide misinformation. However, if you persist diligently and fearlessly with all five principles you will prevail. Either the psychopath will move on elsewhere or, through the course of the normal process, you will have provided yourself with evidential grounds for their removal.

Where a problem is suspected in a senior position where accountability is already difficult, it may be advisable to call in an expert to check the "diagnosis". Whatever the situation, it is imperative, for the prosperity and even the survival of the organisation, to remove an offender from the organisation as soon as possible.

Psychopaths hate a healthy team atmosphere

The structure, teamwork and openness of an authentic collaborative leadership style can quickly expose this sort of problem, as psychopaths are pathologically unable to collaborate in a team. By definition, they are almost totally insecure and so will always be trying to find ways to secure their own position by reducing the power and ability of others. This is why such a personality will sabotage working relationships, destabilize effective teamwork and undermine the team's objectives.

It is important to realise that such personalities will always attempt to undermine a team approach. Teamwork to a psychopath is like garlic to Count Dracula as it prevents them practising their preferred divide and rule tactic and prohibits them from being at the centre of things. Such a person has a hidden terror of other people that has become a fixation about their own survival at everyone else's expense. This means they feel seriously threatened by anyone else's competence or the prospect that others will grow in strength and ability. As such they will always work compulsively to undermine other people's or the group's development and progress. In addition, effective collaboration and teamwork by the rest of the group threatens their craving to control everyone around them. Open teamwork also risks exposing their weaknesses of incompetence, lack of empathy, integrity and their one-pointed self-gratification at the expense of everyone else in the organisation.

The socialised psychopath's skill at politicising and their ability to display emotional sincerity and charm when forming self-serving alliances means that often a comprehensive and remorseless team effort is required to expose and remove the offender.

In practical terms there is no real cure for this disorder as the psychopath has never developed any sense of the self and therefore does not have any motivation for self-improvement. In their view they are not the problem; everyone else is. This being the case it is best to avoid any attempt to treat the individual; even the experts consider effective treatment for psychopathy to be a long way off [10].

In organisational terms, remedial action is, of course, difficult if the psychopath has already achieved the top job. He or she will use any means to maintain their control and will have previously built up a network of compliant "Patrons" and "Pawns" to protect and defend them. Psychopaths will resort to unethical

216

methods and lies without compunction and will exploit any weaknesses found in the group for their own ends in order to maintain their status and power.

Motivational impact on the human givens

Removing a socialised psychopath from your working environment will create a blast of fresh air, and relieve a whole range of stress factors. Not least of these can be an improvement in physical security and self-esteem for all those that had been affected.

Personal relationships and collaborative teamwork will dramatically improve; people will share information more and be supportive of others' success. Individual productivity will improve as the more relaxed and personable atmosphere will improve the team's thinking capacity and their ability to make reasonable and balanced judgments.

Case example: A socialised psychopath at a mental health charity

The new managing director of a sizeable local charity displayed a range of fairly typical symptoms of socialised psychopathic behaviour. The charity was part of a well-established national network of semi-autonomous local charities providing long-term residential care for adults with special needs.

This local operation was based at a large facility but was also spread over several sites and employed, in all, about two hundred full and part time employees.

External appearances

On the surface, the new MDs achievements seemed highly positive. He quickly galvanised the charity into a period of major growth largely through the acquisition of other existing care homes in the locality.

The new MD also set to work regenerating the charity's public profile.

He was adept at creating publicity that attracted corporate sponsorship, new funds and community support. Similarly, he embarked upon a relentless round of networking, media interviews, and press releases, and his charismatic speaking style ensured that he was regularly carrying out public speaking engagements. Another valuable contribution was his ability to attract valuable celebrity endorsements that raised the profile of the charity even more.

All this energetic activity impressed outside supporters such as the social service departments, local business community and the trustees. This promotional activity served to swell the charity funds for his ambitious expansion programme.

This was all well and good. However, stakeholders within the organisation who had to live or work under his new regime experienced a very different side of things. Whilst on the one hand the image of the organisation was of vibrant growth and dynamism, the standard of care and service to the residents was plummeting.

The reality inside the organisation

It wasn't too long after the arrival of the new MD that staff morale began to wane. In the words of one carer "everybody seems to be unhappy". There was a complete loss of team atmosphere with staff members no longer willing to help each other out in the same way as they did before. This negative atmosphere led to a gradual attrition of long-term and experienced staff.

Previously, due to the nature of the work, nearly all the employees were carers who had been with the charity for many years. Although never well paid, there was an intrinsic loyalty to the organisation as the care workers were dedicated to the welfare of their residents and as such considered many of the individual residents as their friends.

Within about two years of the MD's arrival this culture had largely evaporated and only about a fifth of the staff had been there for a period longer than five years. The rest were mostly foreign agency workers or temporary staff. This state of affairs had serious consequences on the actual running of the care side of the organisation.

The new policy had been to replace existing staff members with agency staff, as the MD thought that this arrangement helped flexibility in terms of scheduling. He would lay off experienced and long serving people at will, as soon as there was a dip in room occupancy. This of course would make short term cost savings but he would then hire back in temporary agency staff.

The resultant extensive use of agency staff made life more difficult for those that stayed on, as these temporary workers had to be shown the ropes and were then replaced the next week or month by someone else who, then also had to be trained up.

The knock on effect was that, at the operational level, there was constant crisis management among both staff and middle management. The inbuilt experience of the organisation was rapidly eroded adding greatly to the strain and stress of working for the charity.

But of course the really telling effect was that the rapport, positive attitude and care for the residents suffered. Increasingly the residents found that the people dealing with them were strangers, temporary carers, new to the system, and only passing through. The extra attention to be gained from genuine friendships was increasingly missing.

Many of the temporary staff, especially the agency members, had no recognition that they belonged to a wider team that shared values of care and compassion for the residents as individual human beings with real needs for friendship and attention. But of course this consequence was hardly visible to outsiders. After all the residents were in no position to complain and simply had to suffer in silence, enduring their own personal wordless hell of loneliness and boredom.

So what was going wrong?

Sixteen out of 25 characteristics

In an assessment of the situation an outside specialist observed that the MD displayed about sixteen of the twenty-five traits seen to be typical of a socialised psychopath (See table above).

Fundamentally this was the root cause of the dehumanised operating standards and working conditions for the staff. I have depicted some of these traits in the following paragraphs but in summary the heart and soul of this care organisation began to be eaten away shortly after the MD's arrival. His overweening personal ambition to create a bigger and better known charity was driven with a complete disregard to the feelings and needs of both his employees and the residents.

Manipulation to achieve control and self-centred goals. Every setback or challenge to the progress of "the project", as it became known, was met with a new round of reorganisation that demoralised senior staff and confused everyone at operational level. In effect the sporadic reshuffling led to the gradual replacement of "difficult" individuals (i.e. independently minded) with more compliant subordinates.

Before many months had elapsed employees realised that senior personnel fell into two categories. They were either for the MD's expansion "project" or they were on the way out.

Within two years nearly all the senior long term and experienced managers had left. Almost universally the old hands were replaced with ineffectual box tickers. These replacements seemed incapable of independent thought and displayed more than a whiff of sycophantic hero worship when it came to the relationship they had with the MD.

Capacity to tell lies effortlessly. Although often difficult to pin down as actual lies, employees quickly began to lose trust in the MD. It always seemed so difficult to identify his true intentions for future policy direction or change.

Far from being open and trusting, he kept his cards very close to his chest. Statements as to his intentions were always ambiguous and wrapped up in "nominalisations", that is generalisations that effectively intended to mean what ever the listener felt they meant.

Grand talk of "change" "care" and "compassion" never seemed to translate into any specific or measurable improvements.

On the other hand, sometimes specific, changes would actually occur unannounced even though there had been previous denials that they were intended. This web of misinformation and half-truths wrong footed people and took away their sense of security. Nobody felt they knew what was going to happen next.

Lack of remorse. At no time during this episode did the MD display any signs of remorse or guilt for the trouble and chaos that was being wrought on the operational side of the charity. Indeed he showed no signs that he was even aware of the problems he was creating.

Superficial charm. The MD had an ability to charm those whose support he was after, but tended to be heavy handed with any subordinates within his power. He displayed a casual disregard for the employees' needs for some degree of recognition or status or for any real autonomy in their work.

It was noted that unlike the previous MD, he expended a lot of energy and time cultivating the support and backing of the trustees. He was often wining and dining members of the board of trustees and spent charity money on conferences and strategy days, to which the trustees were all invited. Oddly senior members of staff were not. So the people who had to actually run the operation were not involved in developing strategy or planning for the future.

The effect of this was that the board members became flattered by his attention. Perhaps it was this factor that rendered them completely ineffectual in terms of reining in the MD's ambitions or monitoring the impact he was having at operational level. The outcome was that the MD's charm offensive gave him a free hand. It seemed that the trustees were either oblivious or indifferent to the problems experienced by the employees and the residents.

Evidence of self-importance and pomposity. The previous MD had made do with small even cramped offices. The overall impression to any visitor was that he was camping out in temporary accommodation rather than running a sizeable organisation.

This perception generally arose due to the lack of comfort and space and with paperwork piled up everywhere. In truth, paperwork took second place to the old MD's desire to meet and greet people and his proactive even meticulous enquiries into staff members' welfare and the welfare of the residents they were dealing with. He knew every employee's name and also seemed to be on personal terms with a large number of the residents many of whom seemed to recognise him as an old friend.

The whole atmosphere in the previous MD's offices was one of openness and conviviality and this struck any employee who dropped in to discuss any minor problems that they were confronting. He seemed to have time for everyone and anyone was welcome to drop in if they felt the need to, albeit they would be subjected to a thorough although friendly interrogation about both their area of responsibility and their personal wellbeing. All this helped communication and the coordination of both work and staff.

This approach was in complete contrast to the new arrival.

In physical terms, the new MD isolated himself by removing his administration off the main site and into plush new offices in town remote from the field of work. For some reason the premises were expanded to house a larger group of support staff.

Far from being an open drop in centre, security codes were required to even gain entrance to the new offices. At the same time, it was made very clear that he was too busy to stop to chat with employees. He always seemed to have far more important things on his mind.

The MD placed a heavy emphasis on creating the right image for the organisation. Usually this involved featuring the MD either in photos, interviews or video clips (Indeed the only time he ever really spent with the residents was during a photo shoot or during a visit from a VIP). The charity very quickly acquired smart new print material for all internal forms, that were coordinated with the letterheads, leaflets and other promotional material. The new 'vision and mission' statement was stamped across all offices, promotional material and public areas.

A belligerent and bullying manner. When the new MD became frustrated with progress he frequently gave way to bouts of temper. Although he could exude charm and flash a winning smile, he could also be highly aggressive.

Parasitic behaviour. In essence, the whole nature of "the project" was parasitic. The MD excelled at extracting donations from well-wishers and funds from government agencies. But these funds were in effect being spent on building his empire and his own position at the centre of it, not on enhancing the care of those in his charge.

Impulsive and reckless decision-making. The MD displayed this trait by making arbitrary changes to operational procedures that would effect the lives and wellbeing of residents without due consultation and without any formal planning or even really thinking through the consequences himself. Although he had not taken the trouble to find out the subtleties of how his own organisation really functioned, nevertheless he set about imposing his own ideas for changing the workings of it right from the start.

So for instance he carried out an arbitrary deployment of staff from one area to another "to improve flexibility". However all he managed to achieve was to upset people and further damage the level of continuity in relationships between staff and residents. Long serving employees became disconnected from their former charges, to the upset and demoralisation of both residents and carers.

The MD also imposed a range of cost cutting measures that showed a bizarre sense of priority.

For instance, despite more money being "invested" in corporate image and acquisitions there was a withdrawal of a number of staff benefits that had served to oil the wheels of care and service to the residents. Part of the working routine involved carers taking residents out for trips to the shops or to places of interest. The residents enjoyed these treats and they gave everyone a break. Importantly these outings also helped the bonding process, so important to promote a deeper commitment and friendship between residents and staff. During these trips, it had been the habit that the carers would have their meals and drinks refunded by the charity where appropriate. This facility was withdrawn or reduced to a level where the carer had to subsidise their food and beverages.

Similarly, staff members giving the necessary lifts to the residents were put at financial risk, as the MD withdrew vehicle insurance cover. Although some of the existing staff members put up with this, new arrivals and agency staff tended to avoid the risk and so withheld their driving services.

Essentially low paid members of staff were being asked to subsidise the running of the operation out of their own funds. Inevitably, over a relatively short period of time, this meant that there was less and less opportunity for residents to be taken out for a drive and be given external visits.

This penny-pinching measure achieved a significant loss in the quality of care and treatment for the residents whilst on the other hand, there was never a shortage of charity cash for plush offices, senior executive salaries, PR consultants, strategy conferences, entertaining trustees and VIPs and extra office staff.

Essential irresponsibility. The old system was never perfect but had comprised a subtle and intricate web of long-established personal relationships that had enabled a high degree of individual care, compassion and support to a very needy group of people. The MD's superficial understanding of the organisational needs and his reckless unilateral decision-making failed to take into account individual needs or viewpoints and destroyed so much of what had been worthwhile.

Lack of any real ability to empathise. If the MD had genuinely felt for other people he would have found the way to make more sensible decisions about their welfare. He would have consulted them, taken their needs into account and taken the time and trouble to think through problems thoroughly.

Unrealistic long term aims. The MD's expansion project was all based on raising more money to make acquisitions and trying to achieve accountancy based savings largely through the chimera of economies of scale and short term cost savings.

Disastrously, at least for the residents, the charity's unremitting expansion was not founded on any effectiveness at caring for an increased number of people. As the number of residents grew, the organisational skills and the experience required to meet the challenges of caring for more and more people, failed to grow in parallel. If anything the core ability to actually deliver long-term care for vulnerable residents shrank due to the dwindling number of experienced, permanent carers and the perpetual chaos inherent in the MD's restless drive to change things.

A seeming obsession for persistent stimulation and change. Whatever was already working still had to be fixed.

The MD was constantly foisting changes on quite satisfactory procedures and systems for no apparent reason that anyone else could understand. The changes always made matters more difficult and served only to reduce the level of service to the residents.

Never the less anyone who intended to stay with the organisation for any length of time was not in a position to resist the changes. Not that this meant that new changes were followed through with any degree of rigour or persistence. Far from it, in fact most new initiatives were quietly dropped after a period of time.

This tended to happen for two reasons. Firstly, the MD's enthusiasm for them soon waned and his attention moved on to something more exciting; or secondly, employees usually found that the new procedures or processes failed to improve anything and were more trouble than they were worth so found ways to get around them.

Displays of apparent human emotions contrast with a callousness or lack of empathy. Despite the essential nature of the charity being about human care and attention for especially vulnerable people, the MD lacked any real empathy with the needs of either staff or residents. This inability to empathise contrasted starkly with the MD's eloquently expressed concern for others in his promotional literature, speeches and PR campaigns.

His ability to project a caring image fooled many people outside the organisation who thought he must be some sort of saint, tirelessly working for the welfare of others. This naive view of course overlooked the fact that he had persuaded the trustees to award him a substantial increase in salary way above the previous incumbent's.

Difficulty maintaining stable relationships – Progressively, senior colleagues, that is the people he actually had to work with on a daily basis started to leave. This exodus started to occur from fairly early on in the MD's tenure.

The MD's obsessive need for control exhausted and stressed his fellow colleagues. The iron clamp he imposed on their thinking and activity denied his colleagues their own needs for recognition, status and a degree of autonomy and control over their own areas of work and responsibility.

When they began to understand that their views, experience and judgement were evidently not valued and were no longer being taken into account in decision-making, these experienced senior people started to look for work elsewhere.

The MD displayed an aloof and arrogant attitude in the way he habitually made arbitrary decisions without due consultation with his colleagues. He largely ignored their feedback about operational problems, or suggestions for improvements and overrode suggestions or input from others. This arrogance largely prevented him from developing harmonious working relationships with his colleagues who felt they could not connect with him at all and felt constantly undermined and devalued.

Witch hunts and blame culture. Employees at every level soon began to realise that the MD was super sensitive to any criticism or negative feedback about his own work. In his own eyes he could do no wrong.

Whenever something went seriously wrong (Meaning anything that risked damaging the MD's image or the reputation of the charity) there was invariably an exhaustive witch-hunt to identify the "true" culprit. These witch-hunts created a repressive atmosphere and were harrowing to all those concerned. The end result would frequently be an organisational reshuffle that would remove any antagonists who may have been in a position to expose that it was the MD who had made the cock-up.

A fairly happy ending

In the end it was the MD's compulsion for constant stimulation and change and his overriding ambition that saved the organisation from complete disaster. His evident success at expanding the charity, raising funds and establishing a high profile became his platform for launching himself into the role as leader of a larger charity. After only three years in post he stepped effortlessly on to grander things leaving his replacement to pick up the pieces and work out what was going wrong.

11.5 The power of parallel processing

The problem defined: Stressor 25 - Organisational straight-line thinking

Corporate and public sector bureaucracies now dominate the working lives of millions of citizens whether they are employees, customers or 'service users'. Unfortunately the usual experience of having to work in, or be served by such organisations is far from satisfactory. All too often, dealing with or working for these organisations seems to be inherently stressful and frustrating, even soul destroying. An explanation for this commonplace experience is a recent concept known as Organisational Straight Line (OSL) thinking. The term OSL thinking refers to bureaucratic behaviour that has been likened to High Functioning Autistic behaviour (HFA) or Asperger's Syndrome in an individual.

> OSL thinking enmeshes day-to-day activity in a sticky web of paperwork, rules, regulations and interfering 'guidelines'.

A chief characteristic of OSL thinking is that it enmeshes people's day-to-day activity in a sticky web of paperwork, rules, regulations and interfering 'guidelines' all the while drifting the organisation away from its true purpose. Another defining feature is that OSL thinking tends to invoke the 'law of unintended consequences'. In essence this linear type of thinking generates policies or decisions that, although they are designed to solve one problem, somehow manage to overlook the impact that those decisions have on other areas of the organisation or other stakeholders. The net result is confusion, chaos and waste and a loss of direction. As such, OSL thinking seems to be endemic in public institutions these days, with so many of our government services seeming to be in perpetual crisis and often producing outcomes that are the reverse of the organisational purpose.

Although perhaps an extreme example, the Rotherham child abuse scandal shows how bad things can get when OSL thinking takes over. Although this topic is covered more fully in chapter 11 section 7 (Stressor 27), it is pertinent to mention some of the facts here as well. Over a sixteen-year period gangs of criminals sexually abused and even trafficked 1,400 children. Many of the children were from local authority care homes. All the while the police, local council and social services were so preoccupied by their internal processes and conflicting ideological agendas that they proved catastrophically incapable of doing the job they are paid to do and that is to protect the children in their care. The police even went so far as to arrest fathers who were trying to remove their daughters from harm. Similarly the local authority tried to set-up a criminal enquiry into the identity of the 'whistle blower' who 'breached security'. The 'crime' in this case was to give evidence to a Times reporter who broke the news of the scandal to a wider public.

Some of the characteristics of OSL thinking have become so endemic in large corporations and in the public sector that it is worthwhile expanding on them a little to clarify and illustrate the meaning and try and find a remedy. In simple terms, bureaucratic organisations tend to have some or all of the following symptoms of High Functioning Autistic behaviour:

1. Inability to monitor and prioritise different streams of information
2. Obsession with collecting information
3. Difficulty in reacting flexibly towards changes in circumstances
4. Obsessive desire for sameness, repetition and uniformity
5. A strong need to impose their own perspective on other people
6. Inability to empathise with how others feel towards their behaviour
7. Focus on a particular detail at the expense of the larger picture.
8. Greater comfort within an environment dominated by rules, structure and regulations

1. Inability to monitor and prioritise different streams of information:
Unlike a healthy brain that can carry out parallel processing of information, bureaucratic organisations seem only able to think in linear fashion. This

phenomenon is especially apparent when we look at the full breadth of government involvement across its many diverse departmental responsibilities. Essentially this type of OSL thinking is endemic to bureaucracy. An example from the UK is the dire situation with child protection. This is embodied by the furore over 'Baby P' who died through parental neglect despite sixty visits from the local social services, doctors and police over an eight-month period.

In the usual political knee jerk response to let people know that "something is being done about it" Ed Balls, the then Labour Government's Children's Secretary commissioned Lord Laming to carryout a report. Laming (The Protection of Children in England: A Progress Report)[11] put forward fifty-eight new recommendations in an attempt to resolve the problems within the child protection sector. But these recommendations come on top of the hundred or so of his earlier report he submitted in 2000. In both cases the reports were written in response to the high profile death of a single child at the hands of their parents or guardians.

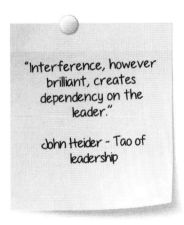

"Interference, however brilliant, creates dependency on the leader."

John Heider - Tao of leadership

A direct result of these reports has been the rocketing of 'child protection' costs and the introduction of an onerous regulations regime. Part of this regime involves comprehensive child protection checks compulsorily carried out by the Criminal Records Bureau into anyone wishing to work with children. In four years the bureau carried out 15 million checks at a cost of £500 million preventing a massive 80,000 people from working with children for sometimes the most spurious and vague of reasons.

This system of bureaucratic record keeping and box ticking has been described[12] as providing only 'ritual security' as it is never going to effectively take the place of rigorous face-to-face appraisals that have been successfully employed for generations with organizations experienced at working with children. Side effects of the regulatory regime have been to

1. Discourage volunteers from wanting to lend a hand,
2. Pile on onerous costs to hard-pressed charities,
3. Undermine adult and parental authority,
4. Generate mistrust and a false sense of security.

Meanwhile this style of regime has done nothing to protect children against the type of 'industrial scale' sexual abuse seen at Rotherham, whilst councils across the country are experiencing difficult and hefty overspends to cope with their child protection responsibilities.

What is missing here is the ability to balance cost and benefit. Essentially all this effort, money and other resources are being expended over only a handful of deaths per year, in total fifty-five children a year die at the hands of their parents and guardians. Perhaps you think this is a heartless way to look at the situation. If so try looking at it this way. Shifting resources towards solving this specific problem has meant reprioritizing resources from somewhere else.

"Rules reduce freedom and responsibility. Enforcement of rules is coercive and manipulative, which diminishes spontaneity and absorbs energy."

John Heider - Tao of leadership

Firstly you have to ask the all-important question; can we really make much of a positive impact on fifty-five fatalities experienced within the confines of family environment in a nation of some 60 million people with the cash and resources available? And how do we go about defending these few children without harming further the primary need for privacy and the integrity of the family life of all the other tens of millions of other people?

Any success is likely to prove fairly meager and at the expense of a further loss of the sovereignty of other families over their own children. The admission to hospital of four hundred or so children every year through stabbings by other children is testimony to the already fragile state of family and parental influence over children's behaviour and aggression. Weaken this further in an attempt to achieve perfect state-provided "child protection" and it will risk leading indirectly to further child on child violence.

In addition, diverting resources from elsewhere to pursue ever greater child protection is likely to have lead to a far greater number of fatalities in other areas. As an example, an estimated 91,030 people die every year at the hands of treatment errors in the NHS[13]. This problem of accidental fatalities has been published in the British Medical Journal and in leading newspapers. Yet there has been no equivalent action by the government in response to these 91,030 fatalities. Instead the financial focus is on protecting fifty-five children.

Unlike a healthy brain that can carry out parallel processing of information, bureaucratic organisations seem only able to think in linear fashion.

How much effort, attention and resource redeployment is required to reduce the NHS death toll by say a mere 10% or 9,000 people. Now if we could do that we would achieve an improvement of 8,945 fatalities over and above the existing total fatalities in the child protection arena.

This is not to suggest a particular policy direction but just to indicate that something crucial is currently missing in this important field of interest. And that is that the various administrative and political organizations involved are carrying out linear thinking that fails to:

- Embrace the wider and longer term view
- Represent a cross spectrum of stakeholder needs
- Take into balance a full range of options
- Fully establish and measure valid criteria for success
- Analyze the marginal costs and benefits arising from pursuing a full range of alternative options

2. Obsession with collecting information: The collection of masses of data on everybody and everything by government departments has become legendary and needs little elaboration here. Intuitively, we know that much of this data is very often a waste of time and a massive waste of resources. It seems that this common policy is driven more by an institutionalised compulsion for collecting things than for any rational or practical purpose.

3. Inability to react flexibly in the usual way towards changes in circumstances: A typical example of this characteristic is the subsequent behaviour of Northern Rock Bank once the government had bailed it out at taxpayers' expense in 2007. A healthy response when someone finds themselves in a deep hole of their own making is to first and foremost stop digging – not so with Northern Rock.

This bank, the fifth largest mortgage provider in the UK, failed precisely because of its own highly-leveraged lending policy and the high-risk mortgages it was offering including mortgages at 125% of household value. Once the credit crisis had started to kick in, the other banks prudently refused to give the company credit and the whole edifice risked collapse.

According to an Audit Commission report, after being rescued by the government in September 2007, the company instead of dropping their high-risk lending policy continued to lend a further £1.8 billion in 100% and even 125% mortgages over the next five months. This was despite 50% of the arrears and 75% of the repossessions at the bank stemming from these types of mortgages. Remember also that this lending policy was carried out at a time when it was obvious to even casual observers, that the problems in the banking sector were adversely impacting house price valuations.

So despite the near crash of the company, the reckless lending policies that got them into trouble in the first place were continued with the result that by June

2008 the company had made further losses of £585 million. This figure is £314 million more losses than the base case scenario used in the recovery plan when the government nationalised the company[14].

4. Obsessive desire with sameness and repetition: This type of thinking has been prevalent in bureaucracies for generations. Just one example is that civil servants, teachers, doctors and even MPs are each employed under the same payment terms and employment conditions for their profession, right across the country. Individuals within each of these professions are given the same payment terms and conditions regardless of local variations in the cost of living, working circumstances, demand and supply of the relevant candidates for the job and, of course, individual variations in performance, experience and capability.

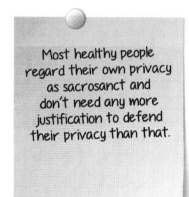

Most healthy people regard their own privacy as sacrosanct and don't need any more justification to defend their privacy than that.

5. A strong need to impose their own perspective on other people: Institutionalised political correctness, now rife amongst public sector organisations, is the organisational equivalent of the typically autistic impulse to impose ideological perspectives on everyone else.

An example of this tyrannical approach to management is the avalanche of literally thousands of pages of guidelines imposed on the teaching profession every year from the UK Department of Children, Education and Schools. This whole cascade of paper is entirely counterproductive as it damages teaching in any number of ways. Typically this type of bureaucratic interference:

1. Exhausts the teachers.
2. Undermines their professional status.
3. Impinges the autonomy and control that they have over their work.
4. Takes away a lot of the fun of teaching.
5. Threatens their job security (compliance being so important).
6. Damages the intrinsic meaning attached to the work that they are doing.
7. Inhibits teachers responding directly to the needs of their children.

When viewed in this way, you can see why the teaching profession in the UK is experiencing massive absenteeism on a weekly basis and a haemorrhaging of employees from the state sector. Perhaps a more helpful stance would be to stop hectoring teachers and instead enable them to apply their own professional creativity.

6. Inability to empathise with how others feel towards their behaviour An example of this impairment is widely manifested with the growing surveillance culture in the UK. The surveillance and invasion of privacy being foisted more and more on private and innocent citizens is allegedly being carried out in the name of counterterrorism, the fight against organised crime and money laundering.

But something crucial is missing here. And that is the ability to recognise that most healthy people regard their own privacy as sacrosanct and don't need any more justification to defend their privacy than that. Being told that we have nothing to fear if we are genuinely innocent is a statement that, apart from being patently untrue, can only come from someone or an organisation incapable of empathising with this need and views the need for privacy as something sinister in itself. This inability to empathise with this intimate biological need is classic Asperger's thinking.

We also see this policy generating 'unintended consequences'. The outcome of heavy-handed surveillance and intrusion, apart from disturbing and upsetting the rest of us has the exact opposite effect on terrorism than the one intended. Government seems to have forgotten that the objective of terrorist activity is to terrorise the host population to an extent that pressurises the government of the day to overreact and impose draconian "security" measures.

The terrorist's aim is precisely to induce the government to impose repressive measures that breach the spirit of the rule of law and restrict freedom. When these sorts of measures occur, the fringe supporters of the terrorist ideology harden into passionate activists and a larger and larger percentage of the population become more and more resistant to the government and status quo. Quasi-totalitarian measures thus act as the unwitting recruiter for the terrorist.

7. Focus on a particular detail at the expense of the larger picture: This straight-line characteristic is another bureaucratic feature. An example here is from a primary care trust hospital where there had been a successful drive to comply with a target to fill vacant bed space. Unfortunately the directive didn't take into account the catering, cleaning, staffing and supply services required to support the higher occupancy rate. So the exercise designed to optimise the use of one existing resource, bed spaces, led to complete overstretch of resources in other departments with chaos and disruption to working practices and scheduling elsewhere. In addition, the hospital was only able to cope with the extra workload by using temporary and expensive agency labour. The lack of the wider view here greatly restricted any cost benefit that might have been achieved by the increase in bed occupancy.

8. Greater comfort within an environment dominated by rules, structure and regulations: A major characteristic of bureaucracy is the cascades of regulations, rules, policy directives, and those euphemistically-labelled 'guidelines' emanating from government departments and the EU. Also typical of bureaucratic organisations are the rigid management structures, standard operating procedures, job descriptions and so on. This type of modus operandi is the organisational equivalent of a comfort zone.

Is organisational straight-line thinking institutionalised stressed thinking?

One important question is whether the phenomenon of OSL thinking is a symptom of stressed organisational thinking or whether these types of organisations attract high functioning autistic people to senior positions within them. Without more research we can only speculate, but it looks at the moment that it is probably a mixture of both aspects.

> Top-down command and control hierarchies precipitate constrained thinking due to an inherently stressful atmosphere.

Top-down command and control hierarchies precipitate constrained thinking due to an inherently stressful atmosphere. This sort of structure also manifests the same low level of interconnectivity in information flows and feedback loops that where they occur in the brain restricts high-level functioning. It may be that it is the mechanistic structure of bureaucratic organisations that is giving the appearance of the organisational equivalence of autistic thinking.

At the same time there is some evidence to suggest that people who feel more comfortable in a highly structured and regimented environment are attracted to this sort of work environment. In other words these types of organisations may be attracting candidates with High Functioning Autistic behaviour (HFA) or Asperger's Syndrome. The presence of a number of employees with this disorder then further reinforces the bureaucratic tendencies for OSL thinking.

Adverse impact on the human givens

Whatever the root cause here, what we can be sure of is, that such defective thinking impacts feelings of autonomy among the affected stakeholders and invades their need for privacy. In addition, OSL thinking impinges other stakeholders' needs for meaning, stretch and competence, whether they are supplicant welfare beneficiaries, functionaries within the organisation itself, clients, or customers, all these regulations, targets, rules and 'guidance' curtail their freedom of action. Within the organisational structure, unintended consequences and the general confusion created by OSL thinking can result in a loss of a real sense of meaning. Any sense of fun or authentic feelings of connectedness with the organisation in question are also threatened or subdued.

As such, OSL thinking has a similar impact on employees, as a range of other stressors including:

Stressor 3	The imposition of goals or targets from a higher authority
Stressor 11	Responsibility without authority or an inadequate control of events
Stressor 13	Insufficient or inappropriate support from management and colleagues
Stressor 16	Disagreement with organisational values or philosophy
Stressor 17	The unequal treatment of equals or the equal treatment of 'unequals'

Case example: Organisational straight-line thinking in a social services department

Tim, a busy Training and Education Officer at a City Hall social services department, was allocated another responsibility to his already stretched area of work. The heads of service had decided unilaterally that he find work experience placements every year for fifty to sixty university students. Peter did not disagree with the policy direction. It seemed a sensible enough idea and totally in keeping with the ethos of bringing on the next generation of social workers with some degree of hands on experience before they actually got qualified. However, good ideas call for more than wishful thinking to make them work. The problem Tim had with the decision was that he was not given either the authority or extra resources to accomplish the job efficiently or effectively.

Essentially he had to cajole or persuade team leaders to volunteer to have a student on their team. But he had no means to enforce this new policy. He also had no buy-in from the team leaders. All the various teams were already stretched and viewed the prospect of a student trainee as another chore that they could well do without. This meant continual and ongoing resistance to Tim's cajoling, persuasion and begging. Although he has never failed to meet his placement quota it has been at the expense of an enormous amount of his time. Ten to eleven weeks of the working year are now taken up canvassing teams and persuading team leaders. But that is not all. Two other factors are adversely impacted.

Firstly, the relationship with the team leaders has become strained as basically they are being badgered to take on extra responsibilities that they don't feel fits with their job descriptions. This ongoing friction means the rest of Tim's job is made more difficult as he relies on joint collaboration and support for the rest of his training and development responsibilities.

Secondly, the students are, out of necessity, basically being squeezed into any available slot. This means that they are not being given opportunities for experience that addresses their exact or preferred training needs. There is inherent uncertainty attached to a prolonged wait for a possible placement that if it does not appear in time will prevent the student from completing their course.

What the senior management failed to do was take a more holistic view of the situation and work with all the relevant departments to create a structure and culture that would enable the fruitful immersion of students into the working life of the various areas. This approach would have benefited all concerned for several reasons.

- The students would enjoy better training
- The teams would receive welcome assistance in their workload, as the student would be able to make a valuable contribution both in man-hours and in new ideas and perspectives
- The students' future clients would receive attention from better-trained social workers
- Tim would be able to focus on his core responsibilities of training and development

Despite lobbying repeatedly for action to be taken to remedy the situation, the senior management have been deaf to any of Tim's pleas. As a result this time-wasting and sub-optimum performance has been going on for five whole years.

This case example demonstrates at least five of the classic characteristics of OSL thinking including:

- The focus by the senior management on a particular detail at the expense of the larger picture
- The imposition of the top management's perception on everyone else over and above the reality on the ground

- A lack of empathy with the problems being created with the various parties affected
- Inflexibility towards changing the circumstances in tune with the demands of the time
- Development of unintended consequences

Remedy

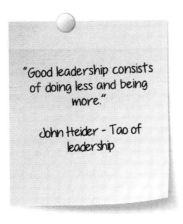

"Good leadership consists of doing less and being more."

John Heider - Tao of leadership

A powerful antidote to this limited way of thinking is to bring as many stakeholders into the decision-making process as possible. Introduce a strong element of bottom-up collaboration and you will enable policies and operating systems to emerge from the talent, training, discretion, knowledge and experience of the dozens of people doing the work at the operational level, not the few 'experts' at the top of the tree dictating one size fits all directives. Using a bottom-up approach in the appraisal of an organisation's strengths, weaknesses, opportunities and threats is the starting point for obtaining all angles to a problem. This approach ensures that decisions are based on relevant real-time data that is drawn from a much wider cross section of views and experience. A collaborative decision-making process will further introduce flexibility, thoroughness and robustness into the final decision.

Of course, another more radical remedy for public sector organisations is to get rid of the regulatory and centralised control aspects altogether. Instead treat employees as mature, responsible adults and devolve responsibility for the relevant function down the line to the people at the operational sharp end. This would mean letting hospitals, schools, doctors' surgeries, local police forces, etc. run themselves with local not central accountability. These operations could then function productively without the interference from centralised bureaucracies whose tendency is always directed towards this sort of low-performance OSL thinking.

One key fact to remember is that the people at the operational end already know and have been trained to do the job. Ministers and civil servants haven't. Any experts working for remote central organisations are inevitably out of touch with the day-to-day operational reality.

11.6 Removing drug misuse

The problem defined: Stressor 26 – Drug misuse

Performance-enhancing drugs, such as cocaine and amphetamines, generate high individual activity and the illusion of higher individual performance. However these higher energy levels are bought at the expense of damaging a number of the user's faculties. These include their ability to:

- Empathise well
- Form and maintain stable relationships
- Integrate the needs of the group with their own goals or personal gratification

The aroused state of mind attained by performance-enhancing drugs also impairs rational thought and other faculties conducive to settled decision-making and sound judgement. Thus working under the influence, regular users can generate other stressors such as negative relationships, over-competitiveness, fast-track career paths and the initiation of rashly thought through changes that create turbulence and further stress (See stressor 27 below).

Although widely regarded as a relatively harmless drug, marijuana is capable of causing the most serious and least reversible neurological damage of any of the common recreational drugs. Part of the problem with marijuana is that by causing the release of dopamine it activates the brain's reward system for doing nothing. Dopamine is nature's method of motivating us to carry out survival activities of one sort or another. As such marijuana tends to induce apathy. This is why addiction to it is one of the hardest to break.

Another problem with marijuana is that roughly a quarter to a third of users suffer from intense anxiety after taking the drug, rendering significant communication, rational thought and decision-making difficult.

Remedy

Encourage teamwork and collaboration as a means to achieve high group performance rather than focussing on driving up individual performance. Educate the staff on the fallacy of 'high performance' drugs and their danger. Use the openness and honesty of the collaborative or teamwork process to expose users. Most organisations already have a policy prohibiting recreational or performance drug use at work, so part of the remedy is to ensure that the rules are enforced rather than paid lip service to.

11.7 Competent decision-making as the platform to launch success

The problem defined: Stressor 27 - Botched decisions due to a manager's subconscious beliefs, insecurities or compulsions

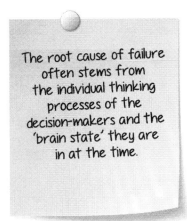

The root cause of failure often stems from the individual thinking processes of the decision-makers and the 'brain state' they are in at the time.

Post mortems on failing companies invariably focus on problems such as the poor marketing strategy, inadequate technology, weak financial control, bad labour relations and so on. But these immediate drawbacks, although they may be instrumental in the failure, are not necessarily the root cause. These more superficial problems tend to arise from poor or absent planning and/or failures in individual decision-making or the group decision-making process.

Inadequate planning and botched decision-making will always limit any organisation's true potential. Eventually a weakness in this key function, if continued unchecked, jeopardises success and even survival[15]. But what is the cause of bad planning and decision-making? One major reason, especially in the small business sector, is lack of training in management and decision-making skills. In certain circumstances inadequate planning also originates from a genuine pressure of time. However these reasons do not hold so well with larger private enterprises and public bodies where management training is, on the whole, taken more seriously and events tend to move more slowly.

Drilling down to the next level we find the root cause of planning and decision-making failure often stems from the individual thinking processes of the decision-makers and the 'brain state' they are in at the time. In other words, affected managers suffer from impaired thinking patterns of one sort or another. Where this is the case emotional impulses, lodged firmly in their brain physiology, are compelling them to act recklessly or mistakenly during the decision-making process.

The unwelcome fact is that a variety of defective thinking patterns (depicted in the box below) contribute immensely to organisational stress as well as triggering operational problems and failure and deserve to be looked more closely.

Defective thinking patterns

• Subliminal fear of change, uncertainty and ambiguity	• Ingrained beliefs and ideologies generating 'cognitive dissonance and confirmation bias
• Compulsive fear of failure	• Over-active dopamine reward system
• Compulsive fear of success	• Depression
• Innate optimism getting in the way of reality	• Wishful thinking

Each defective thinking pattern is covered in more detail below.

Subliminal fear of change, uncertainty and ambiguity

> Where you see the hallmark of 'quick fix' decisions or 'knee jerk' reactions, the cause is often the subliminal fear of uncertainty.

When an individual suffers from a subliminal fear of change, uncertainty, doubt or ambiguity, they find it difficult to handle a significant question or problem if the required solution is not obviously and immediately apparent. Awkwardly, for those affected, a fearful stress response kicks in just at the wrong moment.

The reason for the interference of the stress response is that important decisions usually imply the need for some sort of meaningful change. For instance, integral to such decisions are the management of elements of missing information. Thus, at the outset of the decision-making process there are very often doubts and uncertainty about the likely solution or perhaps uncertainty about the means to achieve the solution and even uncertainty about what the consequences might be when the decision has been implemented. In other words, change and uncertainty are inherent in the decision-making process. This is why, for those unfortunate enough to have a predisposition for fearing uncertainty doubt or ambiguity, significant decisions trigger a stress response.

Where these doubts spark a stress response, the emotional centres of the brain interfere with the rational decision-making process and compel the decision-maker to either act in a desperate hurry to get an answer[16] (See 1.2 The five steps to stress-driven mistakes; Stressed thinking is a C-R-I-M-E) or alternatively freeze them into inaction or denial. In the former case, the rush to arrive at a tangible solution leads to the reckless cutting of corners when it comes to carrying out a thorough and reasoned decision. Where you see the hallmark of 'quick fix' decisions or 'knee jerk' reactions, the cause is often this subliminal fear of uncertainty.

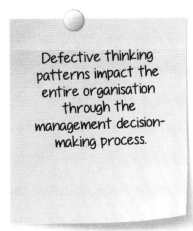

Defective thinking patterns impact the entire organisation through the management decision-making process.

The advantage of the quick fix, at least from the stressed brain's point of view, is that it finishes the uncertainty and so makes the subject feel better. The afflicted person quickly gets to step five – euphoria. The fact that in the rush to get to a solution they have arrived at a third-rate, ill-informed resolution, often based on the most obvious choice open to them at the moment and that this choice will inevitably lead to further problems later on, is totally eclipsed by the euphoria of ending the uncertainty.

A further complication here is that typically, sufferers of this compulsion are unaware of their fear of uncertainty. Such fears are usually so deep-rooted and subtle that they are subliminal. Incidentally some research suggests that, where compulsive behaviour of this type occurs, it may have been compounded by damage to the orbito-frontal cortex. Such damage prevents people from assessing ambiguity or undefined risks in an unemotional way[17]. In these relatively rare cases the problem is probably incurable.

But fear of uncertainty isn't the only reason why people are driven to make decisions emotionally and recklessly. If a decision-maker is suffering from acute pain, depression, or from a compulsive fear of failure, or even fear of success, these conditions can also provoke an emotional arousal at the critical moment when the neo-cortex is required for delivering cool-headed rational thinking based on a realistic perception of the facts and due consultation with relevant stakeholders. The result is, as above, the five steps of stress driven mistakes, and or altered perception, or procrastination, inaction or denial.

Depression, or a compulsive fear of failure, or fear of success can provoke an emotional arousal just when when cool-headed thinking is needed.

The dopamine factor

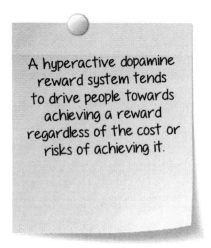

A hyperactive dopamine reward system tends to drive people towards achieving a reward regardless of the cost or risks of achieving it.

Similar to the subliminal fear of ambiguity is the impact the brain reward system can have on decision-making, when it becomes hyperactive[18]. Dopamine is the brain biochemical most associated with pleasure and excitement and is supposed to reward us for getting things right. But what if the reward comes into play before we have actually achieved anything? Unfortunately, if we suffer from this type of hyperactivity it tends to drive us through the decision-making process with little regard for the cost or risks of achieving success. Quite literally the dopamine drives us to become so emotionally excited by the prospect of success that this anticipation or motivation overwhelms any concerns we might otherwise have over potential threats, costs or problems. The result is an impulsive drive towards reckless risk taking that so often turns out to be disastrous.

Case example

The acquisition of a 'cheap' company going into liquidation had seemed like a good idea at the time. Unfortunately, the MD of this £2 million commercial printing firm had a track record of rushed, quick-fix decision-making and it showed in the chaotic organisation of his business. In fact among his staff he had earned the nickname Captain Chaos. When this new opportunity arose to acquire an insolvent fine art printing company, the prospect of early and dramatic success induced an emotional arousal that impelled him to rush in recklessly without following a thorough decision-making process. What was needed was a carefully thought through analysis and planning exercise to merge the two companies' operations. In particular, careful consideration over the two potentially conflicting cultures was crucial to ensure harmonious collaboration between the two workforces and a generally unified effort towards agreed goals.

The inevitable result of the botched takeover was extra costs, more chaos and added confusion. For instance, the rushed due diligence led to a number of 'totally unexpected' costs being uncovered just after, not before, the takeover. The immediate result of this unwelcome discovery was that the quick opportunity to double turnover cost the company £160,000 more than expected. Moreover, the two different cultures proved unable to meld together and all kinds of conflicts arose in scheduling and quality control. Morale, particularly

240

among the highly skilled craftsmen on the fine art side of the business, plummeted and one or two experienced operators became so exasperated they left to work elsewhere.

Fear of uncertainty – further explanation

It might help to explain in more detail why people can be affected by this particular stress response.

Today we are all experiencing a variety of powerful changes in our lives. The rate of change has increased exponentially, in technology, social mores and values, material conditions, family life and so on. Not only are these changes widespread they often come with a reduced level of emotional support from our family and social network. The result is that most of us have, at some time or other, been adversely affected by significant instability, doubt or uncertainty in our lives. We may have even been stressed or even traumatised by such an event. As a result of these earlier experiences, we feel less secure with our place in the wider scheme of things. For those affected, this subliminal insecurity usually originates from infancy and childhood. As this fear is embedded in our emotional memory it continues to impact our family life, our work and our social relationships in adulthood long after the cause of the original insecurity has gone away.

The reason for this is that the amygdala, the part of the brain used for processing and filtering stress stimuli, is also programmed to remember past harmful experiences, but only in a very general sense. As discussed in chapter two, this tiny but important organ uses a rough and ready "pattern matching" process to assess current circumstances and identify any threats. In other words the amygdala is just looking for rough and approximate associations with past events or experiences.

If the amygdala identifies a rough and ready match with past adverse patterns then it tricks us into action by overriding the intellect and other higher mental faculties. Importantly, in these situations the amygdala is unable to distinguish between real and apparent threats or even real and imaginary ones. The key point here, in the context of decision-making, is that if from past experience we have some negative association with uncertainty, change or doubt, then the amygdala's rough and ready pattern-matching mechanism won't be able to differentiate between the current less-threatening situation and the old really threatening one. What happens then is that when we are confronted with a significant decision to make, our instinctive brain alerts us to some perceived threat lurking in our emotional memory and so starts shutting down our rational faculties and kick starts the emotionally driven quick-fix process. Or as professor Camerer of the Californian Institute of Technology comments, emotions are "quick and dirty signals about survival relevant upcoming events".

The near doubling of both staff and turnover led to considerably more work in the already stretched finance office and also put a strain on the existing sales order processing system. The knock-on result here was a significant loss of control over the finances. Invoices weren't chased up and bills were left unpaid. This in turn led to suppliers withholding materials, leading to further processing problems with attendant bottlenecks, delays, missed deadlines and rushed work generating extra scrap. The next knock-on effect was a lot of wasteful rework, a rise in the number of discounts for late delivery and, even more harmful, a high attrition rate of repeat customers.

The upshot of this mess was that the firm made massive losses in the following year. The MD narrowly escaped liquidation by carryout a crash turnaround programme of performance improvements as well as shedding 20% of the workforce and axing 25% of his turnover, that on post-acquisition analysis turned out to be unacceptably low-margin work. And all of this because the MD was over excited at the prospect of success.

The common factor is the impact of emotional arousal

The key factor to remember is that whatever the specific malaise, where a manager or other decision-maker is affected by these types of defective thinking patterns, essentially they are making their decisions under the influence of emotional arousal. Often the more important the decision, the more emotional their thinking processes will become.

As we have seen in chapters one and two, when emotional arousal occurs, our normal faculties become impaired. Just to recap, such a state of mind mars both our ability and or willingness to:

- Think clearly and rationally
- Perceive and assimilate facts accurately
- Access complex long-term memory patterns to utilise past experience
- Have easy access to our imagination for a range of alternative solutions
- Listen to other points of view
- Collaborate supportively with colleagues
- Make sound judgements
- Problem-solve and analyse successfully

Organisational impact

As a direct consequence, these defective thinking patterns impact the entire organisation through the management decision-making process. Not only is there a direct impact on the success or viability of the

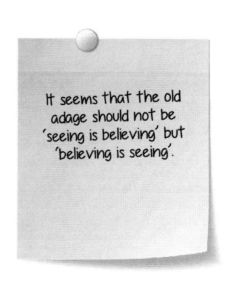

It seems that the old adage should not be 'seeing is believing' but 'believing is seeing'.

242

organisation due to the poor quality decision itself, there is the impact of the decision on the people who have to implement it or live with the consequences of it.

Bad decisions tend to adversely impact the human givens emotional needs. For instance, the need for security is almost immediately harmed as employees become aware that weak decision-making is threatening the viability of the operation. At other times poor decision-making can provoke a sense of a lack of any real meaning where people cannot understand why things are going wrong or are confused over the purpose behind a bizarre decision. Very often rushed decision-making means that relevant stakeholders have not been adequately consulted. In these circumstances there is also an element of attention deficit as well as an impingement of the need for a degree of genuine autonomy and control.

Beliefs as an obstacle to organisational learning and rational decision-making

Beliefs including self-beliefs can be a huge obstacle to successful problem solving, planning and decision-making. The problem arises because there is a particular facet of the brain that filters out evidence from our conscious perception, if this evidence conflicts with our beliefs. The brain is wired in a way so that we literally can't see what we don't already believe. When this deception occurs, we make, what the psychologists term, a 'premature cognitive commitment'. In other words we jump to a conclusion based, not on available new evidence, but on some pre-conception, belief or emotional memory of some past associated event or situation.

> We literally can't see what we don't already believe. This phenomenon has been termed 'premature cognitive commitment'.

An example from the animal world is well known in India. Traditionally, captive baby elephants are kept secure by tying one of their feet to a stake that is hammered into the ground. Although this method is sufficient to stop a baby elephant from running away, it is totally inadequate to stop a fully-grown one from uprooting the stake and ambling off. However, over the childhood years the young elephant develops a premature cognitive commitment to being unable to break free. This conditioning is so strong that as an adult it still 'believes' it is constrained. The grown elephant's past experience conditions it to see the stake and chain as a lot stronger than they actually are.

Cognitive dissonance and confirmation bias

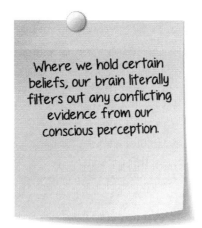

Where we hold certain beliefs, our brain literally filters out any conflicting evidence from our conscious perception.

As you can see, whenever we may be experiencing premature cognitive commitment we are suffering from a serious self-limiting belief. The brain seems programmed to use beliefs to help us make sense of a situation quickly but sometimes this is at the expense of really learning what is going on. The problem occurs because we are comfortable with our beliefs, whereas the process of changing our beliefs or being confronted with their inadequacy can be acutely uncomfortable to us, as it triggers a stress response. This mental stress is known as 'cognitive dissonance'[19].

The relevance to decision-making is that, in a situation where the apparent facts or evidence seem to contradict entrenched beliefs, cognitive dissonance compels us to do one of two things. In effect we get the choice of either doing what is right or doing what is easy - to reduce the pain of the dissonance we either change our belief to match the revealed facts or we try and preserve our belief by conducting what has been termed 'confirmation bias'[20] (sometimes known as 'myside bias'). Unfortunately a lot of the time, as a ruse to escape the stress of having our beliefs challenged, we prefer the second approach.

Just because managers don't know, doesn't stop them from believing they do know.

Seven 'confirmation bias' tactics

Confirmation bias means we actually engage in any one or more, of a range of less-than-useful tactics that help us perpetuate our belief. All this is done at the expense of blinding us to the truth. Such tactics include:

1. Different forms of misperception
2. A hunt for evidence that backs our existing beliefs
3. Rejection, or refutation of the contradictory information
4. Misinterpretation of the information to reinforce our beliefs[21]
5. Seeking support from others who share the beliefs,
6. Attempts to persuade others that our beliefs are valid anyway[22]
7. False or selective recall – remembering only what we want to remember[23]

Premature cognitive commitment and its ugly protégé cognitive dissonance explain why bad news about an organisation is often met with disbelief by senior managers and why, they often find it difficult to accept any negative feedback that disrupts their settled worldview of how they are running things. As a result, negative feedback moves slowly up the hierarchy, if at all. The peculiarity of the brain's filtering system also explains why those who offer differing opinions or expose the facts are often chastised or gagged and termed 'whistle blowers'. The tendency to shoot the messenger further reinforces senior management's isolation from operational reality and further constricts 'bounded rationality' mentioned earlier in chapter six.

When an ideology takes root, the learning stops and executives behave like corporate zombies refusing to see what they don't already believe in.

Diagram 20: Cognitive dissonance

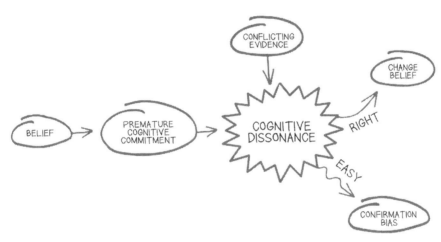

As we know, executives, like the rest of us have cognitive limitations that restrict their view of what is going on in their own organisation. Unfortunately the existence of this 'bounded rationality' doesn't prevent managers from *believing* they know what's going on and from acting accordingly. This delusion is obviously dangerous. Of course it doesn't help matters where these beliefs have become self-serving. And in today's corporations and public sector organisations, senior managers have the self-serving need to protect status and careers with six-figure salaries and pensions to match.

The higher up the organisation they go, it becomes depressingly more difficult for bosses to acknowledge that their beliefs might be at odds with reality. The scale of their adverse reaction is directly proportionate to the amount of status, power, money and reputation under threat.

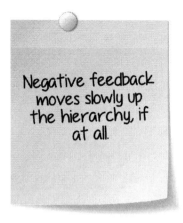

Negative feedback moves slowly up the hierarchy, if at all.

In private enterprises, market factors such as an alert competition and fickle customers and or investors voting with their feet may sooner or later jolt management out of its day dream world or drive the company into bankruptcy. However, public sector organisations and state sponsored charities tend not to have this Darwinian balancing mechanism. Delusion and therefore failure is perpetuated by a weakness in accountability either from below or above. The consequences, as we have seen from a string of public sector projects can be disappointing performance at best and at worst catastrophic failure.

A recent example of catastrophe, already referred to in the introduction and chapter 11 section 5, was at Rotherham Metropolitan Borough Council in the UK. In this, abysmal case of almost inconceivable incompetence the local social services and allied agencies failed to protect over a thousand children from what has been termed 'industrial scale' brutality, perpetrated by predatory gangs of mostly Pakistani sex abusers. Professor Alexis Jay, who wrote a damning independent report on the scandal[24], (incidentally initially met with disbelief by the council) asserts that, "nobody could say 'I didn't know'." Unfortunately given what we now know about 'bounded rationality' and the associated problems of premature cognitive commitment and cognitive dissonance, that is probably what happened - the people at the top subconsciously refused to see anything that conflicted with their existing beliefs.

The Rotherham case shows how beliefs embedded in the culture of an organisation can attract the same drawbacks as with individuals, in terms of their impact on rational thinking. In that instance, like a lot of other councils and public sector authorities in the UK, just one of the prevalent politically correct beliefs is Multiculturalism. The way this manifested in Rotherham was that there was an institutional disbelief that one ethnic group was committing the predatory sex crimes. There seem to have been a couple of other institutional beliefs that got in the way of the facts.

"Just like your finger can hide the sun, so one concept believed in can hide the truth of who you are."

Mooji

One was the belief that the 'sorts of girls' who were being abused were 'asking for it' anyway. (According to Simon Danczuk writing about the scandal in a Times article, the director of children's services implied to him that young girls who were being raped were 'making lifestyle choices'[25].) Another entrenched belief was the typically self-serving one that government-run child protection agencies do a better job of protecting children than their parents can. (Some parents were actually arrested for trying to protect their children from harm).

The use of the phrase 'self-serving' may seem harsh here, but nevertheless it is fully justified. The purpose of the child protection services is to protect children. Believing this to be the case gives important meaning to the work being done by the teams of social workers and their managers. And meaning, as we have seen in chapter three, is an important motivational human need. Where the evidence on the ground suggests that this protection is far from working, then this important sense of meaning is violated. Violating a 'human given', as we know, can quickly trigger a powerful stress response. In other words the sort of cognitive dissonance provoked by this type of situation where the evidence conflicts directly with both the subject's belief and sense of meaning is extremely uncomfortable. The experiencer is faced with evidence that undermines the very purpose of their work, their belief in their own competence (a feeling of competence being an emotional need) and perhaps the validity of their organisation. As a result, the reptilian survival mechanism kicks in and it becomes far easier, quicker and simpler to ignore the evidence, carry on as usual and try and persuade everybody that everything is OK (confirmation bias tactic number six). This is by way of an explanation not an excuse.

People don't like their self-beliefs shaken, it frightens them.

As you can no doubt imagine, with these sorts of ideologies embedded in Rotherham's child protection system, it was chronically unable to see what would have been blindingly obvious to any objective observer in their rational mind – Professor Jay, for one. (Another observer who managed to retain her rational mind was the 'whistle blower' Jayne Senior, a youth service manager who passed on 200 files to the Times in a successful attempt to expose the horrors going on. Typically, the response from the local council was to seek a criminal inquiry into the identity of the whistle blower. A far healthier approach would have been to embrace the information as invaluable bottom-up feedback as to the reality of the situation[26].)

The key lesson is that when an ideology takes root, the learning stops and executives behave like corporate zombies refusing to see what they don't already believe in. The prevalence of ideologies in public bureaucracies is another reason why they are innately disadvantaged when it comes to adapting and refining procedures and processes in response to new information or dynamically changing circumstances.

Premature cognitive commitment also explains why in the political arena, ideological parties and regimes tend to be repressive and obstruct social and economic progress. The fervent belief in their respective 'isms' prevents adherents from processing adverse information that contradicts their belief and instead compels them to embark on an evangelical crusade to persuade others to follow the same beliefs. Other less than useful results include dogged resistance to change, the demonization of opponents, hysterical opposition to alternative ideas and solutions and the persistent advocacy of anachronistic and otherwise highly inappropriate solutions that tend to perpetuate the problems not ease them; all this to escape the pain of adapting to new ideas and new evidence. The good news is that sooner or later ideologically driven causes, movements, parties, governments and institutions are prone to self-destruct. The bad news is that before they go down, they can do untold harm and damage to their stakeholders and anyone else who gets in the way.

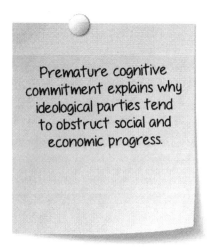

Premature cognitive commitment explains why ideological parties tend to obstruct social and economic progress.

Self-belief is an obstacle to self-awareness and learning

"Remember the truth will set you free – but first it may thoroughly irritate you or frighten you!"

Susan Scott

Unfortunately this belief mechanism works for self-beliefs as well. Our beliefs about ourselves get in the way of seeing the reality about ourselves. The way this works is that from childhood onwards we cultivate self-beliefs that at the time may have helped us come to terms with the complex and sometimes, chaotic or traumatic world we lived in. Unfortunately as life goes on and circumstances change, these beliefs form emotional impressions in the mind that filter out any evidence that contradicts them.

I worked with a business owner once who liked to believe she took a genuine, almost maternal interest in her employees' welfare. In truth she was very personable and charming and often showed attentiveness to her employees' concerns, their families and so on. However the underlying reality was that her business didn't make a lot of money and significantly, the money it did make was largely due to the low wages she paid and her personal persuasiveness in getting people to do a lot of free overtime. The average overtime was about 20 hours a month, but some key staff did a lot more. Now with 100 employees each doing an average 20 hours free overtime she was neatly adding about £200,000 or so of free work to the bottom line profit. This made life quite comfortable for her financially.

> It becomes depressingly more difficult for bosses to acknowledge that their beliefs might be wrong the higher up the organisation they rise.

Instead of taking responsibility to study the systemic reasons for her organisation's poor performance and so make it easier for her people to do their work, the owner preferred to focus her energies on team building exercises, and her 'coaching style' of leadership. These latter activities appealed a lot more to her self-belief about being a compassionate and caring team leader.

Essentially the owner was very good at getting the staff to hold the company together by their excessive input of energy and goodwill and she lived well off their hard work and low pay. Ironically, although the owner was well liked around the business, there was a steady drain of the longer term, experienced employees leaving due to burnout and stress. This attrition of experience had a further deleterious impact on the efficiency of the system.

So, in other words the reality of the working environment was the very opposite of her self-belief of being a 'nice boss'. Drawing her attention to this fact led to something of an emotional arousal; in this instance expressed as self-righteous indignation. People don't like their self-beliefs shaken; it frightens them.

Senior management's self-confidence can be a costly delusion

The type of person occupying the higher reaches of a large organisation usually arrives at this level due in large part to a high degree of self-confidence in their own ability and judgement. As mentioned in chapter six this self-belief in their ability to manage is not necessarily matched by reality. The unsettling implication here for organisational design is that as status rises with promotion, so this self-belief becomes more and more engrained. Thus, once a manager has achieved high office, it becomes even more difficult for inputs of contrary information to penetrate and alter their cherished self-beliefs.

This factor is never clearer than when attempting performance improvements.

I often find that where an executive has cultivated a belief about their own high level of competence, it is very difficult for them to accept that, lagging organisational performance may be due to inadequacies in the system. They after all 'own' the system and as they believe they are so competent it follows that the system must be OK. It is far easier and less painful for them to believe that where things are going wrong that someone somewhere must be 'screwing up'. There follows a search for the culprits rather than a hard look at the weaknesses of their own creation. The whole 'witch-hunt' process creates more organisational stress and further damages the organisation's ability to operate effectively. This denial flies in the face of the sound 'systems thinking' principle that 95% of variations in performance are due to the system and only 5% are due to the people. The search for someone to blame misses huge opportunities for renewal and improvement and perpetuates a cycle of decline and low productivity.

Wishful thinking

Similar to the problem of beliefs, at least in the effect it has on perception and decision-making, is wishful thinking. This term refers more to the existence of a strong desire for a particular outcome; a desire that we have identified with so closely that it too overrides our objective perception. The filtering process seems to be the same as for beliefs, in that an emotional attachment to the desired outcome is so strong that the possibility of it being thwarted provokes a stress arousal. As with other defective thinking patterns, the emotional arousal triggers a rejection of any facts or rationale that conflicts with the desire. So, in the same way as with beliefs, we are more likely to believe in our intended conclusions than believe in any non-intended ones that might be suggested. Similarly, we tend to demand a higher standard of evidence for unpalatable ideas and a lower standard for preferred ones and so on. All other things being equal, when in wishful thinking mode our evaluation of various courses of potential action will tend to predict a positive outcome rather than a negative outcome.

Wishful thinking differs from 'positive thinking' where a clear and rationally positive goal, triggers the sub-conscious mind into finding resources and opportunities that genuinely assist in the achievement of that goal.

Innate optimism getting in the way of reality

We also have to accept that, human beings generally have an innate tendency towards optimism. Although this tendency is quite motivational and gets us up in the morning to get things done, it can also be a major source of trouble with business planning and project forecasting.

Our innate optimism drives us to over estimate the benefits and underestimate both the costs and the time taken to do the work[27]. Well-recognised by venture capitalists this natural tendency has cost untold millions in large-scale government projects in civil engineering, defence contracts and IT. Project overruns in time and money seeming to be almost the norm in the public sector.

Remedies Three categories:		
Self-help	**Third party help**	**Leadership intervention**
• Personal audit for quick fix compulsions	• Psychotherapy, counselling, NLP etc.	• Collaborative leadership
• Confirmation bias inventory	• Learning Transcendental Meditation	• Remove offenders out of harms way
• Reality check on self-beliefs		

Personal audit for quick fix compulsions

Being aware of the problem is more than half the battle here. So, the first step is to find the answer to the question – "Do I have an anxiety about uncertainty?" It helps to work with a partner on this exercise. But whether you are alone or with someone, take some time to reflect and think through past significant decisions and review your thought processes at the time. Answer these questions:

- How did you go about making the decision?

- Did you feel impelled to come up with a rapid answer, not by the pressing circumstances of the situation but by some inner drive?

- Did you derive satisfaction and pleasure during the initial process of research and acquisition of relevant information, thinking things through, analysing, getting collaboration from colleagues and talking the problems through with them?

- Did you also get real enjoyment from the subsequent process of planning and implementing the decision and did you receive a sense of satisfaction from its ultimate accomplishment? OR

- Did you find that you only got a wave of relief or euphoria at the moment you thought you had arrived at an answer? Did you then feel a degree of impatience at not being able to get the decision implemented fast enough?

The need for tough-minded thinking

"Let us consider first the need for a tough mind, characterized by incisive thinking, realistic appraisal, and decisive judgment. The tough mind is sharp and penetrating, breaking through the crust of legends and myths and sifting the true from the false. The tough-minded individual is astute and discerning. He has a strong, austere quality that makes for firmness of purpose and solidness of commitment. Who doubts that this toughness of mind is one of man's greatest needs? Rarely do we find men who willingly engage in hard, solid thinking. There is an almost universal quest for easy answers and half-baked solutions. *Nothing pains some people more than having to think.*"

Martin Luther King

Don't be deluded by a false 'ah ha' moment

Now, there's no harm in feeling good at that euphoric 'ah ha' moment when you get a bright idea or reach a solution. Just don't be seduced into thinking this euphoria is genuine if all you have done is shortcut the process *to get an immediate sense of relief.* The mind might be simply rewarding you for relieving the immediate tension about the uncertainty. It is a very short-term satisfaction – a bit like the alcoholic taking a drink to "solve" his problems.

Delayed gratification is worth the wait

You can tell if you are striking the wrong attitude if, on reflection, you see that your enjoyment during the preliminary analysing and researching stages and the succeeding action stage is *a lot less than at the point where you reach a "quick" decision.*

In other words you are deriving little satisfaction or joy from the process and getting a "hit" only in the *perceived* outcome or in the premature ending of the decision-making process. Believe it or not there is a lot more fun to be had in working with a settled mind through a methodical, thorough, creative and collaborative decision-making process. If you are able to do the job correctly, you are able to enjoy at length the process, the anticipation and the subsequent success of a well thought through and well-planned decision. Can you see that a quick fix might make you feel good at the time of dreaming it up, but it will always cause you all kinds of grief when you have to live with the consequences over a much longer period?

A good motto to adopt is, **never be fearful of <u>not</u> having an answer <u>now</u>, rather, be wary of arriving too hastily at the wrong answer.**

Confirmation bias inventory

As with the impulse for quick-fix decision-making, being aware of the problem is the first and most important step. Self-awareness is a prerequisite for finding a remedy.

Unfortunately being aware of our irrational beliefs is somewhat problematical for the reason that we are very often happily living in our delusion. For this reason working on this problem often requires help or even intervention from a third party and or higher authority who can see that the problem exists.

A useful tool is the 'confirmation bias inventory' (See table 15 towards the end of this section). Used effectively the knowledge you pick up from the inventory may help weaken the instinctive tendency for confirmation bias.

Reality check on your self-beliefs

This simple technique is advocated by Susan Scott in her book 'Fierce conversations'[28] and needs a partner in order to achieve results easily. The partner starts the process by asking you for the one word or phrase that you believe most describes you. When you have made that verbal commitment, he or she can then ask you to think of occasions and situations when you have been, or are the reverse of this. So you might consider yourself to be a 'kind' person. Now spend time thinking when kindness was absent in your life, why did this happen, how many times? Is your view of yourself restricting your ability to learn when you are not being kind? If you can't think of an occasion in your entire life when you have not been kind, your partner needs to ask the supplementary question - *"When would it have been if you did know of an occasion?*

Psychotherapy

Without self-awareness that the issue is a problem, then a change is unlikely. If you are in a position where a subordinate is suffering from one of these tendencies and is in danger of fouling up as a result then one course of action is to recommend psychotherapy or executive coaching with an appropriately qualified coach. There are a number of psychotherapy techniques from different disciplines such as the human givens approach to psychotherapy, clinical hypnotherapy, EFT (Emotional Freedom Technique) and NLP (Neuro-linguistic programming) among others that have a consistent track record of providing clear-cut relief to the problem of these types of defective-thinking patterns.

Such approaches can very often switch off the offending anxiety template or emotional pattern. There is however an important pre-requisite for success. The subject needs to be sufficiently self-motivated to getting the results. Where this commitment is lacking you are unlikely to make much progress.

Coaching and psychotherapy can also be used to help subjects develop their self-confidence. Where people are more self-confident they are less prone to cognitive dissonance and so tend not fall for the trap of filtering out information that supports their beliefs. This fact underlines the importance of the leadership providing the right degree of supportive feedback advocated in Chapter 9 Section 4 (The pivotal role of emotional support and feedback). Encouragement and positive feedback help reduce the ambient level of stress at work and also builds people's self confidence and sense of security within the organisation.

Transcendental Meditation

As mentioned elsewhere, there has been a lot of research done on Transcendental Meditation's ability to develop full brain functioning and so promote greater self-awareness[29]. The relevance here is that greater self-awareness loosens the attachment to personal beliefs and diminishes the tendency to identify so closely with them. Greater self-awareness means having a clearer sense of 'Being' or a clearer sense of the 'observant self' discussed in chapter 4 Section 3.8, a clearer sense of the observant self gives you a better awareness that you are not your beliefs, anymore than you are your thoughts, or your bodily sensations. TM is not a quick fix. If you learn TM, you probably won't come out of your first meditation 'cured'. It takes a twice-daily dip into 'transcendental consciousness' or the 'field of pure intelligence' that you experience doing the actual technique to sort out this perennial mistake of the intellect. Over time the gradual erosion of stress in the nervous system allows you to relax into being more <u>who you are</u> rather than <u>who you think</u> you are or <u>who you think you should be</u> or for that matter <u>who other people think you should be</u>. In a more relaxed state of being it is much easier to discern between your true self and your beliefs.

With the effortless regular practice of TM you experience a growing familiarity with pure awareness or transcendental consciousness and this familiarity helps you separate your beliefs from your core identity. This separation is important because it allows you to feel less threatened when you suddenly discover that your beliefs are being challenged by reality. The reduced 'threat' means less stress arousal, which means that you are a lot less prone to cognitive dissonance and so are more amenable to making the 'right' decision rather than the 'easy' one.

Collaborative leadership

As these problems are so widespread, it is highly advantageous to learn to avoid rushing the planning process and instead take the time and trouble to go through a structured team-based approach to decision-making. Such an approach depicted in Diagram 18 – A structured approach to healthy decision-making, enables the deliberate development of a decision through a sequence of seven steps that involve thorough research, root cause analysis, ongoing consultation with relevant stakeholders and a balanced evaluation of alternative solutions.

One of the benefits of this approach is that it helps to ensure that decisions are made in context, so you can avoid the pitfalls evident with straight-line thinking mentioned earlier. Another is that the collaborative approach using a formal planning structure comprises a powerful aid to reducing personal stress levels.

Diagram 21

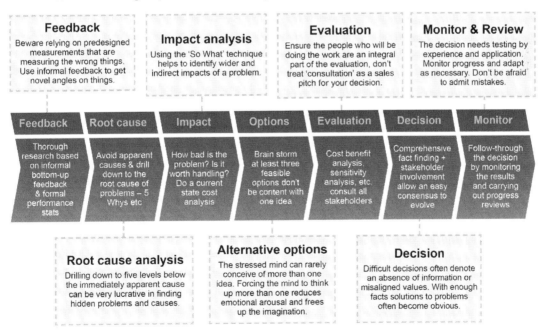

A structured approach to healthy decision-making

A team based approach to planning helps remove emotional arousal and ensures that decisions are made in context so avoiding the pitfalls evident with straight-line thinking such as unintended consequences.

Feedback
Beware relying on predesigned measurements that are measuring the wrong things. Use informal feedback to get novel angles on things.

Impact analysis
Using the 'So What' technique helps to identify wider and indirect impacts of a problem.

Evaluation
Ensure the people who will be doing the work are an integral part of the evaluation, don't treat 'consultation' as a sales pitch for your decision.

Monitor & Review
The decision needs testing by experience and application. Monitor progress and adapt as necessary. Don't be afraid to admit mistakes.

Feedback	Root cause	Impact	Options	Evaluation	Decision	Monitor
Thorough research based on informal bottom-up feedback & formal performance stats	Avoid apparent causes & drill down to the root cause of problems – 5 Whys etc	How bad is the problem? Is it worth handling? Do a current state cost analysis	Brain storm at least three feasible options don't be content with one idea	Cost benefit analysis, sensitivity analysis, etc. consult all stakeholders	Comprehensive fact finding + stakeholder involvement allow an easy consensus to evolve	Follow-through the decision by monitoring the results and carrying out progress reviews

Root cause analysis
Drilling down to five levels below the immediately apparent cause can be very lucrative in finding hidden problems and causes.

Alternative options
The stressed mind can rarely conceive of more than one idea. Forcing the mind to think up more than one reduces emotional arousal and frees up the imagination.

Decision
Difficult decisions often denote an absence of information or misaligned values. With enough facts solutions to problems often become obvious.

The lower stress levels help override the default mechanism of stressed thinking provoked by the various defective thinking patterns. Table 14 (Eight ways team planning reduces confirmation bias) explains both some of the methods used in team planning and their benefits related to confirmation bias. You can also return to Chapter 8 section 1 – Achieving buy-in for strategic change, for more details of a structured approach to group decision-making. Training to help managers develop a working understanding of 'systems thinking' also helps them overcome the prejudice that their people are screwing up, when the reality is that it is the system that is failing.

Table 14

	Eight ways team planning reduces confirmation bias	
1.	**Collaborative problem-solving is inherently <u>less</u> stressful**	A team-based approach to the planning and decision-making process helps people feel instinctively more secure. Collaborative working, so long as it is well structured and fun, comes naturally to people. They are more likely to be calm and relaxed in such a situation and, as such, are in a highly positive brain state. This low-stress state helps supress the emotionally charged survival instinct that can emerge when experiencing cognitive dissonance whilst making a solitary decision. If as a leader, you know how to facilitate the right atmosphere, you are then automatically helping reduce the emotional charge people experience when cognitive dissonance arises. The reduced charge in turn eases the otherwise urgent survival-need to leap to the defence of cherished beliefs or in some emotional way cut short the rational decision-making process. In a lively and supportive team atmosphere, people are much more able to drop their beliefs and pre-conceptions and accept new evidence that contradicts those beliefs.
2.	**A cascade of information overwhelms cherished beliefs**	Team planning helps bring more information to the decision. As you can see, from the structured approach to healthy-decision-making diagram, the first step is the extraction of bottom-up feedback from all stakeholders; most importantly this includes subordinate staff and pertinent stakeholders. The resultant cascade of information about the defects in the system tends to swamp management misconceptions about how the system is working. Executives are less able to ignore overwhelming evidence when everyone else has read it and agreed with it. As a result they feel more secure when dropping their beliefs and falling in with a consensus

\	Eight ways team planning reduces confirmation bias	
		that is based on the group's rational perception of the facts. A feeling of security tends to override their own fear that their cherished beliefs are being destroyed and this factor tends to overwhelm the defensive mechanisms of their personal belief systems.
3.	**Friendly peer pressure**	Group work also adds a new dimension in that peer pressure may not let you get away with ignoring new evidence that contradicts your personal preconceptions or beliefs in quite the same way as you might allow yourself to do on your own. This natural group process of deconstructing premature cognitive commitment is another reason why a secure, non-judgemental and supportive atmosphere is vital to collaborative decision-making. If peer pressure is hostile and critical it is likely to have the opposite effect and get the various antagonists to dig their heals in[30]. The leader's role is to achieve a balance between a challenging and rigorous assessment of ideas and facts on the one hand and a friendly and happy atmosphere on the other, where fear is absent and mistakes are accepted as part of an essential learning curve.
4.	**Progress reviews**	Regular progress reviews that involve team members submitting their thoughts and current plans to the team also help to overcome cognitive dissonance in a constructive way. People are far more likely to push themselves into thinking critically and logically when they know in advance they will need to explain themselves to other team members who are well-informed, genuinely interested in the truth of the situation, and whose views they don't already know[31].
5.	**Future tense not past tense**	The clinical and objective way the feedback is handled in the planning workshops also helps take the sting out of unwelcome news. The emphasis is always on future improvements to the present system not a post mortem as to who screwed up in the first place.
6.	**Timely public exposure**	Part of the sequence of a TBD team-planning programme is to provoke initial public disclosure of rough thoughts at an early stage in the planning process. Again, wherever possible these statements are delivered in a relaxed, secure, non-judgemental atmosphere. Getting team members to announce draft

		ideas at the outset before they have committed time, effort, reputation and emotional investment, means you are getting them to float ideas in public before they are likely to have established a firm belief in or attachment to their position. This enables the managers to be open to changing their ideas in response to (valid) challenging comments. I have seen months of negotiations, rivalry and stubbornness avoided through this simple aspect.
7.	**Non-expert scrutiny and root cause analysis**	Sub-teams of 'non-experts' are used to carryout the initial appraisal of front-line feedback, initiate a rough and ready root-case analysis and put forward the first suggested solutions. In this context, 'non-expert' means, those people who are not usually responsible for the area of work under scrutiny. So we might use the marketing people to look at the feedback about production problems, and the production people to look at finance, and so on. We find that, non-experts are less likely to have preconceptions as to what is 'right' and so are more likely to assess the situation afresh, drill down a bit further beneath the superficial symptoms and expose unwelcome news, pay more objective attention to the evidence when it emerges and come up with novel solutions that break the mould of existing thinking constraints.
8.	**The study phase**	Without learning, nothing much can change, let alone improve. The wealth of data landing on the planning table about the problems, constraints and defects to the system should provide a jolt to the management team as to the need to improve things. But it is not always clear how. There is always the danger that the 'confirmation bias' factor results in managers reverting back to old ways of doing things. As Einstein once said "You can't solve a problem with the same thinking that created it".
		So, an important first step whenever a manager receives an improvement project to get on with, is for him or her to conduct a study in answer to the question – *"What do I need to learn to make a success of this project?"* Answering - *"nothing"* is not an option and can provoke the retort *"Well why have we got this problem then?"* What usually happens however is a sense of relief that however highly paid they are and

Eight ways team planning reduces confirmation bias		
		whatever status they have, the management team are being allowed to admit, even if only tacitly, that that they are not infallible. If handled correctly this aspect can avoid people wasting a lot of time and energy playing impression management games designed to hide their ignorance. With the study phase, managers tend to focus on the need of the time and that is to learn something new that improves the situation. This might be learning a new skill or a different approach to the problem, or trying to discover what the outcome was for similar projects elsewhere (reference class forecasting)[32] or simply finding out new ways to discover the real facts of the situation. Whatever the learning, the organisation is able to move on with a range of improvement projects all being instigated at the same time, each one starting with a study phase. The collective learning provides a powerful and refreshing impetus for the whole organisation.

Remove offenders out of harms way

All the while that, defective thinking patterns are driving or at least subverting the decision-making process, they are a hazard to the organisation and it's purpose. The remedies discussed so far all work to a certain degree but are heavily dependent on the motivation of the affected managers to change their thinking. If you recognise you have a problem of this nature then you may be motivated to do something about it. But what of those who have no idea that their perception and decisions are being distorted in this way?

Under normal circumstances defective thinking reaps the reward of uncompromising failure. This short sharp shock may be painful but serves a useful purpose. If the pain of failure is greater than the pain of cognitive dissonance, those affected have the incentive to reflect on the inner cause of their failure and can hopefully see that on balance the pain of failure is more potent than the pain of having to shift their beliefs or the pain (or tedium) of having to tackle decision-making and planning in a more coherent and structured way. In other words, if we are allowed to, we learn from our experiences and grow in maturity as a result. Perhaps this is why the average age of successful entrepreneurs is now fifty-plus and why, in traditional societies, elders have been regarded with great respect for their wisdom and knowledge.

But in certain circumstances both in the private and public sectors people escape the full consequences of their defective thinking patterns. When this happens, they are essentially enabled to perpetuate their errors of perception or judgement.

In the private sector as we have seen in chapter six, large corporations can become a hiding place for the incompetent who may be otherwise adept at 'impression management' and political manipulation to maintain their positions despite their inadequacy to do the job. In smaller or privately run businesses, I have seen owners protected from 'uncompromising failure' because they have recourse to large amounts of family money to help out when business failure looms. Similarly, success in business involves utilising many skills and qualities and some entrepreneurs, although they may suffer from some degree of defective thinking in one area, also excel in other areas such as sales or negotiations or perhaps they have a high value specialist skill-set such as engineering, or technological inventiveness that otherwise compensates for their weaknesses in general decision-making. In all these circumstances, whatever the reason, learning from mistakes can be avoided seemingly indefinitely.

Perhaps more seriously though, this immunity from failure is a particular weakness in public sector management. There are several reasons for this and they all combine to shield incompetent decision-makers from having to face up to any practical failure arising from their irrational thinking. The monopoly position of most government run activities provides a typically low level of accountability to customers and this insulates managers from the reality of customer attrition. As a result taxpayers money disgorges onto incompetent and competent operations alike with.

Public sector agencies usually work within a cloistered framework of statutory obligations and rights that prolong inefficient or inappropriate practices long after they would have been exposed by dissatisfied customers, leaving to shop elsewhere. In this respect, in the public sector, work doesn't go away when you get it wrong. If anything it multiplies as the law of 'failure demand' (See Chapter 7 Section 1) kicks in and new services are required to cope with the fall-out of failing services elsewhere. In the public sector it seems that defective thinking patterns can be a positive boon to bureaucratic empire building.

The only cure here is, for those senior enough, to fire people who do not respond to any of the above remedies and persist with these defective thinking-patterns or are unwilling to submit themselves to 'treatment'. While people are in this unhealthy state of mind they are a menace to their organisation, to what it stands for and to the people it seeks to serve.

Table 15

Have you ever fallen for these mind traps?
Confirmation bias inventory

It is very tempting to favour one's existing beliefs in the face of conflicting and unwelcome evidence. We have probably all done it at one time or other. To help alert you the next time you are challenged in this way, it is a useful exercise to reflect on when and where you have fallen for this trap before.

Take a while to consider the following twelve questions and their supplementary ones, so as to recall some occasion(s) you have let your beliefs override your reason. In this context, I use the word belief to cover any pre-existing supposition, opinion, assumption, preconception, belief, ideology, hypothesis, theory, premise, attachments and so on that might be getting in the way of you seeing the facts and evaluating them rationally.

It can help to get someone else, who you trust, to ask you these questions and the supplementary ones below and discuss the answers with you.

Have you ever experienced or done any of the following?

1. Suffered from 'selective recall' – This is a tendency to 'forget' information that contradicts your established belief and to remember only information that seems to support your belief? (NB - If you can't answer 'yes' to this or for that matter any other of these questions, are you suffering from selective recall? As a check, ask yourself; "If I could remember an occasion, when I let my beliefs override the facts, when would that have been?" And see what pops up.)

2. Searched for 'facts' that, are consistent with your current ideas? As an example you might have phrased questions in a way to get to the answer you want.

3. Looked for the consequences or outcomes that you would expect, if your belief were true, rather than looking for the consequences that would occur if your belief were false?

4. Thought that the evidence you are looking at supports your existing belief when in fact it is at best neutral to your point of view or even unfavourable?

5. Discounted or criticized evidence as inadequate or flawed in some way because it was set against your beliefs? In other words have you ever set a higher standard of evidence for any belief that goes against yours?

Have you ever fallen for these mind traps?
Confirmation bias inventory

6. Persisted in a belief even after you have seen evidence that the belief is false?

7. Perceived an illusory connection between two events, data or situations because they matched your pre-existing belief?

8. Defended your position because you have previously made a public commitment to it, even though it has subsequently been undermined by new contradictory evidence?

9. During a heated conflict found yourself adopting a more entrenched or extreme position against the other side, when you have been exposed to contradictory evidence (This is known as attitude polarization)?

10. Discounted or ignoring evidence or information that contradicts your belief because you received it some time after you received previous supportive information? (This is known as the 'primacy effect' where we tend to believe or place greater reliance on information we received first[33].)

11. Shifted your position to be similar to others because of the prospect of having to justify yourself to them and then using use confirmatory bias to bolster your own credibility?

12. Given in to 'cost of error bias'? This is where you avoided adopting a course of action that would be too costly to you emotionally. As an example you might decide to ignore or go along with a friend's misbehaviour, of which you disapprove, so as to avoid losing her friendship, which is more valuable to you.

Supplementary questions

Where you give the answer 'Yes' the next important step is to think about the negative consequences to yourself and to others and, if relevant, to the organization. Also reflect on how you felt at the time of making the decision, did you observe an emotional arousal around this issue? What other stressors were active in your life at the time? How do you feel now that you have recognized this trait? Do you need to apologise to anyone?

Where children's welfare or patients' lives are at stake, the merciful thing to do is to end the madness and sack the offenders as soon as possible.

Motivational impact on the human givens

The impact of coherent decision-making on both general motivation and productivity cannot be over-emphasised. Once a manager's own stress has been resolved, he or she is free to access their full inner resources to carry out thorough and exhaustive decision-making and planning. Successful decisions and successful group planning will, depending on the context, go a long way to help meet their own emotional needs and those of their colleagues and subordinates.

Better decisions will provide a safer commercial environment and so help to meet everyone's need for security. Better decision-making that involves listening and bringing in the viewpoints and expertise of the relevant stakeholders leads to greater attention to the needs of colleagues and subordinates. The evidence of more sound judgement actually provides an improved sense of meaning for people, as they see, what they consider to be, coherent and purposeful progress taking place.

Improved decision-making taken from the basis of a settled mind free from stress is almost always likely to be aligned with a wider set of human needs. Such decisions are more likely to enable greater autonomy, more job satisfaction or fun and a more connected and functional community spirit. Quite simply, it makes sense that people enjoy working in successful, well-run organisations considerably more than they do failing ones.

11.8 Your people's brain states are everything

The problem defined: Stressor 28 - People bringing their own stresses to work

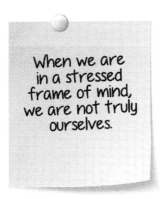

When we are in a stressed frame of mind, we are not truly ourselves.

Most of us get stressed at times and some of us get more stressed than others[34]. This stress may be nothing to do with what management are doing at work but can still mean that we are in a state of emotional arousal as we are going about our daily activities.

When this happens we are effectively bringing our own problems to work – divorce, bereavement, family disputes and worries, financial pressures, chronic illnesses, to name a few common ones. Even half-forgotten traumas can still impact our daily functioning by locking us into a semi-trance state that gets us to react impulsively to certain and otherwise innocuous stimuli. Essentially, when we are in a stressed frame of mind we are not truly ourselves and this prevents us from utilising the full range of our mental and emotional functioning. Instead we can display a range of bizarre or at least irrational behaviours (See table 3). Most of us have experienced this from time to time either in ourselves or we have witnessed it in those around us. When in this state of mind we can snap at colleagues and clients, grumble unduly, be overly cynical or critical of others, procrastinate, give inattention to detail, be clumsy or accident prone, get into unnecessary conflicts, and so on.

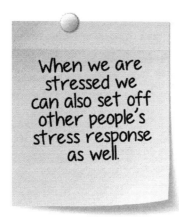

When we are stressed we can also set off other people's stress response as well.

In addition, for some occupations, dealing with members of the public can be inherently stressful. Researchers estimate that 25% of healthcare workers suffer from burnout (mental, physical and emotional exhaustion). This burnout develops from the prolonged and cumulative effects of emotional stress and pressure that arise from personal interaction with members of the public on a daily basis[35]. A large proportion of the remaining 75% of healthcare workers will probably be suffering from varying degrees of stress for the same reason. The result of burnout is substantially lowered productivity, tragic mistakes with diagnostics and prescriptions, compassion fatigue, sickness, absenteeism and premature retirement of skilled and experienced people from the workforce.

This type of problem is not exclusive to healthcare and is prevalent in the teaching profession, police, armed services and anywhere where mediation is required in tense and difficult situations.

Stress is infectious

However an added problem here for optimum working relations and productivity is that stress is infectious. What that means is when we are stressed we can also set off other people's stress response as well. This knock-on effect can happen in two ways.

Happiness may be important on an evolutionary level by helping people cooperate with each other.

Firstly, you have probably experienced that when you are feeling stressed somehow you become entangled in negative interactions with work colleagues and other associates. Snapping at people, dropping a sarcastic remark, generally being grumpy or moody can quickly lead to a reciprocal stress response.

Secondly, and possibly more significantly, stress can be transferred from one person to another subliminally via our hormonal system. On a subtle level people can literally smell fear and this surrogated fear sets-off a stress response[36]. Interestingly no stress response is activated in the receiver, unless there is the presence of some other stressor as well.

This finding about stress being infectious may have important implications for very large organisations. This is especially so for those where there is a high concentration of stressed people such as in prisons, hospitals or even schools. The implication of this is that maybe, instead of building larger and larger hospitals and schools to accommodate high-tech investment and reap the economies of scale, it would be more productive, health-wise and productivity-wise, to downsize a bit.

Happiness is also infectious

On the bright side research shows that happiness is also infectious and is, in fact, far more contagious than unhappiness. Two different areas of study bare this out.

In a path-finding study, scientists at Harvard University tracked 4,700 people over a twenty-year period. The researchers uncovered that apparently the power of happiness can span even physical separation, elevating the mood of a person's spouse, relatives, friends or neighbours by 8% to 34%. Incidentally, the findings also demonstrate that happy people tend to be better off in a number of ways being more productive, more creative and healthier.

"He who excels at resolving difficulties does so before they arise. He who excels in conquering his enemies triumphs before threats materialise".

Sun Tzu
The Art of War[41]

Commenting on the study, Martin EP Seligman, a psychologist from the University of Pennsylvania, has speculated that happiness may be important on an evolutionary level by helping people cooperate with each other. He likens it to an orchestra tuning up. Laughter, singing and smiling help tune the group emotionally, getting people on the same wavelength, so they can work together more effectively as a group[37].

Amazingly, our brains appear capable of transmitting happiness to other brains without recourse to the five senses of perception. EEG readings monitoring coherent alpha and theta brainwave states during particular meditation techniques show commensurate, if diluted, improvements to brainwave coherence in non-participants located even some distance away. Researchers have also observed a decrease in cortisol and an increase in serotonin levels in people situated near to a meditating group[38]. No social or other physical interaction was involved.

As we have seen already in the section on the observant self in chapter 4, there is also a growing body of research that indicates that the broadcasted effect of a meditating group has an impact on both the thinking ability and behaviour of non-participants even at a distance. The research evidence is systematic enough for specific predictions to be made based on a simple mathematical formula as to the number of meditators required to influence a given population size[39]. On the basis of these findings we could soon be hiring groups of meditators to cheer all the rest of us up and prevent acts of aggression, violence and other negativity from breaking out in society in general[40].

Remedy

As we have discussed, there is still a wide body of management opinion that still considers that people's personal stress is outside the management remit and may in any case be beyond their control. However, as we have also seen, if you adopt a policy of low stress at work you can greatly enhance both individual and therefore collective performance. So it follows that, at the very least, it must surely be cost-effective to pass on to employees at all levels the value of a low-stress home lifestyle. This way they are better able to deal with the stress at work but also are less likely to drag it into work with them and infect everybody else.

A lot more is known by conventional science these days about the sort of lifestyle regimes that are conducive to low-stress performance. As such there are now a wealth of opportunities opening up for managers to reduce the overall stress levels in their organisation.

Simple practices such as regular exercise[42], regular meal times, regular sleep patterns, 'interaction with nature', otherwise known as a walk in the countryside,[43, 44] moderation in alcohol, regular social interaction, peer support[45] and so on all help reduce stress and therefore help to improve the productivity and performance of the whole organisation.

> A low-stress place to work is a productive place to work and the employer is the first to benefit from this higher performance.

Specific stress-alleviating tactics such as yoga, Transcendental Meditation (TM)[46], Tai Chi, Network Spinal Analysis (NSA)[47] even regular community singing[48], church attendance[49], and a variety of other valuable ideas could be introduced into employee awareness, if not actually recommended or provided by the employer.

All these tactics and many others have a growing body of evidence that demonstrates improvements in health, mental-health, longevity of life and other parameters associated with a low-stressed physiology.

To some managers the introduction of such ideas in the workplace may sound patronising. However, the overall benefits to the organisation (not to mention the customers, patients or other external stakeholders) of everyone at work functioning a lot nearer their full potential, will be out of all proportion to any cost involved.

The important point here is to adopt those ideas that work for you and that have the nearest fit with your work culture. In different organisations I have seen morning-prayer meetings, workplace chaplaincy and counselling, group practise of TM, yoga sessions, community singing, on-site Indian head massage, and on-site gyms for workouts. Whatever the technique to be adopted the primary leadership function is to answer two fundamental questions.

Firstly, is the tactic, technique, or method to be adopted or recommended by you valid, that is: does it actually work? Sub-questions to pose include:

- Is there any research to back up claims made by the advocates?
- Are the providers suitably qualified and accredited?
- Has the system or tactic got a tried and tested track record in the workplace backed up by independent endorsements?

Just as with any other management initiative, it is important to follow through. So once you have introduced a set of ideas to help stress among employees, monitor feedback from participants on an ongoing basis to find out whether stress levels are genuinely being improved and whether or not this is translating into improved productivity and efficiency.

Secondly, does the tactic fit comfortably with the cultural ethos of the employees? A clash of cultures risks having the reverse effect of what you are trying to achieve. If your intervention manages to cut across cherished beliefs, you risk generating a net gain in stress.

I have heard Richard Branson say that working for companies should be fun, and why not? A bunch of miserable people will be just that; miseries who spread their woes to everyone else around them in whatever line of work they do, be it machine minding in a factory, social work, accountancy, or hotel reception.

On the other hand, a low-stress place to work is a productive place to work and the employer is the first to benefit from this higher performance. If you doubt the wisdom of this statement, revisit the section on the cost of stress. Carry out a stress audit and you will soon identify the real costs that are undermining your organisational performance. Once you know the real cost of the current situation it will be easier to identify the most appropriate remedies and free up the necessary resources to invest in them.

Chapter Twelve

Government influences that constrain success

Stressor summary
Stressor 29 Excessive government regulations
Stressor 30 High taxation

12.1 The hidden impact of regulations on performance

The problem defined: Stressor 29 - Excessive government regulations and intervention

"Politics is the art of looking for trouble, finding it everywhere, diagnosing it incorrectly and applying the wrong remedies."

Groucho Marx

On the face of it organisational leaders, managers and business owners can do little about government regulations and intervention, at least within their own organisations. Even so, the factor requires a mention here, as the impact of this particular stressor these days is universally comprehensive and poses a growing challenge for any business leader or conscientious manager whether in the public or private sector.

Simply put, government intervention through regulations, surveillance and high taxation (See next section about tax) has a tendency to block or impede the initiative, autonomy, enterprise and enthusiasm of everyone affected. Very often, this intervention progressively suppresses the instinctive ability of people to be able to collaborate spontaneously with one another in mutually beneficial problem solving and relationship building.

We are now more aware that centrally imposed targets are stress inducing (See Stressor 3). It appears that regulations have a similar, if diluted, impact as not only do they inhibit the use of our innate resources, including spontaneous problem solving, they are often capable of hampering the fulfilment of several human emotional needs. In very general terms where regulations become a problem it is because they impact one or more of the following needs:

- **Adequate autonomy and control over our lives** – regulations by their very nature tell us how to behave and what to do in given circumstances restricting the use of our own judgement and discretion.

- **Genuine attention from other human beings** – regulations are a blanket prescription imposed regardless of the local circumstances and therefore heedless of our personal feelings, knowledge and observations about the situation.

- **Sense of achievement and meaning from our working lives** – Where regulations cut across our own understanding of what is best in a situation and force us to do what we consider to be wrong, inadequate or pointless then our sense of achievement and meaning is inevitably diminished.

- **Status and recognition** – Regulations can easily be seen to be demeaning. In essence they are imposed by government officials who have made an assumption that we are not to be trusted to either know what to do, or how to behave in given circumstances.

- **Sense of fun out of our work** – Often the tedium of filling in government forms, submitting to audits and inspections, carrying out routine and otherwise pointless chores distracts us from what we want and need to do to improve the situation. This can sooner or later evaporate the fun out of the job.

Government regulations inhibit the use of innate resources, including spontaneous collaborative problem solving,

In the UK a cascade of regulations emanating from Whitehall and The European Union is adding to the daily stress load of the three million companies in the private sector and the millions of people and managers working in the public sector. The extra costs, obstacles, waste, delays and administration incurred in compliance are frustrating to say the least. But this problem is also hitting profits, enthusiasm, professionalism, enterprise, productivity and competitiveness.

All this often hidden damage is occurring with only patchy evidence that there is any significant benefit to society or the economy. Not only is there scarce evidence that the current regulatory regime is effective, over the last few years there have been a series of scandalous incidents all occurring in sectors that are already heavily regulated. These include the food sector, care for the elderly, the NHS, banking and financial services, child protection, agriculture and many more. Always the call is for more and better regulation or more effective regulators when the real point may be that we need to do away with the regulations.

When confronted with a social problem the simplistic obvious answer for most governments is to apply carte blanche regulations. This quick fix response is to ignore the wealth of conscientiousness, experience, professionalism and goodwill of the vast majority of the population. Healthy individuals have a natural and instinctive need to get things right, make a worthwhile contribution to their host group and derive satisfaction and meaning from a job well done. Enabling these instinctive survival mechanisms is far more likely to get consistent results and without the periodic and inevitable lapses in regulations and regulators.

This is not to argue that the protection aspired to by the regulations is not needed. As long as we still have powerful owners, bureaucrats and managers who don't care, then employees and society in general will find themselves at a disadvantage when it comes to a number of factors including safety, security and so on. My main argument is that we need to find a better way than getting central government to impose national standardised regulations. I believe any new approach will involve more widespread collaboration between stakeholders. In this respect the Trade Unions probably have a greater role to play, for too long they have been lost in an ideological struggle for a socialist utopia. As a result they have become effete and useless at the more mundane job of working with employers and employees to create a balanced approach to employee rights and a safer working environment.

> The unions, lost in an ideological struggle for a socialist utopia have become effete and useless at the more mundane job of protecting employees' needs

Larger organisations are much more able to cope with regulations as they have the infrastructure to handle the extra work, but at the smaller end of the scale the costs and frustrations of regulations are becoming critical to business survival.

271

Impact of employment legislation on small business - case study

The night supervisor and two of his female staff at a small print finishing business had begun to meet socially outside working hours and had become over-friendly at work. Unfortunately this led to inappropriate behaviour one night and allegations by two women against the supervisor for sexual harassment. Instead of being able to handle the situation at his own discretion, with appropriate reprimands or sanctions or perhaps attempts at mediation between the parties, the owner had to suspend the supervisor pending a tribunal to be held at some time in the future. The supervisor subsequently signed off sick with stress as he disputed the allegations hotly and never returned to work again.

Whatever the truth of the allegations and the rights and wrongs of the situation, the protracted and heavy-handed quasi-judicial proceedings led to entirely unfortunate and disproportionate consequences.

This small specialist firm went into liquidation.

The company was already struggling with a sales turnover hovering precariously just above break-even point. The loss of the supervisor meant that the night shift could no longer continue in operation. A specialist technician with his skills and experience was impossible to find in the circumstances in that locality in a short space of time. So the night shift workers, including of course the two complainants, had to be laid off. The loss of the night shift revenue put the company below break-even. Faced with this, the owner had no alternative but to go into liquidation. Twelve people lost their jobs and the owner lost his business and with it his retirement savings, his income and his house.

Just about every activity within the private and public sector is becoming increasingly regulated. Every task whether it is arranging a loan, hiring a new employee, designing an office layout, re-equipping a factory, buying a new light bulb or conducting a simple conversation with a colleague such as a performance review or job interview is now potentially fraught with unnecessary tension and worry and or extra work, induced entirely by potential or actual regulative intervention.

Employment regulations suppress the natural ability to express a degree of emotional intelligence and maturity to gauge the correct human response.

There is no room here for a panoramic description of all the implications of government influence on organisational stress throughout society; so a look at one area will have to suffice. As seen with the above case example, a typical area where extensive regulations can induce stress is employment legislation. These various laws are designed to create a useful framework for managers and Human Resource (HR) people to work with. In this respect these regulations help provide a degree of confidence that the relevant professionals are doing the right thing in any given circumstance. However, as is usually the case with government legislation, there are also unintended consequences.

Employment regulations effectively encroach on the need for human beings to enter freely into mutually agreeable working relationships. An added problem is that the complexity of the law is such that a manager has to have fluency in an equivalent of about nine statutes just to avoid stepping into a minefield of potential litigation. It is difficult enough to find sufficiently capable managers to run our businesses, hospitals and government departments without requiring them to be also equipped with extensive legal knowledge. Several possible consequences arise from this situation:

- The people management function tends to become split between operations' managers and HR managers thus duplicating work and complicating working relationships and lines of control.

- Those managers who lack the necessary HR knowledge and understanding unwittingly make disproportionately costly mistakes and end up facing tribunals and litigation, which drag a whole enterprise down.

- Incompetent, risk averse or inexperienced managers resort to robotic box ticking and tight adherence to best practice manuals rather than developing and using their own discretion and judgement to help their working relationships actually work spontaneously and effectively.

- The added burden of regulative activity often results in the cumbersome and expensive outsourcing of the HR function to third-party consultants and insurance companies.

- What tends to get suppressed is the natural ability to express a degree of emotional intelligence, maturity and integrity to gauge the correct human response in any given situation.

> Making something compulsory changes its very nature and therefore changes the emotional impact that it has on us.

Employment regulations tend to create a different mind set to that intended. Instead of focusing on the matter in hand the questions arise in a manager's mind – Have I done what I am supposed to have done in law? Have

I ticked all the boxes? Have I done something that will get me into trouble? Every difficult encounter with an employee becomes a potential threat to career, livelihood and effective operational functioning with its potential to trigger litigation and compensation claims.

It has to be said that much of the employment legislation is well meaning and often makes sense in its own right. However the problems arise due to the blanket imposition in law that curtails the individual manager's need for autonomy and control, to give and receive personal attention and to develop an emotional connection with employees. The compulsory element can easily suppress the sort of natural spontaneity in human encounters that underpin the formation of genuine and productive relationships. We all know that making something compulsory changes its very nature and therefore changes the emotional impact that it has on us. I once saw a rather glum-looking ferryman on the Sandbanks car ferry in Poole wearing a white T-shirt emblazoned with large black letters "THERE ARE NO TOILETS ON THIS FERRY". The sight of it made me laugh, as presumably he had been pestered with endless enquiries in the past.

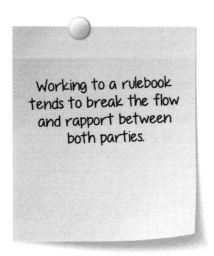

Working to a rulebook tends to break the flow and rapport between both parties.

But his glumness made me think. You see the ferryman's attitude to wearing that T-shirt will vary greatly depending on whether he had been told to wear it by his employer or whether he had decided to wear it of his own accord, to make his own life a bit easier. Who makes the decision makes all the difference between having a bit of fun at the tourists' expense and sullen resentfulness at being made to look an idiot. And so it is with a civil service department in Whitehall telling you how you should act in any given situation. Compulsion changes the nature of your response.

Excessive regulations, in employment law or any other area where they are intended to govern the quality of personal relationships also suffer from the usual law of unintended consequences as detailed in Stressor 25. The problem here is that the compulsory application of rules of conduct tends to undermine the natural trust and openness required for spontaneous and fruitful relationship building. Working to a rulebook tends to break the flow and rapport between both parties. The risk is that both sides are more inclined to work to the minimum required by the statute and are somewhat less inclined to enter wholeheartedly into a working relationship with one another. The inevitable strain is stress inducing, as neither party are genuinely receiving the real human attention they need in the circumstances. Instead, what often happens is that such transactions and interactions tend to get by with just the cursory attention required to go through the motions that satisfy the minimum requirements laid down by law. Both sides are left emotionally dissatisfied by the encounter whatever other outcomes might have been arrived at.

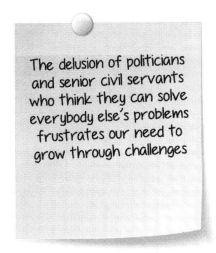

The delusion of politicians and senior civil servants who think they can solve everybody else's problems frustrates our need to grow through challenges

The worst of it is that, as ever, the regulations are vulnerable to being exploited on both sides of the divide by anyone, employer or employee, unethical or ruthless enough to try and take advantage of the situation. The result is that the regulations invariably fail in their intentions of curtailing the excessive behaviour of the minority of rogues. In the meantime the rest of society suffers under the illusion that we are somehow protected. Recent scandals, as mentioned earlier, demonstrate only too clearly that regulations are an inadequate mechanism to protect us from harm. In the case of employment legislation instead of protecting people the regulations distort and suppress the natural relationships of everyone who is simply trying to do a good job, all this for a huge extra burden in time, money and stress.

All in all, the culture of box ticking, compensation claiming and statutory threats for the infringement of a growing number of regulations (literally numbered in their thousands) is having an unbalancing effect on operational activity. Owner-managers, of small businesses in particular, are losing the motivation to employ people. Apparently the average size of UK firms is now getting smaller. This news makes sense as many small business people's original ambition stems from a desire for independence and self-sufficiency. So, having to put up with bureaucratic interference in their own

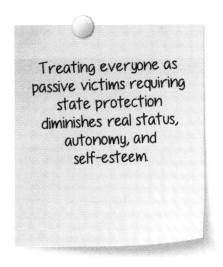

Treating everyone as passive victims requiring state protection diminishes real status, autonomy, and self-esteem

business is somewhat galling. Many small business owners feel a worrying loss of autonomy and control over their own businesses, as do many managers over their areas of responsibility.

But it is not just the bosses that are adversely affected. Government interference in the daily relationships and routines of commercial life emasculates people generally. Crucially such interference takes away our right to solve our own problems and meet our own challenges.

The delusion of politicians and senior civil servants who think they can solve everybody else's problems frustrates our need to grow through challenges; ultimately it stifles many of the inherent inner resources required to meet our own needs. Treating everyone as passive victims requiring state protection also diminishes real status, autonomy, and self-esteem.

> Despite the illusion of protection, recent scandals demonstrate only too clearly that regulations are an inadequate mechanism to protect us from harm.

I suspect that the widespread and growing anger, resentfulness, lethargy and irresponsibility so common in society today are partly the outcome of this regulatory culture. The development of this victim consciousness where everybody has to be looked after by the government partly explains why there are two and half million people on incapacity benefits, up from 740,000 in 1983. The government now "has to" spend £138 billion per year on what is called "social protection"[1]. We need challenges like we need air and government bureaucracy is suffocating us.

Remedy

Internally managers within the organisation are powerless to act against this current threat, at least directly. But that should not be the last word on this. The usual business textbooks so often ignore the whole area of government impact on business life as though it doesn't exist. However, government is probably now the biggest single influence on organisational effectiveness and sustainable business profitability. Yet to read a management or business textbook you would think we operate our economy in a void of free market activity. We don't, and if we continue to ignore this all-important factor it will continue to harm our economy and our emotional well-being.

No man is an island as they say and across the country there are millions of organisational leaders, business owners, managers and workers stuck in frustration, stress and even chaos because of the intervention of bureaucratic government. Every political and regulatory decision made, every plan, every policy document has the potential to significantly impact our working lives, our health, our

> What is required is a collaborative and focussed effort by those people who have at heart the wider interests of society

276

children's upbringing and our prosperity in our old age. But at the moment we just let a small clique of party political activists and senior civil servants get on with the job of running our lives without us bothering to take much notice at all. Our Parliamentary democracy is chronically dysfunctional.

But however dysfunctional our democracy has become, it still remains a democracy of sorts. So there is real potential to improve things so that a much wider and more representative group of people can participate in a rational way in the running of the country. As in a closed organisation, what is required in society at large is a greater degree of collaboration from the grass roots and therefore a more collaborative style and structure of leadership to enable it. It is greater collaboration that will facilitate more "intelligent action" across society and empower higher performance. Although apathy is rife at the moment, new insights from Game Theory suggest that even a small minority of the population can have an impact on the behaviour of the majority[2]. Mercifully, we are not looking for a change in human nature here. What is required is a collaborative and focussed effort by those people who have at heart the wider interests of society and not just the pursuit of their own self-interests or ideological utopias.

According to Game Theory research, collectively a very small proportion of the population can precipitate a change in the behaviour of everyone else by developing the right strategic incentives for cooperative behaviour. Once these 'incentives' are in place, the research suggests "self-regarding behaviour does not always dominate social interaction."[3] More widespread collaboration in political decision-making is the key to both lower stress for all and a better-run government. Another book is required to cover this particular issue thoroughly. However as a summary the quickest and easiest route to more widespread collaboration could simply mean a lot more people taking an active role in their preferred political parties.

> "The difficulty is that politicians believe they must be seen to care. If they abolish a regulation it might look as if they don't care - hence regulatory creep."
>
> John Seddon

Passive viewing of current affairs on the TV and then 50% of us turning up once every five years and putting a cross by our chosen candidate's name provides insufficient attention and activity to provide our political classes with the accountability needed to maintain their optimum performance on our behalf.

As we have seen earlier, effective accountability needs to be current, frequent, specific, clear and direct (See chapter 9.8). At the moment in no way does the electorate provide this necessary level of accountability. Accountability is seriously diluted by the four or five year gap between elections, vague manifestos, the huge size of constituencies, the remoteness and complexity of government and third party pressure from central party organisations, the media and lobbyists that intervene between the voters and their elected representatives. No wonder that currently political party membership is at an all time low. By 2010, total membership of the three main political parties had sunk to only 1.0% of the electorate.

Table 16: Individual UK political party membership figures

Individual party membership figures[4]		
Party	**Numbers**	**Historic membership**
Labour	193,000	Down from 1 million in the 1950s
Conservative	130,000 – 150,000	Down from 3 million in the 1950s
Liberal Democrats	49,000	Down from Liberal party membership of 243,000 in 1960

But even these figures exaggerate the level of actual political participation. A large part of today's membership comprises the 'standing order' category. By this is meant members who are effectively non-participating in every way other than sending off a standing order payment once a year. In addition we have to accept that a significant percentage are also purely 'social members'.

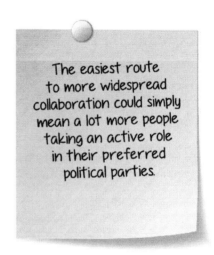

The easiest route to more widespread collaboration could simply mean a lot more people taking an active role in their preferred political parties.

Several reasons are suggested for the drop in participation but four give serious cause for concern in the context of the lack of accountability at political and government level. These are:

- Mass communications particularly the TV are enabling the central party machines to communicate directly with the electorate and so they are less dependent on a grass root membership network and the local constituency parties.

- Parties are less dependent on subscriptions and small donations as they are more proficient at garnering funds from wealthy donors, corporations, institutions, lobby groups and Trade Unions.
- Similarly state subsidies paid to political parties weaken the dependence on individual membership participation.
- Central party leaderships are increasingly seeing a vocal membership as an electoral liability[5].

In the view of the party political machines, it seems that party members are becoming more of a nuisance than an asset. This is the reverse of what is required for a useful level of accountability.

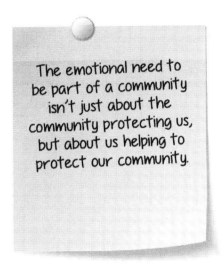

The emotional need to be part of a community isn't just about the community protecting us, but about us helping to protect our community.

So the simple if unwelcome recommendation is to join your preferred party, turn up and participate. Encourage work colleagues and friends to do the same.

As an example of the potential benefits what would have been the impact on the current malaise in the NHS if a mere thirty or forty nurses, doctors and other healthcare professionals had become *active* members in each constituency party in the country? My guess is these few thousand people turning up to discussion groups, and coffee mornings, having chats with and getting to know local candidates and MPs, providing feedback about what was really happening in their local hospital and offering suggestions for improvements would have gone a long way to redress the situation years before the current scandals had broken in the press.

This is not a political point, but a psychological one.

A key emotional need is to feel part of a wider community. For our personal survival that community needs to be healthy and vibrant. For us to be emotionally healthy, being part of a community involves a lot more than being a passive member of it. To be healthy we have to take action and make a contribution. Like several other emotional needs, the relationship only works if it is reciprocal. It isn't just about the community protecting us but about us helping to protect our community.

12.2 How tax impacts motivation and performance

The problem defined: Stressor 30 - High taxation

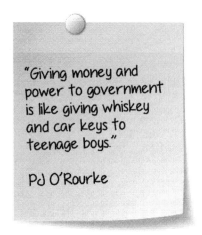

"Giving money and power to government is like giving whiskey and car keys to teenage boys."

PJ O'Rourke

It may seem odd to refer to high taxation as an 'organisational stressor'. This is especially so as the remedy is, in the immediate practical sense, outside the control of individual managers or business owners. However the impact of high tax has such a universal dampening effect on enthusiasm and long-term commitment at work that it is worthwhile giving it a mention here as a stressor.

In addition, high tax also has both a direct and indirect impact on just about every major business decision, so to exclude it from a work on leadership would be leaving a big gap in our understanding. As we have seen, the most effective leadership is holistic leadership, so it is natural to take into account something as intrusive into our daily business lives as the tax government takes from us.

From the perspective of the human givens, high taxation on the rewards received for achieving success further diminishes motivation and raises questions as to the value of doing a thorough and worthwhile job. Government interference takes some of the fun out of management work anyway and dampens the exhilaration of the challenges in business. Add a high and unfair tax bill to this and the creative energy required to build and sustain a first class and profitable business or a successful management career is inexorably sapped.

High tax and spend distorts the balance of political power away from the individual

But that isn't the only problem. In effect, high taxation shifts power disproportionately away from the individual household to the government. As such, the higher the tax level generally, the more it threatens several of our fundamental psychological needs. In particular high tax and high government expenditure threatens the need for a high degree of autonomy and control over our lives. This threat occurs for two powerful reasons.

Firstly, and most obviously, taking the tax from us reduces our capacity to choose how to spend our own money.

Secondly, the spending of our tax money by the government only reinforces further their power of intervention into our daily lives. To adopt Leon Trotsky's infamous phrase, we are basically supplying them with the rope used to hang us with.

A high tax burden also indirectly threatens the core need for individual security and stability. How so? With a high tax take, we all have to work harder for every penny that we get to spend. It also takes far longer to save up for the expensive capital necessaries of life such as a house and retirement provision that we depend on for long-term family security.

High taxation and high government spending creates economic volatility

High tax also impacts our individual security in another way. High tax means that revenue from millions of people is being channelled into the control of a relatively few government functionaries. And in turn this means that power is coalescing towards a single point in our society rather than being dispersed widely among a large number of stakeholders. The larger the tax take the more there is a centralisation of power over hundreds of billions of pounds in the economy.

> High taxation creates economic volatility undermining peoples' need for security

What comes in parallel to this concentration of power is an equal and opposite effect of less diversity in decision-making. There is less variety, less assortment of ideas, a smaller range of viewpoints occurring in the decision-making processes throughout the economy. And when this happens, the impact of key decisions becomes more and more monolithic on the rest of the economy.

The unfortunate by-product here is that any mistakes that are made at the centre of things will rebound and impact on much wider aspects of society than if they were made at local level or individual level. This situation creates volatility. So, under the present circumstances, even slight changes in policy direction create a herd type reaction as people seek to respond to the changes provoking sudden major shifts in existing trends or existing patterns. Sudden changes in direction made by central policy makers are difficult to predict and often wrong-foot people. This volatility helps undermine peoples' psychological need for security.

High taxation weakens feelings of community

The compulsory commandeering of a high proportion of our income and wealth to the government also saps the reciprocal emotional need to both contribute and to feel part of a community. The perceived unfairness of the tax system (by those who have to actually pay the tax of course) inevitably encourages high taxpayers to do everything possible to avoid tax. Some tax avoidance strategies have the immediate problem that they divert the energy and creativity of tens of thousands of professionals away from doing something productive and towards focus on ameliorating the tax take. But inevitably people will also be tempted to fiddle or evade taxes, opt out of income generation altogether or leave the country.

Similarly the high tax take seems to induce an atmosphere of apathy towards those in need. Taxpayers start to feel more and more resentful towards other people's hand-outs or benefits and what they may see as other acts of wasteful government expenditure.

One result of this process is an erosion of goodwill both towards the government and towards those various sections of the community perceived as the beneficiaries. Never has the government done more to help us and never has it been held in such low esteem generally. This erosion of goodwill combined with the natural desire to hang on to your own cash becomes a powerful incentive to try and cheat the system or exit altogether. Emigration or the outward flow of people from the UK is currently running at somewhere between 150,000 to 200,000 people per year. Not surprisingly it is very often the most enterprising and qualified people that are leaving the UK.

"Sir, I own my own business, which moves electronic components around the world and employs some 20 people. My income is around £200,000 a year. Goodbye."[6]

Russell Payne (Letter to the Daily Telegraph in response to the new 50% tax rate imposed in a recent budget)

High taxation threatens our need for status

High tax erodes feelings of status. We become drones working for a welfare system or a socialised economic system. Hard work, initiative and enterprise get scorned and mocked by the "redistribution" lobby so there is a lack of recognition and appreciation here for those that are enterprising enough to take

282

risks, work hard, put their money where their mouth is, and do something innovative and potentially financially rewarding.

High tax and spend social policies threaten the autonomy and control we have over our own lives

The very act of redistributing largesse from one group of people to another is in essence condescension. Benefits on the level seen in recent years remove people's autonomy to solve their own problems. Long-term state hand-outs weaken our sense of meaning or a feeling of competence in our ability to run our own lives.

High tax and high government expenditure threatens our need for a high degree of autonomy and control over our lives.

The social result of the negation of these two important psychological needs is that four million people between the ages of 24 and 60 have never ever done a day's paid work. State-funded welfare is in essence creating a psychic prison for millions of people in the UK. Far from alleviating human misery, the consequent general malaise has led to widespread ill-health among the effected population and an epidemic of mental ill-health, depression and substance abuse leading to yet further strain for our healthcare system.

High tax diminishes individual initiative and effort

High tax damages people's attitudes towards taking the initiative, taking a challenge, and putting in an effort, at least in the economic sphere. Lack of recognition apart; what is the point of taking up the risk and challenge of setting up and building a successful business or career if the government grabs something like 70% - 75% off you?

You may be surprised that the tax level is this high. This estimate of 70% - 75% takes into account the full range of tax that you are hit with if you are fortunate enough to be successful in your endeavours. These include: Top rate of Income Tax currently at 45%, National Insurance both employers' and employees' contribution levied at about 25%, Corporation Tax, VAT at 20% on most of the discretionary items you buy, council tax, duty on fuel and on many luxury items, Capital Gains Tax on savings invested successfully, and Stamp Duty on your house every time you move and on most investments that you might buy with your spare cash. Ultimately, of course, at the end of it all you, or rather your family, get hit with 40% Inheritance Tax on a hefty part of the home that you have spent half a life-time paying a mortgage for.

Tax is wrecking your day

If you are a reasonably successful businessperson or well paid employee in the UK, then one way or another you are probably paying out the equivalent of 70% of your earnings in tax. Let's put this in perspective. Assuming you work an eight-hour day then every day you are in effect working for the government until about 2:30 pm in the afternoon. Only after that are you earning money for yourself and your family.

At the other end of the food chain, what is the point of getting a mind-numbingly futile and boring job in a call centre if the net pay you receive after tax and national insurance for doing forty hours work is hardly any more or even less than the welfare benefits for doing nothing? In these situations it is a relatively rational and healthy reaction to avoid the opportunity of going out to work. Instead there must be a very real pull to just stay at home tucked up in front of daytime telly with a few cans of lager.

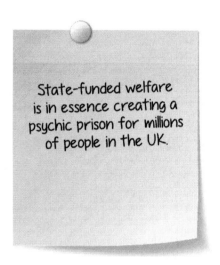

State-funded welfare is in essence creating a psychic prison for millions of people in the UK.

I remember setting up a performance incentive scheme at a window manufacturing company. The scheme involved the firm sharing the value of benefits and savings generated from the performance improvements developed by the team planning process. The staff's enthusiasm for the gain-sharing scheme waned somewhat when we started to explain the tax-take from the bonus. The first surprise was the employer's National Insurance contribution, the original stealth tax. At the time this amounted to 12.8% of the bonus payable, then came the 11% employees National Insurance and finally the 20% income tax. The total tax amounted to 43.8% of their bonus and this for semi-skilled labourers. You could have heard a pin drop in that room when the realisation dawned.

High taxation threatens our privacy and security

A government funded by high tax and command and control regulations and policies depends increasingly on more and more information about our private lives. This, of course, damages another important human need, the need for privacy. So much of our private lives now have to be revealed to satisfy the curiosity of the tax collectors and regulatory agencies. As the tax take grows so does the intrusion.

But it isn't just our privacy that is under threat; security is also threatened here. People are no longer sure that all the information that is being extracted from them will be used in either a fair or ethical way. The esteem of politicians and government bureaucracies has reached an all time low and the essential trust required between the governed and the government is reaching a critical point of dysfunction.

Diagram 22

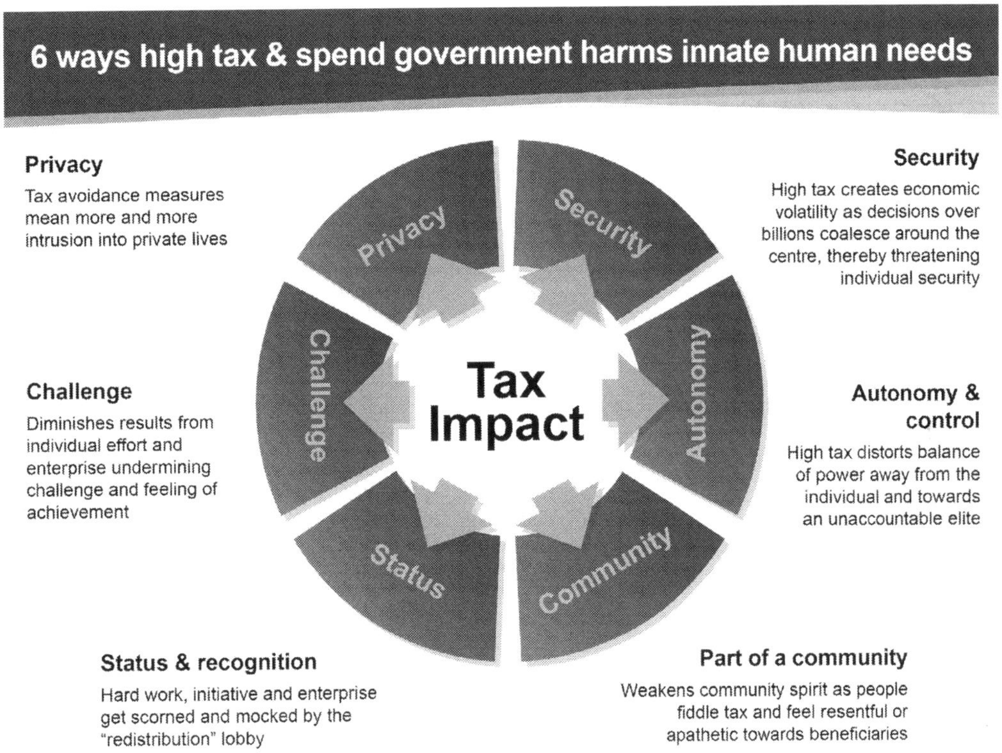
6 ways high tax & spend government harms innate human needs
Privacy
Tax avoidance measures mean more and more intrusion into private lives
Security
High tax creates economic volatility as decisions over billions coalesce around the centre, thereby threatening individual security
Challenge
Diminishes results from individual effort and enterprise undermining challenge and feeling of achievement
Autonomy & control
High tax distorts balance of power away from the individual and towards an unaccountable elite
Status & recognition
Hard work, initiative and enterprise get scorned and mocked by the "redistribution" lobby
Part of a community
Weakens community spirit as people fiddle tax and feel resentful or apathetic towards beneficiaries
Privacy
Security
Challenge
Autonomy
Status
Community
Tax Impact

Remedy

The problem is of such a magnitude now that responsible managers, business owners or indeed public servants should have in their awareness that their ability to earn a living, build a business, accumulate capital for the care of their family and for their own old age is in grave peril from the profligate activity of government. If you think this is extreme, take a look at the statistics.

The UK government has built up a trillion pound deficit and a trillion pound unsupported pension deficit. In effect the Labour government 1997 - 2010 racked up a huge amount of debt equivalent to about £300,000 per household[7] at a time when the average net family income was about £24,792 per year. This is a colossal amount of debt and will hang around our necks for generations.

But perhaps we can get a better perspective of the level of government profligacy when we compare this level of national debt with how individual families manage their personal finances. Compared with the £300,000 (or £323,800 seen in table 14) debt the Government has acquired for each UK household, the average family mortgage is now about £101,000 secured by about £140,000 of equity held in the property. Average unsecured debt is roughly £7,950[8].

Table 17: UK national debt breakdown

UK National Debt Breakdown (2010)	
Category of debt	**Amount in Trillions (£)**
The official public sector debt quoted in the budget	0.89
Unfunded public sector pensions	1.28
Unfunded state pensions	2.7
RBS/Lloyds debt	2.6
Other: including the Local Government Pension deficit, PFI, and nuclear decommissioning	0.4
Total debt (£ Trillions)	7.87*
*With 24.3 million households in the UK then £7,870,000,000,000 equates to about £323,800 of national debt per household.	

Ultimately the reason for this dire state of events is that accountability over government actions has become weakened to the point of chronic ineffectiveness.

For too long the managerial classes have abdicated from the responsibility of participating in such a way in politics as to provide a rational restraining influence on the ambitions of so many politicians and civil servants and self-interested lobby groups. While we were all distracted by our personal affairs and work commitments, they spent our money.

Far from the old adage that the man in Whitehall knows best[9], the government has to relearn the age-old lesson that it must operate under the same rules as everyone else. And it has to be the managerial classes who will have to teach them. Otherwise who else will? Politicians and government have to learn to spend within budget, and that means spending within the confines of revenue raised from the taxpayer.

Accountability in this context means that, just like running our own household budgets, the electorate ensures that the government first works out what it is likely to receive in the way of acceptable and fair tax revenue, and then decides how to spend it. If this means that there is not enough money to go around for some cherished projects, well that's life. National solvency means that those who run the country must learn to prioritise like the leaders of every responsible business or household.

But the question has to be answered; who is going to teach them this crucial lesson if people experienced and trained in management and business economics continue to avoid the issue, as they increasingly have done over the last thirty to forty years? Perhaps the recent spate of government and political scandals over the NHS, bank regulations and MPs' expenses has an up-side. The exposure of so many politicians taking such a cavalier attitude with the taxpayer's money may begin to galvanise the energy of more voters to actually participate in the democratic process and keep a better eye on how their money is being spent.

As with the previous stressor, it is widespread collaboration in the political decision-making processes that is the key to both lower stress for all and a better-run government.

Chapter Thirteen

Pulling the various strands together

13.1 Reinventing management thinking is a key factor in motivating high performance

As a summary of the last seven chapters, each of the thirty stressors is an actual or potential threat to one or more of an individual's biological needs – our human givens. On an individual level, these threats tend to trigger a stress response, so if the stressors are prevalent, stress levels in an organisation as a whole tend to rise. Rising stress levels provoke a range of unproductive thinking and behaviour that adversely impact both organisational costs and performance.

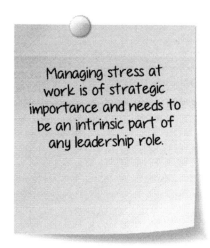

Managing stress at work is of strategic importance and needs to be an intrinsic part of any leadership role.

Stress is so widespread in organisational life these days because many of the stressors are built into the design of the system. In other words, stressors are a side effect of the way we currently structure and manage our organisations.

This is why the usually advocated stress management techniques of one sort or another are inadequate, as they do not tackle the root cause. They are no more than sticking plasters or coping strategies for stressed individuals. This is why 'organisational stress management' is of strategic importance and needs to be an intrinsic part of any leadership role. By reinventing their thinking, managers can embrace this new role, so that stress management principles form an intrinsic part of organisational design, management function and leadership style.

The primary recognition of the new management thinking is that human beings have inherent biological constraints. Disregarding these constraints suppresses innate human talent and resources and so costs the organisation dear in terms of low performance and productivity. Reinventing management thinking is about understanding and working with these biological constraints to liberate the human spirit and unleash the almost infinite creative potential of the workforce.

The first step to removing organisational stress is to learn to trust employees as mature, adult, human beings and so treat them accordingly. First and foremost this involves managers and leaders adopting a collaborative style of leadership that creates a genuine rapport with their groups and a mutually satisfying contract that:

a) Serves to meet people's fundamental human needs at work and

b) Enables them to develop and utilise their innate resources.

Treating people as adult humans is not just about involving them in the decision-making process, but also involves facilitating the development and maintenance of enduring and healthy relationships both between staff members and between staff and management. Powerful functional relationships then act as the glue that holds an organisation together and the platform that maintains the organisational memory through the flux of change.

13.2 How to integrate collaborative leadership into your organisation

Facilitating widespread and effective stakeholder collaboration into the decision-making process is relatively easy and can be very fast. After all you are setting in motion a process that is inherently natural to any healthy stakeholder. So if you set about the transition in the right way you can find that things fall into place both rapidly and seemingly spontaneously.

> "You rarely improve an organisation as a whole by improving the performance of one or more of its parts."
>
> RL Ackoff

To embark on a journey of successful collaborative leadership, there are ten general principles to follow. All of these principles have already been covered in various parts of the book but if developed comprehensively as a programme of change will integrate collaborative leadership successfully into your organisation.

The table over provides you with a quick view as to where to look in the book to pull the various strands together.

Table 18: Integrating collaborative leadership into the system

	Ten principles	Where to find out more
1	Adopt the universal principle of treating other people the way you would like to be treated yourself. This involves a strong element of letting go of control as well as a good measure of humility. For many managers this is perhaps the greatest challenge.	Chapter 6 section 1 on top-down command and control leadership.
2	Maintain full and frank dissemination of information to wherever it can be made use of and to whoever can make use of it.	Chapter 6 section 2 on an atmosphere of mistrust.
3	Structure collaboration into the organisational design. One way to do this is to adopt a seven step structured team planning workshop system and bottom-up feedback process to instigate a regular cycle of performance improvements across the entire organisation (Due to the highly integrated nature of an organic system, piecemeal change doesn't do the trick, the whole system needs to be looked at the same time). You will find that the team planning workshop system helps senior executives overcome bounded rationality, creates buy-in from stakeholders and develops robust non-linear planning and decision-making. Also focus on devolving responsibility and authority for work design and decision-making as far as possible down to the interface with the customer. Minimise pre-specification of job roles and functions enabling work design to be made at the point it is needed, by the people who need it, when it is needed.	Chapter 6 section 1 on top-down command and control leadership, Table 8. Chapter 8 section 1 on major strategic change. Chapter 11 section 7 Table 14 – Eight ways team planning reduces confirmation bias and diagram 18 — A structured approach to healthy decision-making – Competent decision-making as the platform to launch success. Appendix 1 Table 19: - Contrast between top down command and control and collaborative leadership, a summary of the two regimes.
4	Promote leaders that personify the twelve qualities that underpin successful leadership.	Chapter 6 section 1 on top-down command and control leadership, Table 7.
5	Avoid setting and imposing targets, instead instil the principles of continuous improvement across the whole organisation. Establish bottom-up negative	Chapter 7 section 1.

	Ten principles	Where to find out more
	feedback loops that monitor the interaction with the customer and so maintain a clear understanding of customer needs and how to meet them.	
6	Ensure that ambiguities in function, responsibility, authority and reporting are sorted and agreed at the planning stage of any new work or new project, or that there is a forum for sorting these problems out through usage and experience.	Chapter 7 section 2 on boundaries of functions and responsibilities.
7	Ensure that short-term goals emanating from the team planning process fulfil the criteria that differentiate them from centralised targets.	Chapter 9 section 1 on short-term goals.
8	Enable highly effective group decision-making and robust collaborative planning at every level of the organisation by instilling core decision-making and problem-solving skills with all employees.	Chapter 9 section 6 on induction and training. Chapter 11 section 2 on consensus making
9	Adopt the five key criteria for effective accountability – current/prompt, frequent, specific, clear and direct	Chapter 9 section 8 on the positive role of inequality in the workplace, Diagram 19.
10	Rely on the intrinsic motivation of your employees and stakeholders. This means shifting your focus away from direct intervention and more towards establishing a fair and reliable group decision-making process, meeting emotional needs and designing the system to eliminate the 30 stressors that block and inhibit innate human resources. The new aim is to obtain commitment, focus and enthusiasm not compliance.	Chapter 6 section 1 on top-down command and control leadership.

Appendices

Appendix 1

Table 19: Contrast between top down command and control and collaborative leadership

The table summarises the various contrasting characteristics between top down command and control (TDCCL) style leadership and collaborative leadership. These are generalisations only and represent tendencies rather than absolute givens. However the contrast demonstrates amply why collaborative leadership can outperform TDCC especially in larger organisations.

The contrasting characteristics are depicted in six categories:

1. Management structure
2. Motivation
3. Qualities of leadership
4. Decision-making
5. Culture
6. Management and leadership ethic

TDCCL	Collaborative leadership
Management structure	
Rigid hierarchy with fixed lines of reporting and demarcation.	Looser hierarchical structure enables fluid interaction between levels and across functions.
Centralised top-down planning, decision-making, system's design and problem solving exclusively in the hands of the senior management. Essentially TDCCL separates the decision-makers from those who actually do the work.	Devolved planning, system's redesign and problem solving to the lowest possible level so that the people who do the work plan the work. A prerequisite for coherent collaborative leadership is a transparent, accessible and consistently applied team planning or other group decision-making structure. The planning system needs to provide a sound platform for productive group participation in the process.
TDCCL is typified by rigid compliance structures. These include rules and regulations, directives, standardised processes, extreme functional	Control is maintained through enhanced interaction, transparency and openness between stakeholders; gives rise to a 'can do' atmosphere of honesty,

TDCCL	Collaborative leadership
specialisation, best practise rules, budgets, audits, inspections, supervisors, targets, rewards and punishment. Unfortunately this attitude can easily give rise to a 'compliance culture' where the emphasis is on compliance to management demands rather than initiative taking or enterprise to meet customer needs.	openness, enterprise and mutual trust that all helps to serve customer needs and the purpose of the organisation;
Specialisation and demarcation of labour to deliver efficiency and deskilling to reduce labour costs.	Cross-disciplinary skills to help break down demarcation. This enables more fluid teamwork and provides redundancy of function (i.e. extra capacity in the system not immediately required on a day to day basis – particularly problem-solving skills and analytical skills). Redundancy of function gives sprint capacity and facilitates spontaneous bottom-up error detection, proactive problem solving and the spontaneous evolution of improved processes and ideas.
Static view of the organisation combined with a belief that the whole is simply made up of the independent parts. This attitude emphasises the importance of organisational charts and detailed job descriptions that determine the place of things.	Understanding that the interrelationship and interdependence of the individual elements of an organisation are at least as important as the parts themselves. The value is very often found in the 'gap'. It is the gap or interrelationship and interactivity between the various elements that make the whole greater than the sum of the parts. Visual emphasis is therefore on flowcharts, process mapping charts, value-stream mapping charts etc., that clarify the flow of work, responsibilities, interdependencies, interrelationships and value added outcomes.
Motivation	
Entrenched negative attitude about staff becomes self-fulfilling with widely prevalent belief in the inherent irresponsibility of staff members reflected in widespread apathy, sloppy work and	Positive attitude towards staff inspires trust, employee engagement, loyalty, commitment, enthusiasm and enhanced competence.

295

TDCCL	Collaborative leadership
jobsworth attitude especially at junior levels.	
High stress levels and job dissatisfaction all lead to high staff turnover with resultant loss of organisational knowledge, high cost of recruitment, induction and learning curves, the repetition of mistakes over and over again and reduced commitment from new staff.	Low stress levels, highly motivating participation in decision-making and the meeting of emotional needs lead to long-term retention of staff. This ensures the development of deep organisational knowledge that helps prevent the repetition of mistakes and also enhances the evolution of new areas of expertise and core competencies.
Belief that employees need to be motivated by management, in other words motivation is extrinsic - MacGregor's X theory. In essence, employees need to be told what to do and the people in charge know best by virtue of the fact that they are in charge.	Understanding that people are naturally conscientious and motivation is intrinsic – MacGregor's Y theory. 'Human givens' theory understands that people actually need problems to solve and challenges to rise to, in order to remain healthy. Part of our human instinctive survival mechanism means that people also have an intrinsic sense of loyalty and an innate desire to see their host group survive and prosper. This emotional need is a powerful faculty that a leader can tap into if he or she is prepared to let go of apparent (but often illusionary) control.
Belief that individual motivation is more or less fixed. There is a general ignorance of the impact of stress on rational thinking and motivation. Therefore there is little or no need to take this factor into account when designing systems, work function, work targets, shift times and so on.	Recognition that a positive brain state is a crucial ingredient to productive working. Understanding that stress levels can significantly impact motivation, rational thinking and a range of other faculties crucial to highly productive working. As such, organisational stress is seen as the grit in the machine that fouls things up. Thus a primary management role is to avoid or remove stress (organisational stress) from the system.
Qualities of leadership	
The focus of control and power on the leader and the usual attendant secrecy in a	Qualities required by a leader to facilitate dynamic group work include a

TDCCL	Collaborative leadership
TDCC environment can risk attracting those who need to compensate for their own insecurities by having control or power over others – control freaks and socialised psychopaths (estimated at 1:6 of UK managers) or who feel more comfortable working in a rigidly regulated system – those on the Asperger's or autistic spectrum. These personality traits exacerbate anxiety, chaos and confusion and only add to the stress in the working environment.	high degree of self-awareness, social awareness and the ability to genuinely empathise with colleagues and subordinates. As such, the leader has an intuitive understanding as to how to help meet people's emotional needs and how to maintain optimum motivation. Also important in the collaborative leadership role are honesty and integrity and the subordination of self-interest to the wider interests and goals of the group. These qualities resonate with people and further enable openness, trust and loyalty amongst the team.
Senior managers tend to take themselves too seriously and the atmosphere is ponderous and very often humourless.	Collaborative leadership is more fun for both leaders and followers. Teamwork comes naturally to people and is therefore generally enjoyable and can give rise to peak experiences and the development of firm friendships; both of these being key human needs.
Survival and success dependent to a large part on the extreme competence of the leader. This inadvertently induces fragility into the system. A competent senior manager becomes indispensible making the system vulnerable to his or her loss. On the other hand, an incompetent leader can easily damage or even destroy the system.	Survival and success of the system depends on interaction and flow of communication, and decision-making involving a wide body of stakeholders. The system is therefore robust and capable of withstanding substantial loss of parts, (including the loss of the leader) before any breakdown ensues.
Restricted information flow and the stress inherent in an isolated leadership position gives tendency towards 'Organisational Straight Line' (OSL) thinking or linear thinking characterised by the following: Decisions having unintended consequences; there is an obsession with uniformity (standardisation of everything); the organisation collects information seemingly regardless of its efficacy; leaders tend to impose their own perspective or beliefs on everyone else. Diverse views go unheard or are seen as divisive in this environment.	Focus on wholeness - holistic thinking and the use of parallel processing of information engaging a wide body of participation and views tends to capture the salient factors of a situation and lead to robust "right first time" decisions that take into account all relevant stakeholders and cover all eventualities. Random and diverse views tend to be easily accommodated into the whole.

TDCCL	Collaborative leadership
Deference to authority is expected, but beneath the veneer of respect among staff members the more common reality is that there is often little confidence in either the leadership or the leaders' qualities.	Freedom of expression and a climate of continuous improvement enhance healthy challenges to the status quo. This in turn leads to genuine respect for leaders and understanding of their human failings. Generally greater support for leaders during difficult times.
Highly stressed overworked and 'indispensible' senior executives in danger of early burn out, sickness and early retirement at a time of life when their experience could be most valuable. Also a leader's stress levels can produce tyrannical or other defensive behaviour that de-motivates subordinates and triggers further dysfunctional behaviour among them such as sycophancy, political intrigue, hidden agendas, impression-management, ideological attachments and witch-hunts.	Well-balanced managers, enabling others to achieve, produce an environment of focused creativity aligned with the organisation's overall purpose and customer needs. The collaborative style tends to go a long way to meet all twelve of the emotional needs. The consequent low stress levels generate a higher degree of productive working, enthusiasm, commitment and loyalty. Low stress levels also mean that employees are more empathetic towards customer needs and organisational goals.
Leaders are oblivious to the stressful impact that command and control management has on staff members' emotional needs. As a result they tend to set arbitrary goals and targets and deliver team briefings and clear instructions to achieve alignment to organisational objectives and values. Therefore the predominant mode is telling. This approach is stressful because it violates key emotional needs, specifically people's need for a good degree of autonomy and control and the need for attention. Targets and other command and control tactics also invariably violate other needs such as the needs for stretch and challenge, security, recognition, status, and meaning. The result is an increase in stress for all those affected.	Recognition of the inherent self-regulating faculties of employees as well as awareness of the stress created by command and control, target setting etc.; therefore leaders place emphasis on getting full commitment, not compliance. This is achieved through designing the system to enable attention to feedback, removing stressors, facilitating participation in problem-solving, running suggestion systems and team based planning. Therefore predominant mode of action is listening and facilitation of group problem solving. Group problem solving reduces group stress levels by meeting emotional needs including: attention, stretch, a feeling of autonomy and control and a feeling of connectedness to a wider community. Organisational objectives and values are more easily genuinely shared and also tend to emerge from the group process.

TDCCL	Collaborative leadership
	This leadership approach engenders enthusiasm, commitment, higher levels of individual competence and greater interconnectivity between the parts of the organisation.
Leaders are highly assertive, action orientated with a tendency for hands on intervention especially in reaction to a crisis. Reactive troubleshooting can be incessant leading to stress, confusion, turbulence and inherent waste of energy and resources.	Leaders tend to train, study, think and delegate more with attention to root cause analysis, impact analysis and pro-active planning that tends to anticipate events and stakeholder needs before a crisis occurs. Progress is more stable and less trouble-shooting results in less waste and a lot less stress.
Static view of motivation requires little or no psychological skill-set. Reliance on assertiveness and self-confidence of leader, also on their accounting and other intellectual or technical skills.	Primary role of minimising stress in the working environment and the understanding of the variable nature of motivation, requires a skill-set that includes an understanding of the emotional and other biological needs (the human givens) that influence the stress response. Also competence to identify the impact of stress on thinking and work performance and the ability to handle the 30 + potential stress factors that create stress in a working environment. Just as important as technical abilities are a high degree of emotional intelligence specifically social awareness, the ability to empathise and give attention to others.
Decision-making	
A confidential or secret decision-making process controlled and engaged in entirely by senior management. However thorough the actual process, it provides unpredictable results for other stakeholders and therefore can provoke confusion and apprehension as it violates the need for security and the feeling of being part of a wider community. Commitment by staff to the end result is often low.	Structured team based planning process that is transparent, accessible to all stakeholders, easy-to-use and consistent in design. These features enable ease of participation by all parties. The collaborative process engenders lower stress levels that are otherwise often inherent in the ambiguity and uncertainty around decision-making. Lower stress enables participants to undertake deeper analysis involving the assimilation of a wider body of views

TDCCL	Collaborative leadership
	and more reasoned evaluation of a variety of options. One immediate benefit is a much higher level of staff buy-in to new initiatives.
Tendency for upward delegation of decision-making brings undue delays in response to external change. The final decision then meets inherent resistance from employees fearful of not being in control of their own destiny and fearful of real or imagined management intent.	Collaborative decision-making and planning devolved to the lowest operational level and involving multidirectional feedback loops provides timely, adept and flexible responses to environmental change with ready buy-in from junior employees.
Mistakes made during adrenaline-fuelled crisis management perpetuate problems and lead to unintended consequences arising.	The low stress levels inherent in a calm and collected collaborative planning environment optimise use of analytical skills, imagination and creativity, long-term memory, and rational judgement. This further helps provide robust "right first time" decisions, creative thinking and effective anticipation of customer needs.
Docile compliance and conformance is the predominant individual survival strategy leading to abdication of responsibility upwards to senior authority. The inevitable result is senior management are perpetually too busy and taking on far too much. The result at the higher level of the organisation is stress and decision-making paralysis or rushed and botched decision-making – knee-jerk reactions to events rather than a structured, balanced consultative approach to decision-making.	Lively commitment, initiative and enterprise, eager ownership of problems and stimulation of problem solving at the level of problem. The result is faster but more thorough decision-making and a more rapid response to changing customer needs or other circumstances.
Culture	
Ultimately TDCC relies on coercion, however innocuous or mild this is. In essence TDCCL is based on the deeply embedded cultural expectation of implicit submissiveness evoked by the customary boss subordinate relationship. This is always liable to trigger a stress response among employees due to the impact on	Relaxed atmosphere found in a collaborative environment epitomised by a higher degree of creativity and flow, and a higher degree of enthusiasm. People are functioning at a point much nearer their full potential.

300

TDCCL	Collaborative leadership
the individual's need for security and some autonomy and control. Where this occurs you get high stress levels in the work environment that reduce individual enthusiasm, competence, and commitment and decrease group coherence.	
General air of secrecy, often styled as confidentiality, creates anxiety about security and leads to the withholding of bottom-up information about performance and stakeholder needs. This secrecy further restricts the senior management's bounded rationality.	Exhilarating atmosphere of openness, frankness and honesty stimulates active discussion as to areas of weakness and opportunities for performance improvements.
Employees' needs for status, and a challenge are invariably violated to some extent in this type of regime as are the needs for a challenge and some degree of autonomy and control. Impotent subordinates feel they are in a psychic prison; people feel stifled, frustrated and undervalued. Good people tend to leave; dysfunctional people stay on.	Empowered subordinates benefit from emotional satisfaction. Collaborative leadership helps meet full range of biological needs – the 'human givens' that reduce stress and optimise individual competence.
Internal competitiveness and political manoeuvring between both individuals and departments fighting for resources and power within the system leads to waste. Stress levels are aroused by feelings of insecurity and disconnectedness to the wider group.	People collaborate naturally towards common goals directed at the betterment of the whole organisation not just the individual parts or individual careers. Collaborative problem solving focuses on customer or organisational needs and progressively eliminates waste and lifts motivation.
Image driven activity; fear of blame and criticism leads to prevalence of "impression management". This includes an unhealthy 'box ticking culture' whereby there is a focus on risk avoidance to hide incompetence and mistakes and so avoid blame and protect careers rather focus on the customers' or clients' needs.	Substance driven activity; mistakes are naturally embraced as learning experiences enhancing an atmosphere of openness and trust. The absence of criticism means that people's focus is always on achieving authentic results in line with the purpose of the organisation.
Politically correct actions geared to compliance with ideological imperatives.	Spontaneous right action appropriate for the moment and the need of the time

301

TDCCL	Collaborative leadership
This breeds stress through feelings of non-alignment with authentic individual values and probable lack of security – people don't really know where they stand.	and naturally aligned with the group's ethics. Feeling of flow and connectivity with the group all helps improve collaborative working, commitment and enthusiasm.
Atmosphere of compliance and fear of blame can sometimes make major issues taboo. Few people want to be thought of as a troublemaker, by bringing up touchy subjects. Mavericks are discouraged as their unnerving habit of exposing management and organisational weaknesses is seen as a threat to the status quo.	Openness and trust, absence of criticism, the continual improvement principle with the understanding that every situation can be improved, enables head-on tackling of difficult and important issues. Mavericks and free thinkers are seen as an antidote to group think and valued for the original contribution they can make to analysis and solution finding.
A proportion of employees' activity and energy is aimed at fulfilling targets, regardless of the impact these individual targets have on the whole system. Little evidence of any "double feedback loop" – people questioning the why of what they are doing and working to improve things. The need to comply with targets creates stress as it violates a number of emotional needs such as the need for autonomy and control and also the needs for meaning, status and recognition of one's value.	Widespread multidirectional communication of the true facts of the situation, an atmosphere of mutual trust and openness, an absence of criticism when mistakes occur and the authority to question the status quo means that where changes are necessary, activity and energy is quickly realigned with overall organisational needs. The ability to think for oneself, take the initiative and apply enterprise is highly motivating as it meets a number of emotional needs such as the need for autonomy and control, a challenge, a feeling of competence and so on.
Leadership and management ethic	
Limited understanding of the variable factors of human nature impacting performance means that these human factors are ignored in goal setting. Profit and shareholder value tend to become raison d'être of existence in the private sector as does ideological goals in the public sector. So the ends tend to justify the means. The needs for security, attention, meaning and connectedness are violated as employees recognise they are just dispensable pawns in a corporate or	Understanding of importance of satisfying wider human needs to reduce stress and to enhance performance leads to focus on wholeness rather than just limited goals such as bottom line profit or a narrow ideological belief system. The journey therefore becomes indivisible from the destination. People enjoy the ride.

302

TDCCL	Collaborative leadership
political game.	
Egocentric motivation – The leader creates and drives the vision for others to follow.	Group based motivation – The leader facilitates the emergence of a group vision through consensus creating continuous improvement initiatives. These initiatives involve all stakeholders in problem-solving activity and feedback about the environment particularly about customer needs and organisational constraints. Implicit recognition that the leader is an instrument of the group's collective conscious not the driver of it.
Management acts in the belief that the principle variable factor in the system is people's adherence to the protocols running it. The 'system', owned by the senior management is deemed to be a fixed reference point. Thus there is a stressful emphasis on maintaining compliance with protocols and finding individuals to blame when something goes wrong. The belief in the infallibility of 'their' system obstructs even further the ability of management to discover the truth about the faults and weaknesses in the system and means energy, time and resources are expended on finding culprits rather than the root causes of system failure.	Recognition that 90%-95% of problems, arise from defects in the system design and only 5%-10% from the individuals. Variation within a system is seen as almost unavoidable and part of the objective of any improvement is to stabilise it. Hence emphasis is on group engagement in the root cause of system's failure leading to 'continual improvement' of the system design and task specific training of existing members to match the ongoing changes in roles and responsibilities.

Group engagement in meaningful work for the benefit of the host group meets the needs for community connection, stretch, attention, status and recognition, and meaning, hence stress levels are reduced and individual performance improved. |
| Part of the TDCC management function is the establishment of manuals, standard operating procedures and best practice and then ensuring conformance with these. | Recognition that nothing is perfect but that constant improvement is possible drives managers to facilitate employees' self-regulating faculties. Management focuses on obtaining ongoing feedback and suggestions from all stakeholders about defects in the system and how they can be rectified. |
| As the system is a fixed phenomena, so | Recognition that change is the natural |

TDCCL	Collaborative leadership
change management is seen as a discrete art to be applied at some point in time, where a major rethink is required due to major changes in the environment.	order of things and that without change systems collapse into atrophy. Managing change by facilitating ongoing stakeholder feedback in a continual improvement process is therefore all part of a collaborative leader's everyday skill set.

Appendix 2

Notes, research references and further reading

Introduction

1   Numerous recent NHS scandals include the revelations of hundreds of fatalities at Mid Staffordshire NHS Trust and the numerous deaths at the University Hospital of Morecombe Bay NHS Trust maternity unit, subsequently covered up by the NHS's own watch dog the Quality Care Commission.

2   Booker, C. *Our 'child protection' system is an international scandal,* - Children of foreign families resident in the UK are being seized by social workers on an astonishing scale; Daily Telegraph 20th Jul 2013

Cheston, P. *Baby P scandal council Haringey blunders again over child care* - Social workers shamed by Baby P scandal face new condemnation - investigation on blameless parents ruled unlawful by judge; London Evening Standard 14th March 2013

3   Jay Alexis OBE; *Independent enquiry into child sexual exploitation in Rotherham 1997 – 2013*; commissioned by Rotherham Metropolitan Borough Council; report dated 21st August 2014. "Our conservative estimate is that approximately 1,400 children were sexually abused over the full period from 1997 to 2013". The abuse was carried out predominantly by gangs of British Pakistani men. The social services and police already knew of about a third of the children involved, but despite this fact, reports of rape, torture, abduction and sex trafficking were ignored or disbelieved by management. Failure was described as blatant by the report's author. Three previous enquiries had revealed similar findings but were "effectively suppressed". The response to one Home Office researcher, who raised concerns with the Police, is typical of how the pursuit of 'ideological imperatives' can distort an organisation's purpose so that it becomes the reverse of what it is supposed to be doing. The researcher was told not to raise the issue of 'Asian men' again and placed on a two-day ethnicity and diversity course to raise her awareness of ethnic issues.

4   About 46.7 million prescriptions for antidepressants were dispensed in England in 2011. This is a 9.1% increase on 2010 to record levels and makes antidepressants the largest single category of drugs dispensed by the NHS; *Health and Social Care Information Centre bulletin*, January 2014.

Similarly, the rate of antidepressant use in the United States has increased by nearly 400% to record levels over the last two decades, according to a joint report (October 2013) released by the Centre for Disease Control and Preventions and the National Centre for Health Statistics. A National Health and Nutrition Examination Survey found that antidepressants are the most frequently used medication by people in the USA between the ages of 18 and 44.

5   Unemployment in the European Union is estimated at 12.1% or 26.553 million people. This means that a number of people roughly equivalent to the entire working population of Great Britain and the Netherlands combined are unable to work. The hardest hit due to inept government policy and leadership are Greece and Spain who have eye-watering unemployment rates of 27.4% and 26.7% respectively (Eurostat).

The USA, although in a healthier state, still has high levels of unemployment at 6.7%, which means there are still 10.4 million people out of work (Bureau of Labor Statistics Employment situation summary, January 2014).

Chapter One

1   Tyrrell, I. *Trance-Form*, an audiotape produced by the European Studies Institute. ISBN 1 899398 15 5.

2   Athique, M. *Ayurveda: The art of healthy living, Guide to physical, mental and spiritual health and healing.* Mauroof Athique, 20 Annes Grove, Great Linford, Milton Keynes, MK14 5DR, pp. 212 'Negative emotional traits of the three different psycho-physiological types in Ayurveda – Vata (changeable) Pitta (hot) Kapha (solid and steady)'.

3   Sharma, H.; Clark, C. *Contemporary Ayurveda*, Churchill Livingstone, Medical guides to complementary and alternative medicine. ISBN 0 443 05594 7. Chapter 5 'Psychological characteristics of three dosha types in Ayurveda'.

4   Jex, S.M.; Bliese, P.D. *Efficacy beliefs as a moderator of the impact of work-related stressors: A multilevel study*; Journal of Applied Psychology. Vol 84(3), Jun 1999, 349-361.

5   Valentin, A. et al. *British Medical Journal, Errors in administration of parenteral drugs in intensive care units: multinational prospective study, on behalf of Research Group on Quality Improvement of the European Society of Intensive Care Medicine (ESICM) and the Sentinel Events Evaluation (SEE) study investigations.* BMJ 2009; 338; b814 12/3/09.

6   East of England Ambulance Service report showed the service had failed to meet its target response times for 95% of Category A patients in life-threatening situations and details 155 serious incidents including 59 unexpected or avoidable deaths of patients. This figure reflects a near doubling of serious incidents on the

previous year. BBC report 8th January 2014.

Chapter Two

1 Griffin, J.; Tyrrell, I. *Human Givens.* A new approach to emotional health and clear thinking. HG Publishing, ISBN 1 899398 31 7.

2 Martin, P. *The sickening mind, brain, behaviour, immunity and disease.*, Chpt 5 The demon stress, pp. 126 – 134. Harper Collins, ISBN 0 00 655022 3.

3 Goleman, D. *Emotional Intelligence.* Bloomsbury Publishing PLC, ISBN 0-7475-2830-6.

4 Griffin, J.; Tyrrell, I. *Human Givens.* Chpt 9 The APET model: the key to effective psychotherapy. HG Publishing, ISBN 1 899398 31 7.

5 Tian Xu; Ming Wu; Pastor-Pareja, J.C. Stress triggers tumor formation; Yale University, school of medicine on line article, 13th January 2010. Stress induces signals that cause cancer cells to develop.

Chapter Three

1 Maslow, A.H. *Motivation and personality.* New York Harper and Brothers, 1954.

2 Herzberg, F,; Mausner, B.; Synderman, B.B. *The Motivation to Work.* Chapman and Hall, 1959.

3 Adair, J. *Leadership and Motivation.* Kogan Page, ISBN 978 0 7494 5482 1.

4 Griffin,J.; Tyrrell, I. *Human Givens.* HG Publishing, ISBN 1 899398 31 7.

5 Mayo, E. *The human problems of an industrial civilization.* Macmillan,1933.

6 Haslam et al. *Maintaining group memberships: social identity continuity predicts well-being after stroke.* Neuropsychological Rehabilitation, vol 18 2008.

7 Prof Cacioppo. *Loneliness: Human nature and the need for connection.* University of Chicago.

8 Griffin, J,; Tyrrell, I. *Human Givens.* Chpt 5. HG Publishing, ISBN 1 899398 31 7.

9 Wood, S.; de Menezes, L.M. *High involvement management, high performance work systems and well-being.* International journal of human resource management 2011, vol 22 No 7, pp 1585-1608.

10 Putnam, R.D. *Bowling alone: The collapse and revival of American community.* Simon & Schuster 2000.

11   Branscombe, N.R.; Schmitt, M.T.; Harvey, R.D. *The Internal and External Causal Loci of Attributions to Prejudice*. Journal of personality and social psychology, 2009.

12   Loo, R.; Thorpe K.; *Using reflective learning journals to improve individual and team performance*. Team Performance Management, vol 8 Iss: 5/6, pp.134 - 139

13   Griffin, J.; Tyrrell, I. *Human Givens,* Chpt 1. HG Publishing, ISBN 1 899398 31 7.

14   Crawford, M. *The case for working with your hands: Or why office work is bad for us and fixing things feels good.* Penguin, ISBN10: 0670918741.

15   Griffin, J.; Tyrrell, I. Human Givens, Chpt 1. HG Publishing, ISBN 1 899398 31 7.

16   Inzlicht, M.; McGregor, I.; Hirsh, J.; Nash, K. *Neural Markers of Religious Conviction*. Psychological Science, March 2009.

17   Mears, P.; Voehl, F. *Teambuilding a structured learning approach*, Chapter 2, Contributors to continuous quality improvement. St Lucie press, ISBN 1 884015 15 8.

18   Archbishop Sentamu. *Hell is an eternal maxed-out credit card. In heaven there are no debts*. The Times, 24th December 2008.

19   Sharma, H.; Clark, C. *Contemporary Ayurveda, medicine and research in Maharishi Ayur-Veda.* Churchill Livingstone, ISBN 0 443 05594 7.

Chapter Four

1   Humphrey, A.; Groves, P. *Turning downturn into major upturn.* Finance Today, 2003.

2   Griffin, J.; Tyrrell, I. *Human Givens*, HG Publishing ISBN 1 899398 31 7.

3   Heider, J. *The Tao of leadership.* Chpt 27. Wildwood House 1986, ISBN 0 7045 0528 2.

4   Griffin, J.; Tyrrell, I. *Human Givens*, Chpt 5 The human givens and the need for security. HG Publishing, ISBN 1 899398 31 7.

5   Goleman, D. *Emotional Intelligence,* Chpt 7 The roots of empathy, The neurology of empathy, pp 102-104. Bloomsbury Publishing PLC - ISBN 0-7475-2830-6.

6   Egbert, L.D.; Battit,G.E.; Welch, C.E.; Bartlett, M.K. *Reduction of postoperative pain by encouragement and instruction of patients.* New England Journal of Medicine, 270, 825-827.

7   Goleman, D.; Boyatzis, R.; McKee, A. *Primal leadership* Chpt 3. Harvard

Business School Press, ISBN 1-57851-486-X.

8   Levenson, R.; Ruef, A. *Empathy a physiological substrate*, Journal of Personality and social Psychology 63, 2 1992.

9   Deikman, A.J. *The Observing Self.* Beacon Press, Boston, ISBN 0-8070-2951-3. 1982.

10   Davies, P. *God and the new physics*. Penguin Books, 1984.

11   Capra, F. *The Tao of Physics.* Flamingo 1983, ISBN 0 00 654489 4.

12   Nader, T. *Human Physiology, expression of Veda and the Vedic literature.* 4th edition, Maharishi Vedic University, Netherlands, ISBN 81-7523-017-7, 2000.

13   *Patanjali's Yoga Sutras* (circa 300 BC), translated by Rama Prasada, Munshiram Manoharial, Publishers Pvt Ltd, New Delhi, 1995, ISBN 81-215-0424-0.

14   Walton, K.G.; Cavanaugh, K.L.; Pugh, N.D. *Effect of group practice of the Transcendental Meditation program on biochemical indicators of stress in non-meditators: A prospective time series study.* Journal of Social Behaviour and Personality 2005;17(1):339-376. Reductions of behavioural indicators of stress such as changes in cortisol and serotonin levels in control subjects 20 miles away.

15   Pugh, N.D.; Walton, K.G.; Cavanaugh, K.L. *Can time series analysis of serotonin turnover test the theory that consciousness is a field?* Society for Neuroscience Abstracts 14: 372, 1988. "Group practice (of Transcendental Meditation) actually reduces the effects of stress, in those in the vicinity, in a manner similar to the reduction within the individual meditator when he practices the Transcendental Meditation programme." – Walton.

16   Travis, F.T.; Orme-Johnson, D.W. *Field model of consciousness: EEG coherence changes as indicators of field effects.* International Journal of Neuroscience 1989 December; *49(3-4)203-11*. Synchronised changes in EEG patterns generated between meditators and non-meditating subjects.

17   Orme-Johnson, D.W.; Dillbeck, M.C.; Wallace, R.K. *Inter-subject EEG coherence: Is consciousness a field?;* International Journal of Neuroscience 16: 203 – 209, 1982. Synchronised changes in EEG coherence seen between meditators and non-meditating subjects at a distance

18   Orme-Johnson, D.W.; Alexander, C.N.; Davies, J.L.; Chandler, H.M.; Larimore, W.E. *International peace project in the Middle East: The effect of the Maharishi Technology of the Unified Field,* Journal of Conflict Resolution, 32(4): 776-812, 1988. Findings: Improved quality of national life as measured by composite indices comprising data on war intensity in Lebanon, newspaper content analysis of Israeli national mood, Tel Aviv stock index, automobile accident rate in Jerusalem, number of fires in Jerusalem, and maximum temperature in Jerusalem. Significant improvement in each variable in the index (Israel, 1983). Decreased war deaths (Lebanon, 1983).

19   Hatchard, G.D.; Deans, A.J.; Cavanaugh, K.L.; Orme-Johnson, D.W. *The*

Maharishi effect: A model for social-improvement. Time series analysis of a phase transition to reduced crime in Merseyside metropolitan area. Psychology, Crime & Law, Volume 2 Issue 3 1996. pp 165 – 174. (See chapter 11 references for further information.)

20   MC Dillbeck, CB Banus, C Polanzi, GS Landrith III, *Test of a field model of consciousness and social change: the Transcendental Meditation and TM-Sidhi Programme and decreased urban crime.* The Journal of Mind and Behaviour 9(4): 457-486, 1988. Findings: Improved quality of city life: Decreased crime rate (Cities and Metropolitan Areas, U.S., 1973-1979). Decreased violent crime (Washington, D.C., 1981-1983).

21   Dillbeck, M.C.; Kavanaugh, K.L.; Glenn, T.; Orme-Johnson, D.W; Mittlefehldt, V. *Consciousness as a field: the Transcendental Meditation and TM-Sidhi Programme and changes in social indicators.* The Journal of Mind and Behavior 8(1): 67-104, 1987. Findings: Improved quality of life in cities and territories. Decreased crime (Union Territory of Delhi, 1980-1981. Metro Manila, 1984-1985. Puerto Rico, 1984). Improvements on monthly quality of life indices in territories and states: Metro Manila Region, 1979-1981, including crime, foetal deaths, and other deaths, State of Rhode Island, U.S., 1978, including crime rate, motor vehicle fatality rate, mortality rate for other causes, auto accident rate, unemployment rate, pollution, beer consumption rate, and cigarette consumption rate.

22   Griffin, J.; Tyrrell, I . *How dreaming keeps us sane, or can drive us mad. Dreaming reality.* HG Publishing, ISBN 1 899398 36 8.

23   Keltner, D. *Born to be good: The science of a meaningful life.* WW Norton 2009. Discusses research carried out at the Social Interaction Laboratory, University of California about how the vagus nerve seems particularly adapted to promote altruistic activity. The research suggests that human capacity for virtue, cooperation and a moral sense are actually old in evolutionary terms. Born to be good means that our evolution has equipped us with qualities of self-sacrifice, generosity, kindness, fun, play, reverence which are required for group survival and of course gene replication.

24   Hardy, J.B. *The Hidden Game revealed.* e-book, www.johnberlinghardy.com.

25   Colman, Pulford, Rose, *Team reasoning and collective rationality: Piercing the veil of obviousness,* Acta Psychologica 19th May 2008.

Chapter Five

1   Burns, T.; Stalker, G.M. *The Management of Innovation.* London Tavistock, 1961.

2   Morgan, G. *Images of organisations*, Chapter 3. Sage publications Inc. ISBN 0 7619 0632 0.

3   Seddon, J. *Systems thinking in the public sector, The failure of the reform regime and a manifesto for a better way*; Triarchy Press 2008; ISBN 978 0 9550081 8 4. Senge P.M., *The fifth discipline, The art and practice of the learning organisation;* Random House 2006; ISBN 978 1 9052112 0 3

4   Womack J.P. Jones, D.T. *Lean Thinking, Banish waste and create wealth in your corporation.* Simon and Schuster, 2003, ISBN 13: 978 0 7432 3164 0.

5   Timpson, J. *Upside down management, A common sense guide to better business.* Wiley, 2010, ISBN 978 0 470 68945 5.

6   Stewart, R.F. *Informal history of SRI planning research work carried out from the 1950's by SRI's Long range planning service (LRPS) and the TAPP study (Theory and Practice of Planning).* Also private conversations with Albert Humphrey former research consultant at SRI with the TAPP study and founder of Team Action Management. See chapter 11 ref 15 for further details.

7   Semlar, R. *Maverick, The success story behind the world's most unusual workplace, Arrow* . ISBN 0-09-932941-7.

8   Spector, R.; McCarthy, P. *The Nordstrom way to customer service excellence, A handbook for implementing great service in your organisation.* John Wiley & Sons Inc, ISBN 0 471 70286 2.

9   http://sociocracyuk.ning.com/

10   Jones, A. *A life in service.* Human Givens Journal, vol 16, No 2 – 2009.

Chapter Six

1   Seddon, J. *Systems thinking in the public sector, the failure of the reform regime and a manifesto for a better way.* Triarchy Press, 2008 ISBN 978 0 9550081 8 4.

2   Crizzle, A. Hillcroft House survey, *UK Management Culture of Fear, HR magazine,* April 2013. Survey of 1,000 UK employees about performance appraisal processes and results, leadership qualities of direct line managers and overall job satisfaction levels reported 93% (up from 49% in 2008) would strongly consider leaving their employer. Survey indicated this lack of effective skills could lead to increased levels of conflict and stress in the workplace, poor working relationships and poor performance.

3   Morgan, G. *Images of organization.* Chpt 4 Learning and self organization, organizations as brains. Sage Publications, 1997, ISBN 0 7619 0634 7.

4   Anderson, C.; Kilduff, G. *Why do dominant personalities attain influence in face-to-face groups?* The competence – signalling effect of trait dominance.

Journal of personality and social psychology, February 2009.

5   Christian E. Gimsø 'Narcissus and Leadership Potential - The measurement and implications of narcissism in leadership selection processes'; Doctoral dissertation May 2014, BI Norwegian Business School. The findings indicate that narcissistic candidates are more likely to get selected as leaders.

6   Bromhall, C. 2004. The eternal child, Chpt 2 How evolution has made children of us all. Random House, ISBN 0091894425.

7   Griffin, J.; Tyrrell, I. Human Givens. Ch 5, p122 – 123. HG Publishing ISBN 1 899398 31 7.

8   Stewart, R.F. Informal history of SRI planning research work carried out from the 1950's by SRI's Long range planning service (LRPS) and the TAPP study (Theory and Practice of Planning). See chapter 11 ref 15 for further details.

9   Wood, S.; de Menezes, L.M. 2011. High involvement management, high performance work systems and well-being, International journal of human resource management, vol 22 No 7, pp 1585-1608.

10   Bromhall, C. 2004. The eternal child, Chpt 2 How evolution has made children of us all. Random House, ISBN 0091894425.

11   Klucharev, V. Reinforcement learning signal predicts social conformity, The Donders Centre for Cognitive Neuroimaging in Nijmegen, The Netherlands, Neuron vol 61, page 140.

12   Wiltermouth, S.S.; Heath, C. Synchrony and Cooperation, , Psychological Science, vol 20, p 1. Stanford University in California.

13   Haidt, J.; Seder, J.P.; Kesebir, S. Hive Psychology, Happiness, and Public Policy; University of Virginia, Journal of Legal Studies, DOI: 10.1086/529447.

14   de Waal, F. Professor of primate behaviour at Emory University, Atlanta, New Scientist 28th January 2009.

     de Waal, F. Our Inner Ape, Riverhead Trade, ISBN13: 9781594481963.

15   Camerer, C.F.; Fehr, E. When Does "Economic Man" Dominate Social Behavior? Science 6 January 2006: Vol. 311. no. 5757, pp. 47 - 52 DOI: 10.1126/science.1110600. Game theory is now beginning to understand that self-regarding behaviour does not always dominate social interaction.

16   Mujica-Parodi, L. reported in New Scientist prior to publishing research findings, Smell of fear, Stony Brook University, New York, December 2008 US Defence Advanced Research Projects Agency project… (See references Ch 4, ref 46).

17   Fowler, J.H.; Christakis, N.A. Dynamic spread of happiness in a large social network: Longitudinal analysis over twenty years in the Framingham Heart Study BMJ 2008; 337: a 2338, doi: 10.1136/bmj.a2338 4/12/2008 "Clusters of happy and unhappy people are visible in the network.

18   Pugh, N.D.; Walton, K.G.; Cavanaugh, K.L. Can time series analysis of serotonin turnover test the theory that consciousness is a field? Society for

Neuroscience Abstracts 14: *372*, 1988... (See references Chpt 4, ref 15).

19 Timpson, J. *Upside down management, A common sense guide to better business*, Wiley, 2010, ISBN 978 0 470 68945 5.

20 Humphrey, A.; Groves, P. 2003. *Turning downturn into major upturn*, Finance Today.

21 Bicheno, J. *The new lean toolbox, towards fast, flexible flow*. PICSIE Books, ISBN 0 9541 2441 3.

22 Dyer, J. *Collaborative Advantage*, Oxford University Press.

23 Semlar, R. *Maverick, The success story behind the world's most unusual workplace*. Arrow , ISBN 0-09-932941-7.

24 Griffin, J.; Tyrrell, I. *Human Givens*. HG Publishing, ISBN 1 899398 31 7.

25 Goleman, D.; Boyatzis, R.; McKee, A. *Primal leadership*. Harvard Business School Press, ISBN 1-57851-486-X.

26 Goleman, D. *Emotional Intelligence*. Bloomsbury Publishing PLC – ISBN 0-7475-2830-6.

Chapter Seven

1 Seddon, J. *Systems thinking in the public sector, the failure of the reform regime and a manifesto for a better way*. Triarchy Press, 2008, ISBN 978 0 9550081 8 4.

2 Seddon, J. 2003. *Freedom from Command and Control a better way to make the work, work*. Vanguard Education Ltd.

3 Van Vulpen, M. *Go with the flow: the common sense way to run our public services*, Human Givens Journal Vol 16, No 1 2009, pgs 24 – 30, interview with Professor John Seddon.

4 Ali Baba-Akbari Sari, research fellow, Trevor A Sheldon, professor of health sciences, pro-vice chancellor, Alison Cracknell, specialist registrar, Alastair Turnbull, consultant physician, *Sensitivity of routine system for reporting patient safety incidents in an NHS hospital: retrospective patient case note review*, British Medical Journal BMJ 2007;334:79 (13 January), doi:10.1136/bmj.39031.507153.AE (published 15 December 2006) This study indicates that preventable mistakes in NHS hospitals might be killing or directly contributing to the deaths of 91,030 people a year. Although only an estimate this figure is up from an earlier estimate of only 20,000 in 1997 and a subsequent estimate of 34,000 in 2005. It seems the more money that is spent on the NHS the more people are inadvertently killed. Incidentally this estimate does not include any cases where the patient was in hospital for less than a day, had

mental health problems or gave birth; neither does it include patients in ambulance trusts and general practice or patients affected by hospital-acquired infections. So the real mortality rate for preventable errors is going to be somewhat higher. There were 9.1 million hospital stays in England in 2005/6 out of which 910,303 people are estimated to have suffered harm due to a range of mistakes. These errors include errors during surgery, misdiagnosis, falls, infections, equipment failures, wrong dosage of drugs and medical complications. In 15 per cent of cases the harm inflicted resulted in impairment or disability that lasted for more than six months and increased the average stay in hospital by eight days. The researchers estimated that up to a half of these mistakes were preventable.

Further report by Rebecca Smith, Medical Editor in the *Daily Telegraph*, 'Hospital blunders kill 90,000 patients', 30th Nov 2007.

5   Semlar, R. *Maverick, The success story behind the world's most unusual workplace*. Arrow , ISBN 0-09-932941-7.

6   Jay, A. *Corporation Man.* Who is he, what he does, why his ancient tribal impulses dominate.Pelican, 1971, 9780 1402 19111.

7   Griffin, J.; Tyrrell, I. *Human Givens*, page 122. HG Publishing ISBN 1 899398 31 7.

8   Stanford, N. *Guide to organization design,* The Economist in association with Profile Books, Creating high-performing and adaptable enterprises, p. 10–14. ISBN 978 1 86197 802 8.

9   Semlar, R. *Maverick, The success story behind the world's most unusual workplace*, Chpt 14 - Too big for our own good. Arrow , ISBN 0-09-932941-7.

Chapter Eight

1   Kerridge, D. *Dr Deming's cure for a sick system,* Journal for quality and participation, Dec 1996.

2   Kate Wighton, Interview with Russell Foster, Professor of Circadian Neuroscience at Oxford University, article *Waiting for that life-changing idea? Just sleep on it,* Times Online, 22nd November 2008.

3   *A prospective study of the effects of the Transcendental Meditation programme in two business settings, Anxiety, Stress and Coping;* International Journal 6: 245-262, 1993. The study on managers and employees showed increased relaxation and less stress among the TM meditators. Basically, TM practitioners displayed : more relaxed physiological functioning, a greater reduction in anxiety, reduced tension on the job. The study included comparisons with non-meditating control

subjects who had similar job positions in the same companies.

4   Eppley, K.; Abrams, A.; Shear. J. *Differential effects of relaxation techniques on trait anxiety: a meta-analysis.* SRI (Stanford Research Institute), Journal of Clinical Psychology, 1989, 45(6): 957-974. Researchers carried out a meta-analysis of 104 independent studies on the effects of different trait relaxation techniques. The meta-analysis demonstrated that Transcendental Meditation is more effective than other techniques of meditation or relaxation.

5   *Transcendental Meditation and improved performance on intelligence-related measures: A longitudinal study,* Personality and Individual Differences 12: 1105-1116, 1991. Longitudinal effects of the Transcendental Meditation and TM-Sidhi programme on cognitive ability and cognitive style, published in *Perceptual and Motor Skills 62: 731-738, 1986.*

6   Lyubimov, N.N. *Electrophysiological characteristics of mobilisation of hidden brain reserves;* Abstracts of the International Symposium 'Physiological and biochemical basis of brain activity' (pg 5). St Petersburg, Russia, 22nd – 24th June 1994.

Lyubimov, N.N. *Mobilisation of the hidden reserves of the brain;* programme abstracts of the 2nd Russian-Swedish symposium 'New research in neurobiology' Moscow, Russia, 19th – 21st May 1992.

7   *The Transcendental Meditation technique and creativity: A longitudinal study of Cornell University undergraduates;* published by the Journal of Creative Behavior 13: 169-190, 1979.

A psychological investigation into the source of the effect of the Transcendental Meditation technique, (Ph.D. dissertation, York University) published in Dissertations Abstracts International 38, 7-B: 3372-3373, 1978.

8   Haratani, T. et al. *Effects of Transcendental Meditation on the mental health of industrial workers.* Japanese Journal of Industrial Health 32: 656, 1990.

Haratani, T. et al. *Effects of Transcendental Meditation on the health behavior of industrial workers.* Japanese Journal of Public Health 37 (10 Suppl.): 729, 1990.

9   Miskiman, D.E. *The Treatment of Insomnia by the Transcendental Meditation Program, Scientific Research on the Transcendental Meditation Program,* Graduate Department of Psychology, University of Alberta, Edmonton, Canada, published in Collected Papers, vol. 1, ISBN 90 71750 04 3 eds. D.W. Orme-Johnson and J.T. Farrow. New York: MERU. Press, 1977d.

Miskiman, D.E. *Long-term Effects of the Transcendental Meditation Program in the Treatment of Insomnia, Scientific Research on the Transcendental Meditation Program,* Graduate Department of Psychology, University of Alberta, Edmonton, Canada, published in Collected Papers, vol. 1, ISBN 90 71750 04 3 eds. D.W. Orme-Johnson and J.T. Farrow. New York:

MERU Press, 1977b.

10   *The Transcendental Meditation technique and creativity: A longitudinal study of Cornell University undergraduates,* Journal of Creative Behavior 13: 169-190, 1979.
A psychological investigation into the source of the effect of the Transcendental Meditation technique (Ph.D. dissertation, York University) published in Dissertations Abstracts International 38, 7-B: 3372-3373, 1978. The TM group scored significantly higher on figural originality and flexibility and on verbal fluency using Torrance Tests of creative thinking.

11   *Influence of Transcendental Meditation upon autokinetic perception,* Perceptual Motor Skills 39: 1031-1034, 1974.
Longitudinal effects of the Transcendental Meditation and TM-Sidhi programme on cognitive ability and cognitive style, Perceptual and Motor Skills 62: 731-738, 1986. Results show that practice of the Transcendental Meditation technique improves field independence for the practitioner. This improvement is an important finding as it was previously thought that these basic perceptual abilities do not improve beyond early adulthood.

12   Orme-Johnson, D.W. *Medical care utilization and the Transcendental Meditation program,* Psychosomatic Medicine 1987, 49:493-507. A retrospective study was published in The American Journal of Managed Care vol 3 No 1 January 1997. Data collected by US health insurance company showed that a national TM meditating cohort of 2,000 people went to the hospital 56% less often for sickness or surgery than the control group of 600,000 people. The TM group needed 50% fewer doctors visits.

13   Anderson, J.W. et al. *Blood pressure response to Transcendental Meditation: a meta-analysis,* published by the American Journal of Hypertension 2008 21:310-316. A meta-analysis carried out by an independent team confirmed that the TM programme leads to clinically important reductions in blood pressure; this conclusion was robust when only the highest quality research was analyzed. The authors conclude that sustained blood pressure changes of the magnitude produced by TM would be associated with substantially decreased risk of heart attack and stroke, the leading cause of mortality worldwide

14   Maharishi Mahesh Yogi, *Wholeness on the move,* Maharishi University of management. Maharishi Prakashan, 1SBN 81 7523 001 0.

15   Harung, H. PhD, *Invincible leadership,* MUM Press, Fairfield Iowa, 1999.

16   Wood, S.; de Menezes, L.M. *High involvement management, high performance work systems and well-being.* International journal of human resource management 2011, vol 22 No 7, pp 1585-1608.

17   Fisher, K. *Leading self-directed teams,* McGraw-Hill Inc, ISBN 0-07-021071-3.

18   Ralph, D. *The effectiveness of self-directed teams at Wesley Jessen,* MBA Dissertation, Bournemouth University Business School, 1998

19   Deming W.E. *The new economics for industry, government and education*, MIT Press edition, ISBN 0 262 54116 5.

Chapter Nine

1   Hall, K., Savery, L.K. *Stress management, Management Decision*, Vol 25 no 6 1987 pp 29-35, Research carried out in Western Australia demonstrated that incompetent delegation led to lack of autonomy which was stressful to the managers concerned. It was found that stress was often created by the actual hierarchical structure not facilitating sufficient autonomy to fulfil the task. There was a resultant delay in projects and undermining of managers' authority within their own departments.

2   Sirota, D.; Mischkind, L.A. ; Meltzer, M.I. *Stop de-motivating your employees*, Harvard Management Update, Vol. 11, No. 1, January 2006.

3   Goleman, D.; Boyatzis, R,; McKee, A. *Primal leadership* Ch 4 The leadership repertoire. Harvard Business School Press, ISBN 1-57851-486-X.

4   Blanchard, K & J. *The one minute manager*. Harper Collins 2004 ISBN 0007811365

5   Goleman, D. *Emotional Intelligence.*, Chap 10 – the artful critique page 154. Bloomsbury Publishing PLC – ISBN 0-7475-2830-6.

6   Baron, R. *Countering the effects of destructive criticism: The relative efficacy of four interventions*, Journal of Applied Psychology, 75, 3 (1990).

7   Levinson, H. *Feedback to subordinates, Addendum to the Levinson Letter*, Levinson Institute, Waltham MA 1992, from Daniel Goleman Emotional Intelligence pages 153-154.

8   Blanchard, K & J. *The one minute manager*. Harper Collins 2004 ISBN 0007811365

9   Stewart, R.F. *Informal history of SRI planning research work carried out from the 1950's by SRI's Long range planning service (LRPS) and the TAPP study (Theory and Practice of Planning)*.

10   Greenglass, E.R.; Burke, R.J.; Konarski, R. Department of Psychology, York University, Ontario, Canada, *The impact of social support on the development of burnout in teachers: Examination of a model* 10.1080/02678379708256840 Work & Stress Journal, Volume 11, Issue 3 July 1997, pages 267 – 278.

11   7.3 million UK employees work at weekends to clear workloads according to research by MetLife Employee Benefits. 29% of workers saying partners, friends and family resent their failure to switch off from work. Newsquest Media Group April 2013.

12   Durmer, J.S.; Dinges, D.F. *Neurocognitive Consequences of Sleep deprivation*, Seminars in Neurology, Medscape Today, 21st April 2005 "Deficits in daytime performance due to sleep loss are experienced universally and associated with a significant social, financial, and human cost".

13   Walker, M.; Mander, B.A.; Santhanam, S. University of California at Berkeley, findings presented at the annual meeting of the American Association of the Advancement of Science (AAAS) in San Diego, California, 21st Feb 2010.

14   Valentin, A et al, *Errors in administration of parenteral drugs in intensive care units: multinational prospective study*, on behalf of Research Group on Quality Improvement of the European Society of Intensive Care Medicine (ESICM) and the Sentinel Events Evaluation (SEE) study investigations, British Medical Journal, 2009; 338; b814 12/3/09.

15   Tang, F.L. et al, *Journal of Clinical Nursing*, 2007; 16:447-57

16   Åkerstedt T. *Work injuries and time of day-national data*. Shift International News. 1995;12:2.

17   Costa G., Shift Work and Health: Current Problems and Preventive Actions; *Safety and health at work*; 2010 December vol 1, Issue 2, Pages 112-123

18   Straif K.; Baan R.; Grosse Y.; Secretan B.; El Ghissassi F.; Bouvard V.; Altieri A.; Benbrahim-Tallaa L.; Cogliano V. *Carcinogenicity of shift-work, painting, and fire-fighting*. Lancet Oncology; 2007;8:1065–1066.

Kolstad HA. *Nightshift work and risk of breast cancer and other cancers –a critical review of the epidemiologic evidence*; Scandinavian Journal Work Environmental Health; 2008;34:5–22.

19   Figueiro, M.; Rea, M. *Lack of short-wave light during the school day delays dim light melatonin onset (DLMO) in middle school students*; Neuroendocrinology Letters, vol 31, issue 1, 2010; Lighting Research Centre, Renslelaer Polytechnic Institute, Troy, New York.

20   Sharma, H.; Clark, C. *Contemporary Ayurveda*, Chpt 9 The rhythms of nature. Churchill Livingstone, Medical guides to complementary and alternative medicine, ISBN 0 443 05594 7.

21   Dembe, AE., Erickson, JB., Delbos, RG., Banks, SM. *The impact of overtime and long work hours on occupational injuries and illnesses: new evidence from the United States;* Center for Health Policy & Research, University of Massachusetts Medical School, Occupational & environmental medicine 2005;62:588-597. Working in jobs with overtime schedules was associated with a 61% higher injury hazard rate compared to jobs without overtime. Working at least 12 hours per day was associated with a 37% increased hazard rate and working at least 60 hours per week was associated with a 23% increased hazard rate.

22   Dr S Cohen, Carnegie Mellon University, Pittsburgh, 2009

23   Schwartz, T. *For real productivity, less is truly more,* Harvard Business Review blog, Monday May 17 2010, blogs.hbr.org/Schwartz/2010/05.

24   Dr Freeman, Journal of Schizophrenia Research. March 2009 Vol 108 Issue 1 Pages 280-284.

25   Leger, D. *The cost of sleep related accidents: a report for the National Commission on sleep disorders research,* Sleep 11:100-109.

26   Foster, R. Professor of circadian neuroscience at Oxford University, presentation to Cheltenham Science Festival, June 2007,

27   Cooper C., *Work email is making us a 'generation of idiots'. Time to switch off.* Guardian article 14th May 2015.

28   Eppley, K.; Abrams, A.; Shear, J. *Differential effects of relaxation techniques on trait anxiety: a meta-analysis.* SRI (Stanford Research Institute), Journal of Clinical Psychology, 1989, 45(6):957-974. A meta-analysis of studies on methods used to reduce trait anxiety showed Transcendental Meditation to be more effective than other techniques of meditation or relaxation.

29   *The Transcendental Meditation technique and the prevention of psychiatric illness,* Vasa Hospital, University of Gothenburg, Sweden. 1977 Epidemiological Study conducted by the Swedish National Health Board. The Study covered 335,000 psychiatric hospital admissions over a three-year period in 115 hospitals and 39 polyclinics and indicates that the TM Technique is not only safe but also has considerable value in the prevention of psychiatric illness.

30   Miskiman, D.E. *The Treatment of Insomnia by the Transcendental Meditation Program,* Scientific Research on the Transcendental Meditation Program, Graduate Department of Psychology, University of Alberta, Edmonton, Canada, Collected Papers, vol. 1, ISBN 90 71750 04 3 eds. D.W. Orme-Johnson and J.T. Farrow. New York: MERU Press, 1977d.

       Miskiman, D.E. *Long-term Effects of the Transcendental Meditation Program in the Treatment of Insomnia,* Scientific Research on the Transcendental Meditation Program, Graduate Department of Psychology, University of Alberta, Edmonton, Canada, Collected Papers, vol. 1, ISBN 90 71750 04 3 eds. D.W. Orme-Johnson and J.T. Farrow. New York: MERU. Press, 1977b.

31   Orme-Johnson, D.W. *Medical care utilization and the Transcendental Meditation program,* Psychosomatic Medicine 1987, 49:493-507.

32   Miszczak, J.; Achimowicz, J. *Hybrid analysis of spontaneous brain activity in different states of conscious experience,* Military Institute of Aviation Medicine, Warsaw, Poland, presentation to 5th Annual Meeting on EEG and Clinical Neurophysiology entitled 'Electrophysiological Manifestation of Brain Processes' Esztergom, Hungary 1-9 October 1982.

33   So, K.T.; Orme-Johnson, D.W. *Three randomized experiments on the longitudinal effects of the Transcendental Meditation technique on cognition,* Intelligence, 1st Nov 2001. Regular experience of the wakeful hypometabolic

state produced by the Transcendental Meditation program develops general cognitive ability.

34 Barnes, V.A. et al. *Transcendental Meditation program.* Annals of New York Academy of Sciences 1032:211-215, 2005. Faster Recovery from Stress.

Barnes, V.A. et al. *Impact of Transcendental Meditation on cardiovascular function at rest and during acute stress in adolescents with high normal blood pressure.* Journal of Psychosomatic Research 51, 597-605, 2001.

35 Gelderloos, P. *Field independence of students at Maharishi School and a Montessori school.* Perceptual and Motor Skills 65: 613–614, 1987.

36 *Private notes* from Albert S. Humphrey, former research consultant on the Theory and Practice of Planning at SRI in California during the 1960s.

37 Meier, D. *The accelerated learning handbook, A creative guide to designing and delivering faster, more effective training programs.* McGraw-Hill, ISBN 0 07 135547 2.

38 Blanchard, K.; Zigarmi, P.; Zigarmi, D. *Leadership and the one minute manager.* Harper Collins Publishers (United Kingdom), 2000 ISBN 97 80007103 41 6.

Chapter Ten

1 Mayo, E. *The human problems of an industrial civilization,* Macmillan 1933.

2 Nieuwenhuis, Marlon; Knight, Craig; Postmes, Tom; Haslam, S. Alexander; *The Relative Benefits of Green Versus Lean Office Space: Three Field Experiments.* Journal of Experimental Psychology: Applied, Jul 28 , 2014,

3 Tchijevsky, A.L. Transaction of Central, Laboratory Scientific Research on Ionification (*The Commune,* Voronej, 1933).

Krueger, A.P.; Sfgel, S. *Ions in the air.* Human Nature 1(7):46-52, July 1978.

4 Figueiro, M.; Rea, M. *Lack of short-wave light during the school day delays dim light melatonin onset (DLMO) in middle school students;* Neuroendocrinology Letters, vol 31, issue 1, 2010; Lighting Research Centre, Renslelaer Polytechnic Institute, Troy, New York; field study findings consistent with results from controlled laboratory studies.

5 Hawkins, L.H. *Air ions and office health,* Building Services and Environmental Engineer, April 1981.

6 Jukes, J. et al, *The impact of improved air quality on productivity and health in the workplace,* Facilities Management. December 2006.

7 Kerr K.G. *Air ionisation and colonisation /infection with methicillin-resistant Staphylococcus aureus and Ancinetobacter species in an intensive care unit.*

Intensive Care Med (2005) DOI 10.1007/s00134-005-002-8.

Chapter Eleven

1   Flin, R. *Rudeness at work, a threat to patient safety and quality of care*, BMJ 2010; 340: c2480.

2   Pearson, C.; Porath, C.; *On the nature, consequences and remedies of workplace incivility. No time for "nice"? Think again.* Academic Management Executive 2005; 19:7-18.

3   Belbin, R.M. *Team roles at work*, Butterworth-Heinemann 1993. Belbin identifies eight team roles – shaper, plant, coordinator, monitor evaluator, resource investigator, implementer, team worker, and completer-finisher

4   Ibid

5   Carter, R. *Mapping the Mind*, Phoenix Books, 2000.

6   Buckholtz, J.W.; Treadway, M.T. et al, Mesolimbic dopamine reward system hypersensitivity in individuals with psychopathic traits, *Nature Neuroscience* 13, 419–421 (2010) doi:10.1038/nn.2510, Published online 14 March 2010,

7   Deeley, Q.; Surguladze. S. et al, Facial emotion processing in criminal psychology, *British Journal of Psychiatry* (2006) 189: 533-539. Doi: 10.1192/bjp.bp.106.021410.

8   Goleman, D.; Boyatzis R.; McKee, A. *Primal leadership*. Harvard Business School Press, ISBN 1 – 57851 – 486 – X, 2002, pp 34 – 52.

9   Porter, S.; Ten Brinke, L.; Wilson, K. *Crime profiles and conditional release performance of psychopathic and non-psychopathic sex offenders*, Legal and Criminological Psychology, vol 14, 1, pp 109 – 118.

10   Gray, N. et al. *Forensic psychology: Violence viewed by psychopathic murderers*, Nature 423, 497 – 498 29 May 2003.

11   Lord Laming. *The Protection of Children in England: A Progress Report.* A report ordered by the House of Commons, The Stationary Office, March 2009. ISBN 9780102958928.

12   Furedi, F., Bristow, J. *Licensed to Hug: How Child Protection Policies Are Poisoning the Relationship Between the Generations and Damaging the voluntary sector*; Civitas: Institute for the Study of Civil Society; June 2008 ISBN 978-1-906837-16-7

13   Ali Baba-Akbari Sari, research fellow, Department of Health Sciences, University of York, Trevor A. Sheldon, Professor of health sciences, pro-vice chancellor, Department of Health Sciences, University of York, et al. See chapter 7 reference 4 for further details.

14   National Audit Office, *HM The Treasury: The nationalisation of Northern Rock.* 20th March 2009, HC 298 2008-09 ISBN 9780102954708.

15   Stewart, R. F. *Informal history of SRI planning research.* Work carried out from the 1950's by SRI's Long range planning service (LRPS) and the TAPP study (Theory and Practice of Planning). The TAPP study carried out action-based research into why companies fail, concluding that lack of formal planning was a significant factor; private notes from Albert S. Humphrey formerly senior research consultant at SRI and founder of Team Action Management, which is a team-based planning system based on the LRPS work and the TAPP findings.

16   Ming Hsu; Bhatt, M.; Adolphs, R.; Tranel, D.; Camerer, C.F. *Neural Systems Responding to Degrees of Uncertainty in Human Decision-Making,* Science Journal 9 December 2005: Vol. 310. no. 5754, pp. 1680 – 1683.

17   Bechara A, *Journal of Gambling Studies.* 30th October 2004 Department of Neurology, University of Iowa study.

18   Buckholtz, J.W. et al, *Mesolimbic dopamine reward system hypersensitivity in individuals with psychopathic traits,* Nature Neuroscience 13, 419–421; 2010.

19   Festinger, L.; *A Theory of Cognitive Dissonance*; California: Stanford University Press 1957 Cognitive dissonance was observed to be the mental stress or discomfort experienced by someone who holds two or more contradictory beliefs, ideas, or values at the same time, or is confronted by new information that conflicts with existing beliefs, ideas, or values.

      Festinger, L. *Cognitive dissonance*; Scientific American 207 (4): 93–107; 1962.

20   Nickerson, Raymond S. *Confirmation Bias: A Ubiquitous Phenomenon in Many Guises.* Review of General Psychology 2 (2): 175–220; June 1998.

21   Redelmeir, D. A.; Tversky, A. *On the belief that arthritis pain is related to the weather,* Proceedings of the National Academy of Sciences 93 (7): 2895–2896, 1996.

22   Harmon-Jones, E. *A Cognitive Dissonance Theory Perspective on Persuasion;* The Persuasion Handbook: Developments in Theory and Practice, James Price Dillard, Michael Pfau, eds. 2002. Thousand Oaks, CA: Sage Publications, p.101.

23   Oswald, Margit E.; Grosjean, Stefan (2004), *Confirmation Bias,* in Pohl, Rüdiger F., *Cognitive Illusions: A Handbook on Fallacies and Biases in Thinking, Judgement and Memory,* Hove, UK: Psychology Press, pp. 79–96, ISBN 978-1-84169-351-4, OCLC 55124398

      Hastie, Reid; Park, Bernadette; *The Relationship Between Memory and Judgment Depends on Whether the Judgment Task is Memory-Based or On-Line,* in Hamilton, David L., *Social cognition: key readings,* New York: Psychology Press; 2005; p. 394, ISBN 0-86377-591-8, OCLC 55078722

Stangor, C.; McMillan, D. *Memory for expectancy-congruent and expectancy-incongruent information: A review of the social and social developmental literatures,* Psychological Bulletin (American Psychological Association) 111 (1): 42–61; 1992

24   Jay Alexis OBE, *Independent Inquiry into child sexual exploitation in Rotherham 1997 – 2013*; commissioned by Rotherham Metropolitan Council; report dated 21st August 2014; "... In just over a third of cases, children affected by sexual exploitation were previously known to services because of child protection and neglect. It is hard to describe the appalling nature of the abuse that child victims suffered. They were raped by multiple perpetrators, trafficked to other towns and cities in the north of England, abducted, beaten, and intimidated. There were examples of children who had been doused in petrol and threatened with being set alight, threatened with guns, made to witness brutally violent rapes and threatened they would be next if they told anyone. Girls as young as 11 were raped by large numbers of male perpetrators..."

25   Danczuk S. Member of Parliament for Rochdale; *Rotherham is not an isolated incident*; Daily Telegraph article on-line 31st August 2014. Danczuk describes this classic case of how harmful premature cognitive commitment can be, when it is combined with general incompetence, a low degree of empathy and the usual bounded rationality and politically correct ideology seen in the public sector. "... Sit before children's services managers and you're likely to hear endless waffle about guidelines, policies, procedures, strategy and thresholds. But they won't mention the kids. Worse still, management never refers to practitioners or seeks advice from those at the coalface. Experience has no currency. Cold, remote theory rules. In the wake of the Rochdale grooming scandal, a Serious Case Review was critical of the health workers whose outreach work had uncovered an endemic child abuse problem. Amazingly, they were criticised for having the wrong qualifications. Once you start heading down this road, where management exists in a bubble and an organisation's values come from textbooks rather than the people they serve, then you end up with situations like Rotherham. Where political correctness and cultural sensitivity are more important than child rape. ..."

26   Kenber B. investigative reporter; *Times article* 5th June 2015

27   Lovallo, D., & Kahneman, D.(2003, July). *Delusions of success: How optimism undermines executives' decision.* Retrieved August 25th 2008 from Harvard Business School

28   Scott S.; *Fierce conversations – Achieving success at work and in life, one conversation at a time;* Viking Penguin 2002; ISBN 0-670-03124-0

29   Alexander C.N.; Alexander V.K.; Boyer R.W.; Jedrczak A.; *The subjective experience of higher states of consciousness and the Maharishi technology of the unified field: Personality, cognitive, perceptual, and physiological correlates of growth to enlightenment;* 1984; Scientific Research on Maharishi's Transcendental Meditation and TM-Sidhi programme, Collected papers vol 4;

ISBN 90-71750-05-1

30 Baron, J. *Thinking and deciding* (3rd ed.), New York: Cambridge University Press, 2000; ISBN 0-521-65030-5, OCLC 316403966

31 Shanteau, J.; Sandra L. Schneider, ed. *Emerging perspectives on judgment and decision research;* Cambridge University Press; p. 445. ISBN 0-521-52718-X. 2003.

32 Kahneman, D.; Tversky A. *Intuitive Predictions: Biases and Corrective Procedures,* 1979 TIMS Studies in Management Science, Volume 12 (Elsevier/North Holland).

33 Nickerson, R.S.; *Confirmation Bias: A Ubiquitous Phenomenon in Many Guises;* Review of General Psychology 2 (2): 175–220; 1998.

34 Jex, S.M.; Bliese, P.D. *Efficacy beliefs as a moderator of the impact of work-related stressors;* Journal of Applied Psychology. Vol 84(3), Jun 1999, 349-361.

35 Mateen, F.J.; Dorji, C. *Health-care worker burnout and the mental health imperative.* Lancet 2009 Aug 22;374(9690):595-7.

36 Lilianne Mujica-Parodi, *Smell of fear;* New Scientist prior to publishing research findings, , Stony Brook University, New York, December 2008 US Defence Advanced Research Projects Agency project.

37 Fowler, J.H.; Christakis, N.A. *Dynamic spread of happiness in a large social network: Longitudinal analysis over twenty years in the Framingham Heart Study;* BMJ 2008; 337: a 2338, doi: 10.1136/bmj.a2338 4/12/2008 "Clusters of happy and unhappy people are visible in the network, and the relationship between people's happiness extends up to three degrees of separation (for example, to the friends of one's friends' friends)..."

38 Pugh, N.D.; Walton, K.G.; Cavanaugh, K.L. *Can time series analysis of serotonin turnover test the theory that consciousness is a field?* Society for Neuroscience Abstracts 14: 372, 1988. Findings: As the numbers of a meditating group increase, there is a correlation between a decrease in a nearby subject group's cortisol levels (a hormone associated with stress) and an increase in their serotonin levels (a hormone associated with mental well-being). "We have hypothesized that group practice of the TM-Sidhi program can affect society, and this study helps to understand the effect. Group practice actually reduces the effects of stress, in those in the vicinity, in a manner similar to the reduction within the individual meditator when he practices the Transcendental Meditation program." Dr Walton.

39 Hatchard, G.D.; Deans, A.J.; Cavanaugh, K.L.; Orme-Johnson, D.W. *The Maharishi effect: A model for social-improvement. Time series analysis of a phase transition to reduced crime in Merseyside metropolitan area.* Psychology, Crime & Law, Volume 2 Issue 3 1996. Pp 165 – 174. "Time series analysis was used to test the hypothesis that Merseyside crime rate was reduced by a group practising Maharishi Mahesh Yogi's Transcendental Meditation and TM-Sidhi programme. Previous research suggests that a phase transition to increased

orderliness evidenced by reduced crime rate should occur when the group size approaches the square root of 1% of the total population. Analysis of Merseyside monthly crime data and coherence group size from 1978 to 1991 shows that a phase transition occurred during March 1988 with a 13.4% drop in crime when the group size first exceeded the $\sqrt{1}$ % or Maharishi Effect threshold (p < 0.00006). Up to 1992, Merseyside crime rate has remained steady in contrast to the national crime rate, which increased by 45%… Demographic changes, economic variables, police practice, and other factors could not account for the changes." The authors.

40   Scientific Research on Maharishi's Transcendental Meditation and TM-Sidhi programme collected papers – vol 4, pp 2479 – 2762 MERU Press, ISBN 90-71750-051.

41   SunTzu, *The art of war*, translated by Samuel B Griffith, Oxford University Press, 1963.

42   Coulson, J.C.; McKenna, J.; Field, M. *Exercising at work and self-reported work performance,* International Journal of Workplace Health Management. 2008 vol: 1 Issue: 3 Page: 176 – 197.

43   Berman, M.G. et al. *The Cognitive Benefits of Interacting with Nature,* University of Michigan, Psychological Science –December 2008.

44   Lavidis N.; Associate Professor R Einstein, Queensland University School of Biomedical Science press release concerning the launch of a new scent, Seranascent 20th August 2009. The actual combination of feel good chemicals released by pine trees, lush vegetation and cut grass can make people feel relaxed.

45   Martin, P. *The sickening mind, brain, behaviour, immunity and disease,* Flamingo and Imprint of Harper Collins, ISBN 0 00 655022 3, pp157 – 163. "The message that emerges loud and clear from scientific evidence accumulated since the mid 1970s is that having a reasonable quantity and quality of social relationships is essential for mental and physical wellbeing."

46   Haratani, T. et al. *Effects of Transcendental Meditation on the mental health of industrial workers.* Japanese Journal of Industrial Health 32: 656, 1990.
      Haratani, T. et al. *Effects of Transcendental Meditation on the health behavior of industrial workers.* Japanese Journal of Public Health 37 (10 Suppl.): 729, 1990.

47   Blanks, R.H.; Boone, W.R.; Schmidt, S.; Dobson, M. *Network Care: A retrospective outcomes assessment.* 1996
      Dobson, M.; Boone W.R.; Blanks, R.H.; *Women and Alternative Health Care: A retrospective study of recipients of Network Care.* 1996 Association for Reorganizational Healing Practice Washington, DC 20036

48   Rinta, T.; Welch, G. *Should Singing Activities Be Included in Speech and Voice Therapy for Prepubertal Children?* Journal of Voice, vol 22, Issue 1, Pages 100-112, Literature review includes section on singing and its psychological impact.

49   Hall, D. *Religious Attendance: More Cost-Effective Than Lipitor?* Journal of the

American Board of Family Medicine, 9:103-109 (2006), Department of General Surgery, University of Pittsburgh Medical Centers. Meta-analysis demonstrates weekly attendance at religious services accounts for an additional 2 to 3 life-years compared with 3 to 5 life-years for physical exercise and 2.5 to 3.5 life-years for statin-type agents.

Chapter Twelve

1   *The official yearbook of the UK*, Office for National Statistics, 2005, Her Majesty's Stationery Office (HMSO), ISBN 0 11 621738 3.

2   Camerer, C.F.; Fehr, E. *When Does "Economic Man" Dominate Social Behavior?* Science 6 January 2006: Vol. 311. no. 5757, pp. 47 - 52 DOI: 10.1126/science.1110600. Game theory is now beginning to understand that self-regarding behaviour does not always dominate social interaction. With the right strategic incentives a minority of "other-regarding individuals"* can generate a "cooperative" aggregate outcome if their behavior generates incentives for a majority of "self-regarding people"** to behave cooperatively. In strategic games, players with high degrees of strategic thinking can mimic or erase the effects of others who do very little strategic thinking.

*Other-regarding individuals value per se the outcomes or behaviors of other persons either positively or negatively.

**Self-regarding people do not care per se for the outcomes and behaviors of other individuals.

3   Ibid

4   McGuiness, F. *Membership of UK political parties,* House of Commons Library, Social and general statistics, SN/SG/5125 3rd December 2012.

5   Ibid

6   Russell Payne, letter to the Daily Telegraph, 24th April 2009.

7   Denham, M. *The Real National Debt: A Decade of Reckless Growth;*

Tax payers alliance; Research Note 78: 19 October 2010. The official national debt quoted in the budget is £890 billion. However added to this are unfunded public sector debts.

8   Aviva family finances report January 2012; Aviva PLC GN 20553 01/2012.

9   Jay, D.; *The socialist case*. Faber and Faber, 1937.

Made in the USA
Charleston, SC
28 October 2015